The Archaeology
of War

The Archaeology of War

from the editors of
ARCHAEOLOGY
M A G A Z I N E

With an Introduction by
Mark Rose

HATHERLEIGH PRESS
New York • London

The Archaeology of War
A Hatherleigh Press Book

ISBN 1-57826-214-3

Project Credits

ARCHAEOLOGY Staff
Editor-In-Chief: Peter A. Young
Executive Editor: Mark Rose
Editorial Intern: Alexander Benenson

Hatherleigh Press Staff
President & CEO: Andrew Flach
Publisher: Kevin Moran
Managing Editor: Andrea Au
Art Director & Production Manager: Deborah Miller
Assistant Editor: Alyssa Smith
Cover Design: Deborah Miller
Interior Design: Deborah Miller, Michael Wood
        and Jacinta M. Monniere

Printed in USA

About the Archaeological Institute of America

The Archaeological Institute of America (AIA), publisher of ARCHAEOLOGY Magazine, is North America's oldest and largest organization devoted to the world of archaeology. The Institute is a nonprofit educational organization founded in 1879 and chartered by the United States Congress in 1906. Today, the AIA has nearly 10,000 members belonging to more than 100 local societies in the United States, Canada, and overseas. The organization is unique because it counts among its members professional archaeologists, students, and many others from all walks of life. This diverse group is united by a shared passion for archaeology and its role in furthering human knowledge.

Contents

INTRODUCTION
War and Archaeology:
A New Voice xv
by MARK ROSE

Part I: ROOTS OF WAR

Prehistory of Warfare 3
Humans have been at each others' throats since the dawn of the species.
        by STEVEN A. LEBLANC

  MURDER OR WAR? 7
      by ALEXANDER BENENSON

Unearthing a Violent Past 11
Archaeologists have found evidence of warfare between prehistoric villages around the world.
        by ALEXANDER BENENSON

Icons of War 14
Ancient artworks attest the military might of early rulers of Egypt and Sumer.
        by MARK ROSE

Life and Death in a
Maya War Zone 17
Within a Yucatán pyramid lie the grim traces of a violent change in rulership—the remains of a slaughtered royal family.
    by CHARLES SUHLER *and* DAVID FREIDEL

Battlers at the Bottom
of the World 23
Maori warriors built fortifications not unlike those of their Celtic counterparts.
        by BRIAN FAGAN

Part II: ANCIENT WARFARE

Egypt's New Kingdom
Warrior Kings 29
*Pharaohs took to the field to defend or expand
their empires.*

by MARK ROSE

Was There a Trojan War? 32
*Troy's chief archaeologist weighs in on the Western
World's most mythic battle.*

by MANFRED KORFMANN

EVIDENCE FROM HITTITE RECORDS 34
by J. D. HAWKINS
EVIDENCE FROM HOMER 36
by JOACHIM LATAC

Warriors of Paros 38
*Soldiers' burials offer clues to the rise of Classical
Greek city-states.*

by F. ZAFEIROPOULOU AND A. AGELARAKIS

Fallen Heroes 42
*Bones of Pericles' soldiers come to New York for
analysis.*

by MARK ROSE

◉ EYEWITNESS: Alexander
at Granicus 49
compiled by MARK ROSE

The Spoils of Actium 51
*An ancient war memorial provides startling details
about the ships in Antony and Cleopatra's fleet during one of history's mightiest naval engagements.*

by WILLIAM MURRAY *and* PHOTIOS M. PETSAS

RATING ANCIENT WARSHIPS 54
by WILLIAM MURRAY
MONUMENTS TO WAR 58
by ALEXANDER BENENSON

Rescuing an Old Dig 60
*Women warriors from beyond the Danube and
complex burial rituals are among the unexpected
finds at a Roman military cemetery.*

by HILARY COOL

WERE SARMATIANS THE SOURCE
OF ARTHURIAN LEGEND? 64
by C. SCOTT LITTLETON

Chinese Chimes and Chariots 66
Cavalry in the afterlife? You can take it with you.

by JARRETT A. LOBELL

Part III: FROM THE MIDDLE AGES TO THE AGE OF EXPLORATION AND CONQUEST

A Day of Much Slaying 71
A mass grave of slaughtered soldiers reveals the brutality of late medieval warfare.
by MARK ROSE

LANCASTER VS. YORK 73
by MARK ROSE

The Ship that Terrorized Europe. . . 76
Viking raids were made possible by the elegant, efficient longship.
by ALEXANDER BENENSON

Suppression of the Cathars 79
A fairy-tale landscape in southern France belies a brutal crusade.
by JAMES WISEMAN

Reconstructing Medieval Artillery . 84
Archaeologist Peter Venming takes a hands-on, experimental approach to his studies of centuries-old arms.

☞ EYEWITNESS: The Crusades and the Fall of Constantinople. 89
compiled by MARK ROSE

The *Mary Rose* 93
Resurrecting the pride of Henry VIII's fleet
by ALEXANDER BENENSON

QUALITY CARGO 94
by ERIC A. POWELL

Death March of Hernando de Soto. . 96
Archaeologists chart the conquistador's trail of human destruction from Florida's Gulf Coast to the mouth of the Mississippi.
by DAVID H. DYE

Pizarro's Family and His Head 101
A conquistador's family, from cradle to grave
by MARK ROSE

☞ EYEWITNESS: Cortés and the Night of Sorrows 104
compiled by ALEXANDER BENENSON

Relics of the Kamikaze 107
Excavations off Japan's coast are uncovering Kublai Khan's ill-fated invasion fleet.
by JAMES P. DELGADO

FACING THE KHAN'S WRATH 110
by JAMES P. DELGADO

Digging Napoleon's Dead. 114
A mass grave in Lithuania is gruesome evidence of the catastrophic French retreat from Moscow.
by JARRETT A. LOBELL

Napoleon's Lost Fleet. 118
Divers discover what really happened at the battle of the Nile.
by ANGELA M.H. SCHUSTER

☞ EYEWITNESS: The Battle of the Nile 122
compiled by MARK ROSE

The Great Wall's Patchwork History 124
Satellite images show centuries of construction preceded the Ming Dynasty's fortifications.
by ALEXANDER BENENSON

Part IV: THE WARS OF NORTH AMERICA

The Forgotten
Fight for America. 129
The centuries-long struggle for control of the continent before 1776

    by MARK ROSE

Anatomy of a Massacre. 136
An unpublished 1950s excavation and more recent skeletal analysis yield graphic new details about the slaughter of a British garrison during the French and Indian war.

    by DAVID R. STARBUCK

Turtle Dives Again. 142
Re-creating George Washington's revolutionary submarine

    by TOM GIDWITZ

BENEDICT ARNOLD GUNBOAT. 147
    by JESSICA E. SARACENI

Remains of a Sumptuous Feast. . . . 148
Excavations at Valley Forge reveal how soldiers coped with insufficient supplies and food.

    by NATHANIEL RALSTON

The Guns of Palo Alto. 151
Battlefield surveys indicate that Mexican maps distorted the opening engagement of the Mexican-American war. Why?

    by CHARLES M. HAECKER

Doing Time 157
How Confederate POWs weathered captivity

    by DAVID R. BUSH

UNION SOLDIERS IDENTIFIED. 161
    by JESSICA E. SARACENI

Civil War Espionage 164
A dig at a Union cannon foundry unearths artifacts and a tale of international intrigue.

    by ANDREW SLAYMAN

Iron Warships of the Civil War . . 166
The ironclads, monitors, and submarines of the Civil War laid the foundation for all modern warships.

    by ALEXANDER BENENSON

GEORGIA ON MY MINE 169
    by ERIC A. POWELL

Fire Fight at Hembrillo Basin 172
Buffalo Soldiers hold their ground in a nighttime skirmish with the Apache.

    by KARL W. LAUMBACH

Part V: WAR IN MODERN TIMES

In Flanders Fields 183
Uncovering the carnage of World War I
by NEIL ASHER SILBERMAN

👁 EYEWITNESS: Trench
Warfare in World War I 189
compiled by MARK ROSE

A Long Road Home 192
The remains of a WWII pilot found in the mountains of Papua New Guinea are buried in Arlington National Cemetery.
by WILLIAM BELCHER *and* HELEN M. WOLS

THE GREAT MIA HUNT 194
by WILLIAM BELCHER

World War II POWs 198
Discoveries and excavations have yielded new information on the treatment of prisoners in Europe, Asia, and the United States.

UNEARTHING SOVIET MASSACRES 198
by SPENCER P.M. HARRINGTON

BONES AT THE RIVER KWAI 199
by DOMINIC G. DIONGSON

FRITZ RITZ 200
by JESSICA E. SARACENI

GARDEN UNDER GUARD 200
by ERIC A. POWELL

Remembering Chelmno 201
Heart-wrenching finds from a Nazi death camp
by JULIET GOLDEN

Proving Ground
of the Nuclear Age 206
The mangled artifacts and lunar landscape of the Nevada Test Site are a vivid testament to the advent of atomic weaponry.
by WILLIAM JOHNSON *and* COLLEEN BECK

Diving at Ground Zero 210
The ships of Bikini Atoll are a grim reminder of the atomic age.
by JAMES P. DELGADO

Cold War Memories 214
A critical period is commemorated in a new National Historic Site.
compiled by MARK ROSE

Part VI: ARCHAEOLOGY AND WAR

Battles over Battlefields 221
The fight to save Civil War sites from developers
by STEVE NASH

PARK SERVICE RETIREES
PROTEST CUTS 226
by STEVE NASH

Who Owns the Spoils of War? . . . 228
As Germany and Russia spar over the return of wartime booty, historians and legal scholars take a fresh look at what really happened 50 yearss ago.
by KARL E. MEYER

LIMITS OF WORLD LAW 234
by KARL E. MEYER

Probing a Landscape of Death 237
Eva Elvira Klonowski's mission to recover and identify the victims of ethnic cleansing.
by BRENDA SMILEY

Museum Under Siege 243
Efforts to rescue the collections of Afghanistan's National Museum
by NANCY HATCH DUPREE

Spoils of War 251
The plundering of Iraq's cultural institutions demonstrates yet again how warfare fuels the global trade in looted antiquities.
by NEIL BRODIE

TELL IT TO THE MARINES 256
by JANE WALDBAUM

The Archaeology of Battlefields. . . 257
A pioneer in the field discusses a new way to investigate warfare.

About the Authors 260

Further Reading 264

Acknowledgments 268

Index 270

WAR AND ARCHAEOLOGY: A NEW VOICE

by MARK ROSE

We grasp our battle-spears: we don our breastplates of hide.
The axles of our chariots touch: our short swords meet.
Standards obscure the sun: the foe roll up like clouds.
Arrows fall thick: the warriors press forward.
They menace our ranks: they break our line.
The left-hand trace horse is dead: the one on the right is
*   smitten.*
The fallen horses block our wheels: they impede the
*   yoke-horses!*

This description of battle by the Chinese poet Ch'ü Yüan (332-295 B.C.) is just part of the vast literature of war. Homer tells of the deeds of the Greek and Trojan warriors. The Book of Judges tells of Deborah and Barak's victory over the Canaanites. The Greek warrior-poet Archilochus, in the sixth century B.C., laughs at a close

Courtesy Mark Rose

In the works of Sir Walter Scott, with their glorified notions of medieval warfare, the villain could be counted on to die inexplicably before mortal combat ensued.

call while fighting barbarians: "One of the Saians is thrilled with that unblemished shield left unwillingly behind in the bushes. But I saved myself, so what do I care about the shield, the hell with it; I'll obtain an equally good one."

Then there are the bare facts from history books and official accounts. Marcus

Agrippa defeated the fleet of Antony and Cleopatra on September 2, 31 B.C., securing control of the Roman Empire for Augustus. The Thirty Years War, which devastated Europe, began after two Habsburg councilors were thrown out a castle window—the Defenestration of Prague—in 1618. When ANZAC troops, soldiers from Australia and New Zealand, evacuated Gallipoli in 1916, their dead and wounded numbered around 115,000.

There are also the impressions and memoirs of contemporaries and participants. The chronicler Jean de Waurin wrote of the battle at Towton, where armies of the rivals Henry VI and Edward IV faced off in 1461, "So followed a day of much slaying between the two sides, and for a long time no one knew to which side to give the victory so furious was the battle and so great the killing: father did not spare son and son did not spare father." Four centuries later, Ulysses S. Grant and Robert E. Lee confronted each other. Grant won through his relentless pursuit and destruction of the enemy, but of one engagement he wrote a simple, telling line: "I have always regretted that the last assault at Cold Harbor was ever made." Why was Cold Harbor too much? The final push "cost us heavily and probably without benefit to compensate." Worse, Lee balked at terms for retrieving the wounded, delaying recovery parties for 48 hours, by which time all but two had died.

Poetry, official accounts and histories, and personal commentaries. The written testimony of war is vast and varied. But is it objective truth? All authors write with a purpose in mind and in the context of their own culture and time. Is there an independent voice, one that tells of war not through a biased lens but with a clear eye? There is. It is archaeology.

Archaeology tells us that conflict and war have likely been with us for as long as we have been human. Steven A. LeBlanc has advocated this idea so much that his colleagues now know him as "Dr. Warfare." In *The Archaeology of War* he contends, "There is no reason to think that warfare played any less of a role in prehistoric societies for which we have no such records, whether they were hunter-gatherers or farmers." The archaeological evidence bears him out. Stone projectile points have been found embedded in the bones of a 13,000-year-old woman from Sicily, the 9,300-year-old Kennewick Man from Washington, and Ötzi, the 5,000-year-old "Iceman" from the Alps. And whole farming villages were massacred: at Germany's Talheim 7,000 years ago, and at Crow Creek in South Dakota where excavations revealed the remains of 500 men, women, and children killed around 1325 A.D.

As one might expect some archaeological evidence for war comes from tombs. The discovery of a collective burial on Paros, Greece, for example, has illuminated the transition from battles fought as individual duels by chieftains and nobility, as described by Homer, to the mass formations by citizen-soldiers. Study of the remains of these individuals, and those from a collective burial of Athenian soldiers who died during the fifth-century B.C. Peloponnesian War, will open a window on ancient training and tactics. The same can be said for the 33 bronze war chariots discovered in a tomb in China

The turret of the innovative Civil War ironclad Monitor *was raised in 2002.*

from the Warring States period, the time of the poet Ch'ü Yüan.

Burials and bones are not the only keys archaeologists are using to understand war. They are also "reading" ancient monuments, such as the grandiose display of captured rams that Augustus erected in northwestern Greece to commemorate his defeat of Antony and Cleopatra's fleet. The now-empty sockets in the stone that held the rams have given insight into the warships of the time. In Rome itself, newly discerned traces of an inscription on the Colosseum indicate that it was built with spoils, and possibly slaves, from the sack of Jerusalem in 70 A.D.

Archaeology is also exploring questions that lie on the border between legend and history. Recent excavations at Troy have inevitably raised the century-old question, was there really a Trojan War? Elsewhere, does evidence show that women warriors were among the garrison of the Roman frontier in northern Britain? And did Sarmatians from the Eurasian steppe serving in Britain bring with them the legend that would become King Arthur?

Archaeologists are also investigating wars that are now long forgotten. Throughout eastern North America, they are searching for and uncovering evidence of many conflicts in the centuries before the Revolutionary War: Fort Caroline, a French outpost brutally eradicated by the Spanish in 1565; the "Plundering Time" in Maryland in 1645; and the *Elizabeth and Mary*, part of a fleet that attacked Québec City in 1690. At Fort William Henry, the 1757 massacre, once sensationalized in *Last of the Mohicans*, is being reassessed on the basis of archaeological discoveries.

New approaches, such as battlefield archaeology, are now used on a routine basis. Careful recording and analysis of bullets, cartridges, and other gear left behind on the landscapes of war has rewritten history. Thanks to this research we now know what really happened at Palo Alto, site of a battle between Mexican and U.S. forces in 1846, and at Hembrillo, where "Buffalo Soldiers" of the U.S. cavalry fought the Apache.

Blending archaeological and forensic techniques is another innovative way to understand war. For example, put to rest thoughts of medieval warfare as the honorable combat by knights of the sort found in the pages of Sir Walter Scott's *Ivanhoe*. The battlefield at Towton yielded a mass burial that tells of medieval war from the foot soldier's perspective: skulls found there averaged four and had as many as 13 wounds. In modern contexts, forensics are aiding in the recovery of MIAs from past conflicts—WWII, Korea, and Vietnam—and in documenting war crimes in recent ones.

The treatment of captured enemies and of civilian populations during war is now being put under the archaeological magnifying glass with subjects ranging from Johnson's Island, a Civil War camp for Confederate officers, to Chelmno, a Nazi death camp in Poland. Such studies are revealing how different populations were treated, like the German soldiers held at the "Fritz Ritz" and the Japanese Americans interred at a "relocation center" in Idaho.

Some of the most impressive advances in understanding the past have come when archaeologists have rolled up their sleeves and re-created the weapons of war. How effective was medieval artillery? Very. Catapult-like trebuchets built the "old way" have proved reliable and accurate. In 1776, the experimental one-man submarine *Turtle* nearly sank the British flagship in New York harbor. Using period materials and tools, a team has built a new *Turtle*, demonstrating just how innovative it was and how close it came to succeeding.

Equally spectacular have been archaeological recoveries of Civil War vessels that revolutionized naval warfare. In 2002, the gun turret of *Monitor* was brought to the surface, 140 years after the vessel sank. And, in 2000, the Confederate submarine *Hunley* was raised intact. The first submarine to sink an enemy vessel, *Hunley* itself went down with all hands after its successful attack on the USS *Housatonic*, part of the fleet blockading Charleston.

The extraordinary efforts made to bring up *Monitor* and *Hunley* contrast with the daily loss of Civil War battlefields to subdivisions and commercial development. Archaeologists and citizen-activists are struggling to stay ahead of the bulldozers. More recent evidence—of both warfare and the impact on society of even the possibility of war—is also in need of study and preservation. Here archaeologists are taking the lead in investigating the ships sunk during atomic bomb tests at Bikini Atoll, in recording the remains at Nevada's Nuclear Test Site, and in creating the Minuteman Missile National Historic Site.

Cold War archaeology brings home the point that the intersection of warfare and archaeology is part of the present. Even today the fate of artworks taken at the end of WWII is debated. Among them are ancient artifacts, such as the "Treasure of Priam" that Heinrich Schliemann excavated at Troy in 1873. Does it belong to Russia or Germany? Does Turkey have a claim to it? And what of artifacts and archaeological sites in times of war now? The looting of museums and the ruins of ancient cities in Afghanistan and Iraq are clarion calls for better efforts to protect our universal cultural heritage. As a small step toward that, the Archaeological Institute of America is now educating U.S. troops about archaeology before they are sent abroad. And, even as soldiers are educated about archaeology, the new speciality of battlefield archaeology promises to give us a greater insight into warfare.

From the flint weapons of prehistory to the ballistic missiles of today, archaeologists are unearthing and documenting the dramatic history of warfare. *The Archaeology of War* presents their discoveries, experiments, reassessment, and insights and what their findings tell us about human conflict.

PART I:

Roots of War

Prehistory of Warfare

HUMANS HAVE BEEN AT EACH OTHERS' THROATS SINCE THE DAWN OF THE SPECIES.

by STEVEN A. LEBLANC

In the early 1970s, working in the El Morro Valley of west-central New Mexico, I encountered the remains of seven large prehistoric pueblos that had once housed upwards of a thousand people each. Surrounded by two-story-high walls, the villages were perched on steep-sided mesas, which suggested that their inhabitants built them with defense in mind. At the time, the possibility that warfare occurred among the Anasazi was of little interest to me and my colleagues. Rather, we were trying to figure out what the people in these 700-year-old communities farmed and hunted, the impact of climate change, and the nature of their social systems—not the possibility of violent conflict.

One of these pueblos, it turned out, had been burned to the ground; its people had clearly fled for their lives. Pottery and valuables had been left on the floors, and bushels of burned corn still lay in the storerooms. We eventually determined that this site had been abandoned, and that immediately afterward a fortress had been built nearby. Something catastrophic had occurred at this ancient Anasazi settlement, and the survivors had almost immediately, and at great speed, set about to prevent it from happening again.

Thirty years ago, archaeologists were certainly aware that violent, organized conflicts occurred in the prehistoric cultures they studied, but they considered these incidents almost irrelevant to our understanding of past events and people. Today, some of my colleagues are realizing that the evidence I helped uncover in the El Morro Valley is indicative of warfare endemic throughout the entire Southwest, with its attendant massacres, population decline, and area abandonments that forever changed the Anasazi way of life.

When excavating eight-millennia-old farm villages in southeastern Turkey in 1970, I initially marveled how similar modern villages were to ancient ones, which were occupied at a time when an abundance of plants and animals made warfare quite unnecessary. Or so I thought. I knew we had discovered some plaster sling missiles (one of our workmen showed me how shepherds used slings to hurl stones at predators threatening their sheep). Such missiles were found at many of these sites, often in great quantities, and were clearly not intended for protecting flocks of sheep; they were exactly the same size and shape as later Greek and Roman sling stones used for warfare.

The so-called "doughnut stones" we had uncovered at these sites were assumed to be weights for digging sticks, presumably threaded on a pole to make it heavier for digging holes to plant crops. I failed to note how much they resembled the round stone heads attached to wooden clubs—maces—used in many places of the world exclusively for fighting and still used ceremonially to signify power. Thirty years ago, I was holding mace heads and sling missiles in my hands, unaware of their use as weapons of war.

We now know that defensive walls once ringed many villages of this era, as they did the Anasazi settlements. Rooms were massed together behind solid outside walls and were entered from the roof. Other sites had mud-brick defensive walls, some with elaborately defended gates. Furthermore, many of these villages had been burned to the ground, their inhabitants massacred, as indicated by nearby mass graves.

Certainly for those civilizations that kept written records or had descriptive narrative art traditions, warfare is so clearly present that no one can deny it. Think of Homer's *Iliad* or the Vedas of South India, or scenes of prisoner sacrifice on Moche pottery. There is no reason to think that warfare played any less of a role in prehistoric societies for which we have no such records, whether they were hunter-gatherers or farmers. But most scholars studying these cultures still are not seeing it. They should assume warfare occurred among the people they study, just as they assume religion and art were a normal part of human culture. Then they could ask more interesting questions, such as: What form did warfare take? Can warfare explain some of the material found in the archaeological record? What were people fighting over and why did the conflicts end?

Today, some scholars know me as "Dr. Warfare." To them, I have the annoying habit of asking un-politic questions about their research. I am the one who asks why the houses at a particular site were jammed so close together and many catastrophically burned. When I suggest that the houses were crowded behind defensive walls that were not found because no one was looking for them, I am not terribly appreciated. And I don't win any popularity contests when I suggest that twenty-mile-wide zones with no sites in them imply no-man's lands—clear evidence for warfare—to archaeologists who have explained a region's history without mention of conflict.

Virtually all the basic textbooks on archaeology ignore the prevalence or significance of past warfare, which is usually not discussed until the formation of state-level civilizations such as ancient Sumer. Most texts either assume, or actually state, that for most of human history there was an abundance of available resources. There was no resource stress, and people had the means to control population, though how they accomplished this is never explained. The one archaeologist who has most explicitly railed against this hidden but pervasive attitude is Lawrence Keeley of the University of Illinois, who studies the earliest farmers in Western Europe. He has found ample evidence of warfare as farmers spread west, yet most of his colleagues still believe the expansion was peaceful and his evidence a minor aberration, as seen in the various papers in Barry Cunliffe's *The Oxford Illustrated Prehistory of Europe* (1994) or Douglas Price's *Europe's First Farmers* (2000). Keeley contends that

"prehistorians have increasingly pacified the past," presuming peace or thinking up every possible alternative explanation for the evidence they cannot ignore. In Keeley's *War Before Civilization* (1996), he accused archaeologists of being in denial on the subject.

Witness archaeologist Lisa Valkenier suggesting in 1997 that hilltop constructions along the Peruvian coast are significant because peaks are sacred in Andean cosmology. Their enclosing walls and narrow guarded entries may have more to do with restricting access to the huacas, or sacred shrines, on top of the hills than protecting defenders and barring entry to any potential attackers. How else but by empathy can one formulate such an interpretation in an area with a long defensive wall and hundreds of defensively located fortresses, some still containing piles of sling missiles ready to be used; where a common artistic motif is the parading and execution of defeated enemies; where hundreds were sacrificed; and where there is ample evidence of conquest, no-man's lands, specialized weapons, and so on?

A talk I gave at the Mesa Verde National Park last summer, in which I pointed out that the over 700-year-old cliff dwellings were built in response to warfare, raised the hackles of National Park Service personnel unwilling to accept anything but the peaceful Anasazi message peddled by their superiors. In fact, in the classic book *Indians of Mesa Verde*, published in 1961 by the park service, author Don Watson first describes the Mesa Verde people as "peaceful farming Indians," and admits that the cliff dwellings had a defensive aspect, but since he had already decided that the inhabitants were peaceful, the threat must have been from a new enemy—marauding nomadic Indians. This is in spite of the fact that there is ample evidence of Southwestern warfare for more than a thousand years before the cliff dwellings were built, and there is no evidence for the intrusion of nomadic peoples at this time.

Of the hundreds of research projects in the Southwest, only one—led by Jonathan Haas and Winifred Creamer of the Field Museum and Northern Illinois University, respectively—deliberately set out to research prehistoric warfare. They demonstrated quite convincingly that the Arizona cliff dwellings of the Tsegi Canyon area (known best for Betatakin and Kiet Siel ruins) were defensive, and their locations were not selected for ideology or because they were breezier and cooler in summer and warmer in the winter, as was previously argued by almost all Southwestern archaeologists.

For most prehistoric cultures, one has to piece together the evidence for warfare from artifactual bits and pieces. Most human history involved foragers, and so they are particularly relevant. They too were not peaceful. We know from ethnography that the Inuit (Eskimo) and Australian Aborigines engaged in warfare. We've also discovered remains of prehistoric bone armor in the Arctic, and skeletal evidence of deadly blows to the head among the prehistoric Aborigines have been well documented. Surprising to some is the skeletal evidence for warfare in prehistoric California, once thought of as a land of peaceful acorn gatherers. The prehistoric people who lived in southern California had the highest incident of warfare deaths known anywhere in the world. Thirty percent of a large sample of males dating to

the first centuries A.D. had wounds or died violent deaths. About half that number of women had similar histories. When we remember that not all warfare deaths leave skeletal evidence, this becomes a staggering number.

There was nothing unique about the farmers of the Southwest. From the Neolithic farmers of the Middle East and Europe to the New Guinea highlanders in the twentieth century, tribally organized farmers probably had the most intense warfare of any type of society. Early villages in China, the Yucatán, present-day Pakistan, and Micronesia were well fortified. Ancient farmers in coastal Peru had plenty of forts. All Polynesian societies had warfare, from the smallest islands like Tikopia, to Tahiti, New Zealand (more than four thousand prehistoric forts), and Hawaii. No-man's lands separated farming settlements in Okinawa, Oaxaca, and the southeastern United States. Such societies took trophy heads and cannibalized their enemies. Their skeletal remains show ample evidence of violent deaths. All well-studied prehistoric farming societies had warfare. They may have had intervals of peace, but over the span of hundreds of years there is plenty of evidence for real, deadly warfare.

When farmers initially took over the world, they did so as warriors, grabbing land as they spread out from the Levant through the Middle East into Europe, or from South China down through Southeast Asia. Later, complex societies like the Maya, the Inca, the Sumerians, and the Hawaiians were no less belligerent. Here, conflict took on a new dimension. Fortresses, defensive walls hundreds of miles

Murder Or War?

In 2001, an X-ray revealed that Ötzi, the 5,000-year-old "Iceman" found near the Italian-Austrian border a decade earlier, had been shot in his left shoulder with a flint arrowhead. (See page 1 of the photo insert.) Though it stopped short of any major organs, the small arrowhead probably severed nerves in his shoulder, making his left arm useless and limiting his chance of survival. But bruises on his torso and a gash on his hand indicate that the arrowhead was only part of the story. Blood identified as coming from four other men was found on his clothing and tools, suggesting multiple attackers had assailed him from several different sides.

Even earlier examples of attacks, likely with the intent to kill, have been found. In 1997, researchers found a small fragment of flint in the 13,000-year-old pelvis of a woman found in a cave in San Teodoro, Sicily. The fragment's size and shape indicate it was from an arrowhead rather than a spear. The bone showed signs of having healed around the fragment suggesting that the woman survived the attack. Ancient violence was not limited to the Old World. The 9,300-year-old Kennewick Man, discovered in eastern Washington in 1996, appears to have suffered an injury similar to the woman in Sicily. He was hit in the pelvis with a stone-tipped dart launched from an atlatl or spearthrower. His wound also seems to have healed completely, though it would have caused a significant amount of pain and inflammation and would have limited his mobility.

It is impossible to know whether Ötzi or the others were isolated victims or casualties in larger conflicts. However, all three discoveries indicate that prehistoric humans used technology not just for hunting animals, but also for engaging in combat with each other.

by ALEXANDER BENENSON

long, and weapons and armor expertly crafted by specialists all gave the warfare of these societies a heightened visibility.

There is a danger in making too much of the increased visibility of warfare we see in these complex societies. This is especially true for societies with writing. When there are no texts, it is easy to see no warfare. But the opposite is true. As soon as societies can write, they write about warfare. It is not a case of literate societies having warfare for the first time, but their being able to write about what had been going on for a long time. Also, many of these literate societies link to European civilization in one way or another, and so this raises the specter of Europeans being warlike and spreading war to inherently peaceful people elsewhere, a patently false but prevalent notion. Viewing warfare from the perspective of literate societies tells us nothing about the thousands of years of human societies that were not civilizations—that is, almost all of human history. So we must not rely too much on the small time slice represented by literate societies if we want to understand warfare in the past.

The Maya were once considered a peaceful society led by scholarly priests. That all changed when the texts written by their leaders could be read, revealing a long history of warfare and conquest. Most Mayanists now accept that there was warfare, but many still resist dealing with its scale or implications. Was there population growth that resulted in resource depletion, as throughout the rest of the world? We would expect the Maya to have been fighting each other over valuable farmlands as a consequence, but Mayanist Linda Schele concluded in 1984 that "I do not think it [warfare] was territorial for the most part," even though texts discuss conquest and fortifications are present at sites like El Mirador, Calakmul, Tikal, Yaxuná, Uxmal, and many others from different time periods. Why fortify themselves, if no one wanted to capture them?

Today, more Maya archaeologists are looking at warfare in a systematic way, by mapping defensive features, finding images of destruction, and dating these events. A new breed of younger scholars is finding evidence of warfare throughout the Maya past. Where are the no-man's lands that almost always open up between competing states because they are too dangerous to live in? Warfare must have been intimately involved in the development of Maya civilization, and resource stress must have been widespread.

Demonstrating the prevalence of warfare is not an end in itself. It is only the first step in understanding why there was so much, why it was "rational" for everyone to engage in it all the time. I believe the question of warfare links to the availability of resources.

During the 1960s, I lived in Western Samoa as a Peace Corps volunteer on what seemed to be an idyllic South Pacific island—exactly like those painted by Paul Gauguin. Breadfruit and coconut groves grew all around my village, and I resided in a thatched-roof house with no walls beneath a giant mango tree. If ever there was a Garden of Eden, this was it. I lived with a family headed by an extremely intelligent elderly chief named Sila. One day, Sila happened to mention that the island's trees did not bear fruit as they had when he was a child. He attributed the decline to the possibility that the presence of radio transmissions had affected production, since Western Samoa (now known as Samoa) had its own radio station by then. I suggested that what had changed was not that there was less fruit but that there were more mouths to feed. Upon reflection, Sila decided I was probably right. Being an astute manager, he was already taking the precaution of expanding his farm plots into some of the last remaining farmable land on the island, at considerable cost and effort, to ensure adequate food for his growing family. Sila was aware of his escalating provisioning problems but was not quite able to grasp the overall demographic situation. Why was this?

The simple answer is that the rate of population change in our small Samoan village was so gradual that during an adult life span growth was not dramatic enough to be fully comprehended. The same thing happens to us all the time. Communities grow and change composition, and often only after the process is well advanced do we recognize just how significant the changes have been—and we have the benefit of historic documents, old photographs, long life spans, and government census surveys. All human societies can grow substantially over time, and all did whenever resources permitted. The change may seem small in one person's lifetime, but over a couple of hundred years, populations can and do double, triple, or quadruple in size.

The consequences of these changes become evident only when there is a crisis. The same can be said for environmental changes. The forests of Central America were being denuded and encroached upon for many years, but it took Hurricane Mitch, which ravaged most of the region in late October 1998, to produce the dramatic flooding and devastation that fully demonstrated the magnitude of the problem: too many people cutting down the forest and farming steep hillsides to survive. The natural environment is resilient and at the same time delicate, as modern society keeps finding out. And it was just so in the past.

These observations about Mother Nature are incompatible with popular myths about peaceful people living in ecological balance with nature in the past. A peaceful past is possible only if you live in ecological balance. If you live in a Garden of Eden surrounded by plenty, why fight? By this logic, warfare is a sure thing when natural resources run dry. If someone as smart as Sila couldn't perceive population growth, and if humans all over Earth continue to degrade their environments, could people living in the past have been any different?

A study by Canadian social scientists Christina Mesquida and Neil Wiener has shown that the greater the proportion of a society is composed of unmarried young men, the greater the likelihood of war. Why such a correlation? It is not because the young men are not married; it is because they cannot get married. They are too poor to support wives and families. The idea that poverty breeds war is far from original. The reason poverty exists has remained the same since the beginning of time: humans have invariably overexploited their resources because they have always outgrown them.

There is another lesson from past warfare. It stops. From foragers to farmers, to more complex societies, when people no longer have resource stress they stop fighting. When the climate greatly improves, warfare declines. For example, in a variety of places the medieval warm interval of circa 900–1100 improved farming conditions. The great towns of Chaco Canyon were built at this time, and it was the time of archaeologist Stephen Lekson's *Pax Chaco*—the longest period of peace in the Southwest. It is no accident that the era of Gothic cathedrals was a response to similar climate improvement. Another surprising fact is that the amount of warfare has declined over time. If we count the proportion of a society that died from warfare, and not the size of the armies, as the true measure of warfare, then we find that foragers and farmers have much higher death rates—often approaching 25 percent of the men—than more recent complex societies. No complex society, including modern states, ever approached this level of warfare.

If warfare has ultimately been a constant battle over scarce resources, then solving the resource problem will enable us to become better at ridding ourselves of conflict.

There have been several great "revolutions" in human history: control of fire, the acquisition of speech, the agricultural revolution, the development of complex societies.

...One of the most recent, the Industrial Revolution, has lowered the birth rate and increased available resources. History shows that peoples with strong animosities stop fighting after adequate resources are established and the benefits of cooperation recognized. The Hopi today are some of the most peaceful people on earth, yet their history is filled with warfare. The Gebusi of lowland New Guinea, the African Kung Bushmen, the Mbuti Pygmies of central Africa, the Sanpoi and their neighbors of the southern Columbia River, and the Sirionno of Amazonia are all peoples who are noted for being peaceful, yet archaeology and historical accounts provide ample evidence of past warfare. Sometimes things changed in a generation; at other times it took longer. Adequate food and opportunity does not instantly translate into peace, but it will, given time.

The fact that it can take several generations or longer to establish peace between warring factions is little comfort for those engaged in the world's present conflicts. Add to this a recent change in the decision-making process that leads to war. In most traditional societies, be they forager bands, tribal farmers, or even complex chiefdoms, no individual held enough power to start a war on his own. A consensus was needed; pros and cons were carefully weighed and hotheads were not tolerated. The risks to all were too great. Moreover, failure of leadership was quickly recognized, and poor leaders were replaced. No Hitler or Saddam Hussein would have been tolerated. Past wars were necessary for survival, and therefore were rational; too often today this is not the case. We cannot go back to forager-band–type consensus, but the world must work harder at keeping single individuals from gaining the power to start wars. We know from archaeology that the amount of warfare has declined markedly over the course of human history and that peace can prevail under the right circumstances. In spite of the conflict we see around us, we are doing better, and there is less warfare in the world today than there ever has been. Ending it may be a slow process, but we are making headway.

Unearthing a Violent Past

ARCHAEOLOGISTS HAVE FOUND EVIDENCE OF WARFARE BETWEEN PREHISTORIC VILLAGES AROUND THE WORLD.

by ALEXANDER BENENSON

T wo of the most graphic examples of prehistoric village warfare are the mass graves excavated at Crow Creek, South Dakota, and Talheim, Germany. The remains found at these sites bespeak brutal strife and call into question modern idealized images of prehistoric people as noble savages or pacificists.

Uncovered in 1978, the Crow Creek mass grave held nearly 500 men, women, and children. (See page 1 of the photo insert.) The largest Native American mass burial site ever, it was discovered by archaeologists working to stabilize a portion of the river bank eroded by waves long a Missouri River reservoir in central South Dakota. Many of the bones, dated to around A.D. 1325, bore traces of fatal wounds or mutilation after death. Who were the killers? What had provoked them to such violence?

Those interred at Crow Creek were members of a group of Native Americans that scholars call the Initial Coalescent

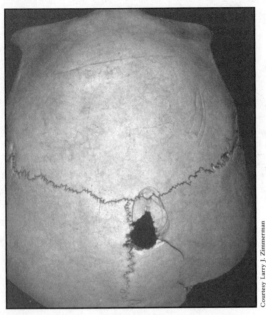

Courtesy Larry J. Zimmerman

Many of the remains from Crow Creek show evidence of trauma such as this skull fracture.

tradition peoples, ancestors of today's Arikara people. In the face of frequent droughts and scarce resources, they had migrated from what is now Iowa, Nebraska, and northern Kansas. The Missouri offered a steady source of water and rich soil to grow corn, squash, and beans. Excavations of sites in this area show a population boom throughout the late thirteenth and early fourteenth centuries. As many as 8,000 people are thought to have settled along the 80 miles of river upstream from Crow Creek around this time. By 1325, there were probably close to 15 villages established in the area, but the new prosperity would prove to be a double-edged sword for the villagers at Crow Creek.

The people depended on agriculture for survival, but the explosive population growth led to increased competition, for access to

water and arable land, and perhaps even warfare. The Crow Creek village, situated between two streams, was prime real estate. Archaeological evidence and aerial photography show its residents had begun work on an extensive fortification system, including a six-foot-wide, six-foot-deep, 1,250-foot-long trench that guarded the one approach to their village not protected by natural obstacles. Archaeologists believe that the need for resources eventually prompted a neighboring tribe village to attack Crow Creek. It probably took place in late fall or early winter, just as concerns about the availability of food would have reached their height. Archaeologists think the attackers crossed the village's unfinished trench and, once inside, set fire to the earthlodges. A close examination of the bones paints a grisly picture of what happened next.

Some skulls have fractures from blows. Other marks indicate that the attackers mutilated the bodies, cutting off hands and feet, and in some cases the head. Scalping marks were also found on the frontal bones of several skulls. Tooth marks from scavenging animals show that the bodies were not buried right away, although remnants of an earthen burial covering and ceremonial fire were found on top of the grave. The mass grave contains fewer female remains than would be expected, indicating that many of the younger women were probably taken by the killers.

Evidence of pathology on the bones provides a window into the lives of the Crow Creek villagers. Many of the bones show growth-check lines, caused by malnutrition or even starvation. In addition some 100 bones exhibit a honeycomb pattern typically associated with scurvy, which could have been caused by a deficiency in vitamin C. Other pathologies on the bones are consistent with iron and protein deficiencies. About half of the upper jawbones found show signs of some kind of inflammation, often the result of a starchy, corn-rich diet. The evidence suggests that maintaining a reliable source of quality nutrition was a lifelong struggle for people in and around Crow Creek, a struggle that would have only been made more difficult by the rapid population growth. Malnourished, and possibly on the verge of starvation it is easy to see how a desperate nearby village could have been driven to turn on its neighbors.

The burial site, along with the remains of the settlement, all sit on what is now the Crow Creek Sioux Reservation. The Sioux (Lakota/Dakota) people were extremely concerned about the excavation of the remains. To ease their worries, archaeologists hired several Sioux excavators and sought the advice of a Lakota holy man, who built a sweatlodge near the burial site. The excavation proceeded only after he had received spiritual confirmation from the *wanagi* guardian spirits that disturbing these dead was permitted. The reburial of the remains on the site involved several traditional Lakota ceremonies and Christian rituals. The next day, an Arikara holy woman conducted a small, private ceremony at the site in honor of her ancestors.

IN 1983, A MAN IN TALHEIM, southern Germany, inadvertently dug up bones while gardening. The bones turned out to be human,

and in the vicinity of 7,000 years old. A weeklong excavation ensued, revealing a small ten-by-five-foot chamber filled with the remains of at least 34 Middle Neolithic farmers. But what was most surprising was the story that their fractured skulls and scattered arms and legs told. These villagers had been viciously murdered. Some of their bones had breaks that had healed—suggesting the people were no strangers to violence.

The skeletal evidence indicates the inhabitants of Talheim, who belonged to the Linear Pottery culture, were killed in a variety of ways. Some skulls had oval-shaped holes punched out of them, the size and shape of which match precisely with that of the sharpened edge of the polished stone axes associated with the Linear Pottery culture. Other skulls have deep, rounded depressions. These men and women had been bludgeoned to death. Two skulls showed injury from flint arrowheads.

The bodies had been thrown hastily into the grave, some face first, some lying sprawled out on their backs, their arms and legs intertwined. This is in stark contrast to the normal Linear Pottery graves that usually contain only one person carefully arranged in a crouching position.

The motivation for the massacre is difficult to discern. Evidence such as the use of polished, stone axes suggests that the killers might have been other Linear Pottery farmers rather than the indigenous forest-dwelling foragers, often cited as the farmer's greatest threat. The attack was probably prompted by competition for local resources.

Icons of War

ANCIENT ARTWORKS ATTEST THE MILITARY MIGHT OF EARLY RULERS OF EGYPT AND SUMER.

by MARK ROSE

At the end of the fourth and in the early third millennium B.C., early kings and city-states vied for power in Egypt and Mesopotamia. From this period come two iconic artifacts from the beginnings of state warfare: the Narmer Palette and the Standard of Ur.

In the winter of 1897–1898, the British archaeologist James Quibell made an extraordinary discovery, a cache of ritual objects from an early temple at Hierakonpolis, about 60 miles south of Luxor. Among the objects was an elaborately carved gray stone palette, an oversize ceremonial version of the type of stone used for grinding cosmetic pigments. A victorious King Narmer, identified by hieroglyphs, is shown on the palette with his defeated enemies. (See page 2 of the photo insert.)

On one side, Narmer wears the red crown of Lower Egypt (the Delta region) in a procession to view executed enemies. These prisoners, with their arms bound, are shown laid out in two rows with their severed heads and genitals between their feet. In the center of the palette is the circular grinding area around which loop the necks of two animals, perhaps signifying the joining of Upper and Lower Egypt. At the bottom, the king is represented by a mighty bull able to destroy people and cities that oppose him. On the other side, Narmer wears the white crown of Upper Egypt (the Nile Valley) and raises his mace to smite an enemy. Nearby, the falcon god Horus presents Narmer with the people and land of the papyrus plant; and below, the bodies of vanquished enemies.

Significantly, this is the earliest representation we know that shows a king wearing both crowns of Upper and Lower Egypt. On that basis, the palette was interpreted as commemorating the unification of Egypt, apparently accomplished through the conquest by Narmer, based in the southern city Hierakonpolis, of a northern rival in the Delta around 3100 B.C. We now know, however, that many of the cultural and economic underpinnings of Egyptian civilization were coming together in the centuries before Narmer, so it is simplistic to view him as the great founder of Egypt. It may be he was one of several kings who effected the unification over a period of time, and perhaps that was sometimes accomplished by military might. So a more cautious reading of the palette is in order. Nonetheless, it is a compelling, and frightening, statement of the power wielded by the king.

BEGINNING IN 1926, Leonard Woolley excavated the Royal Cemetery of Ur, a Sumerian city-state in what is now southern Iraq. The elaborate burials were of Ur's elite, likely the royal family, who were accompanied in death by sacrificed officials, guards, and slaves, as well as by finely crafted objects of gold, silver, and semiprecious stone. Mesopotamia at the time of the Royal Cemetery, about 2600–2400 B.C., was a mosaic of city-states—Ur, Umma, Lagash, Kish, Mari, Eshnunna, and others—each ruled by its own dynasty. These city-states often came into conflict with one another over matters ranging from border disputes and control of water to questions of dynastic power and status. The last resort, when negotiations and bullying failed, was war, which the city-states prosecuted with well-equipped armies.

In the Royal Cemetery, Woolley discovered one of earliest representations of a Sumerian army. It appears on a rectangular box inlaid with shell, red limestone, and lapis lazuli, set in bitumen (a naturally occurring asphalt). The box, which measures 19.5 inches in length and 8.5 inches in height, is known as the Standard of Ur. (See page 1 of the photo insert.) Woolley thought it had been mounted on pole and was carried in processions, hence the name, but it could also have been the sounding box of a musical instrument. Whatever its function, the scenes on the box were intended to show the prosperity and power of Ur and its ruling dynasty. One side (known as the "Peace" side) shows, in an upper row or register seated figures at a banquet, drinking and listening to a musician playing a lyre. In two lower registers, men lead animals and bring goods in a veritable parade of wealth. The opposite, or "War" side, is also arranged in three registers. In the topmost, a large figure in the center, presumably the king, watches as soldiers bring naked captives before him; behind the king are more soldiers and his chariot. The middle register shows (on the left) a line of foot soldiers with spears, cloaks, and helmets and (on the right) enemy soldiers being killed. The bottom register depicts an attack by four-wheeled chariots, each manned by a driver and a fighter, and pulled by four donkeys. Beneath the wheels of the chariots can be seen the crushed, lifeless bodies of the foe.

We don't know particulars of the battle scenes on the Standard of Ur—if, indeed, they show a specific historical event. But we do know of a long border conflict between the city-states Lagash and Umma from the same period. Our sources include another commemorative relief, known as the Vulture Stele, and ancient texts. The Vulture Stele, now in fragments, was found at Lagash and dates from around 2525–2450 B.C. Carved on one side of the largest piece is a group of soldiers drawn up for battle and marching over the corpses of slain enemies. The men are equipped similarly to the soldiers of Ur but carry large rectangular shields as well. On the reverse side, captured enemies are shown in a giant net held by the patron god of Lagash. A second fragment, showing vultures eating the dead on the battlefield, gives the stele its name.

The evidence from the city-states of Sumer shows that even at this early time, rulers were able to field armies that numbered in the thousands of soldiers. Some of these at least went into battle with standard-ized gear and moved in infantry formations. Others, perhaps an elite group, formed a separate chariot corps.

Life and Death in a Maya War Zone

WITHIN A YUCATÁN PYRAMID LIE THE GRIM TRACES OF A VIOLENT CHANGE IN RULERSHIP—THE REMAINS OF A SLAUGHTERED ROYAL FAMILY.

by CHARLES SUHLER *and* DAVID FRIEDEL

We found burial 24 quite by accident, having walked over it for weeks as we worked on the west face of a 1,700-year-old pyramid on the North Acropolis of Yaxuná, a Classic Maya site in northern Yucatán. Near the end of the 1996 field season, Don Bernardino, one of our field crew, noticed a small hole near one of the trenches. We peered in and saw a large corbel-vaulted chamber, its floor covered in fine, pale dirt—a sealed royal tomb. We were already two weeks into the excavation of the burial of an Early Classic king in an adjacent pyramid, the first sealed royal tomb in northern Yucatán discovered by archaeologists. Finding a second was an embarrassment of riches for one season, but manageable. We immediately began digging.

The tomb chamber was a little more than six feet long and less than five feet wide, with a stairway at one end leading to its entrance. Forensics expert Sharon Bennett cleared the sediment away, which revealed a pile of human bones and polychrome ceramic vessels. We suspected that the bones were those of sacrificial victims placed in the antechamber of a king's burial, like those found at the entrance to the late seventh-century tomb of Pacal at Palenque in Chiapas. But where a second chamber should have been there was nothing.

At the bottom of the pile of bones were the remains of the tomb's principal occupant, a male more than 55 years old. He had been decapitated, his head tossed atop the heap of bodies. The contorted positions of many of them suggested they had been thrown down the stairs. Near his shoulders was an obsidian blade for bloodletting; near his feet, the charred remains of a polished white shell crown. This type of royal headdress, known as a *sak-hunal* or "white oneness," usually consisted of a white cloth band adorned with greenstone talismans. Near the crown we found a small burnt jade carving of a quetzal bird, presumably a jewel from a diadem.

The bones of an adolescent girl and a young woman, neither of whom had borne children, flanked the man's skeleton. Each also wore a sak-hunal. The bones of an infant lay in the girl's lap; the young woman cradled a doll-like goddess effigy in her left arm. Other artifacts in the tomb included jade jewels, carved bones, small mosaic pieces, and little pots and pitchers from a set used to prepare ritual enemas. Altogether, the tomb contained the remains of 11 murdered men, women, and children.

We wondered who these people were and why so many had been placed in a tomb chamber usually reserved for a single person. Then it dawned on us. We had stumbled onto the dark side of Maya history. Like the murder of the Romanovs after the Bolshevik Revolution, the sacrifice of the royal family in burial 24 had accompanied a violent change in rulership.

LOOKING OUT OVER THE LOW, scrub forest and green, fallow fields surrounding the site today, it is hard to imagine the nobles, warriors, merchants, and artisans who once lived in the dense scatter of buildings here. Ten miles south of Chichén Itzá, Yaxuná was founded sometime in the Middle Preclassic, around 500 B.C. The largest known pyramid in Yucatán dating to that period anchors the city's southern end. Fifty miles inland, Yaxuná was a waystation on an overland trade route linking the peninsula's central cities—Calakmul, El Mirador, and Nakbé—with the salt beds of the north coast. The site had natural wells for water, level ground for crops, and abundant surface stone for construction. Until the rise of Chichén Itzá in the eighth century A.D., Yaxuná was the largest city in the central northern lowlands. Its strategic location, however, was not without drawbacks, for Yaxuná became a valuable pawn in the power struggles of the lowland Maya world.

We came to Yaxuná in 1987 looking for evidence of urban warfare dating to the time of Chichén Itzá's rise to preeminence. Little did we suspect that more than a decade of work would yield signs of no fewer than six deliberate destruction events between the fourth and thirteenth centuries. Nowhere was this more apparent than in the charred building remains, broken pottery, and desecrated burials in the site's North Acropolis. The event that ended the lives of those found in burial 24, dated to the late fourth or early fifth century A.D., is the earliest known in the long sequence of violent acts of conquest.

Most of the damage can be linked to two major wars: a pan-peninsular struggle between Tikal, in the Petén region of Guatemala, and a site represented by a snake-head emblem glyph, quite possibly Calakmul in southern Campeche, in the fourth, fifth, and sixth centuries; and a conflict that pitted Chichén Itzá against an alliance of Puuc cities to the west and Cobá to the east, during the ninth and tenth centuries.

Data collected during earlier surveys and excavations at the site suggested that Yaxuná had little if any relationship with Chichén Itzá. George Brainerd of the University of California, Berkeley, who excavated the site during the 1940s and 1950s, was surprised by its apparent lack of Sotuta ceramics, typified by red slatewares and large, wide-necked, black-on-cream vessels, which were produced in abundance at Chichén Itzá. Yaxuná did, however, have links with many other cities of the northern Yucatán. Earlier in this century Mayanist J. Eric S. Thompson had noted the presence at Yaxuná of several Puuc-style buildings, recognizable by their distinctive columned facades, suggesting that the site had strong ties to cities such as Uxmal, Sayil, and Kabah, 70 miles to the west. A 60-mile *sacbé,* or stone causeway, linking Yaxuná with Cobá to the east was built at the beginning of the seventh century.

Warriors from Cobá had seized Yaxuná at the beginning of the Late Classic, about A.D. 600. We found destroyed public buildings dating to this period, as well as Cehpech ceramics typical of Cobá and the Puuc cities in the fill just above the destruction layer. Justine Shaw, one of our graduate students, believes that the new overlords must have harnessed most of the local labor for construction of the sacbé, since few new structures were built at the site during this time. For the rest of the Late Classic period, Yaxuná appears to have remained a frontier outpost of Cobá.

We believe that in the ensuing Terminal Classic period, at the beginning of the ninth century, Cobá strengthened its relationship with the Puuc cities in an attempt to consolidate its control of the peninsula. As a crucial link between Cobá and its allies, Yaxuná was quickly refurbished. Rather than building anew, however, its rulers simply refaced existing structures, ignoring their original Preclassic or Early Classic designs. By the late ninth century, however, Chichén Itzá had defeated the alliance. We believe that the magnificent set of murals adorning Chichén Itzá's Temple of the Jaguars depicts this victory.

We knew from earlier surveys that there were no obvious fortifications at Yaxuná. We did hope to find evidence of urban warfare and conquest in a change of ceramics from the Cehpech of Cobá and the Puuc cities to the Sotuta types of Chichén Itzá. We began excavating the remains of a small Puuc-style palace on the North Acropolis in 1992. A three-room structure decorated with a columned facade and reliefs with war symbolism, including shields and battle standards, the palace had been built midway up the south face of an Early Classic pyramid.

As we cleared the area in front of it we realized that the palace had been deliberately destroyed. Ornamental blocks had been pulled from its facade. Beneath and around them were thick concentrations of smashed vessels with lug handles mixed with marl, a white limy dirt. We had seen such destruction years earlier during excavations at the Late Preclassic site of Cerros in Belize. James Garber, Robin Robertson, Maynard Cliff, and other colleagues from that project described this type of destruction as a termination ritual, a reverential release of sacred power undertaken prior to the construction of a new temple over an old one. At Cerros, evidence of these rituals included concentrations of intentionally smashed ceramic vessels, typically loop-lugged jars, buried in layers of distinctive white marl banked against the walls of platforms and pyramids.

As we cleared the debris from the exterior of the palace, James Ambrosino, another of our graduate students, began excavating the interior. During the 1995 field season, he had discovered the remains of a noblewoman entombed beneath the floor of the palace's west room. In her right hand she held pieces of a small metal mirror inlaid with mosaic, a symbol of accession to high office. Her burial, however, had been violated, apparently during the destruction of the palace; debris and white marl had fallen into the tomb. The bones of her upper torso and head had been scattered, and her burial offerings smashed. Some of the stonework had been removed, causing the masonry roof to cave in; the tomb had then been set on fire.

In the palace destruction debris we found, for the first time at Yaxuná, Sotuta ceramics and green obsidian knife blades characteristic of Chichén Itzá. We surmised from this that warriors from Chichén Itzá had destroyed the palace and the tomb. We began to suspect that we were dealing with an urban battlefield, and that this termination ritual was an act of war, rather than reverence.

As the excavation progressed, we attempted to define the relationship between the palace and the pyramid against which it was built. Behind the palace we encountered the remains of an Early Classic temple atop the pyramid. A pair of offering vessels had been placed in a trench dug through its floor: a black-slipped jar in the western end and a red-slipped jar in the eastern. The black jar had a black stone ax jammed inside it beneath which was a set of bright greenstone jewels. The red jar had a lid of worked pottery and contained a single greenstone portrait jewel depicting a god or a king, a large square plaque made of red spondylus shell, and several shell and jade beads. The offerings had been sealed in the trench and a dance platform built atop the temple remains. It was during the excavation of a terrace extending from the dance platform that we came upon burial 24. The tomb chamber had been built over a portion of the central stairway that once led up to the Early Classic temple. Stratigraphically, the cached vessels and burial 24 belonged to a single destruction-construction event.

As soon as we discovered the tomb, we understood the significance of the ax over the jewels in the black pot. In Maya glyphs, an image of an ax is read *ch'ak*. As a verb, it is *ch'akah,* to ax or decapitate and, more generally, to destroy, as in *ch'akah kun,* to ax or destroy a seat of power. A related concept is *ch'aktel,* scaffold, which can be spelled with the ax glyph. Classic Maya imagery indicates that both decapitation sacrifices and royal accessions were performed on scaffolds. We suspect that such a scaffold may have been built atop the dance platform.

Red shell of the kind used to make the beads found in the red cache vessel is called *k'an* in Mayan. This word means precious and, more generally, the color yellow, but k'an also names the birthplace of the resurrected Hun-Nal-Yeh, the primordial Maya maize god. According to some versions of the Maya creation story, Hun-Nal-Yeh, after being beheaded by gods of the underworld, was reborn from his own severed head as a handsome young man, dressed by beautiful girls for triumphal dancing. That the sacrifice of those in burial 24 may have signaled the birth of a new dynasty at the site is an intriguing speculation.

Who would have murdered Yaxuná's royal family during the late fourth or early fifth century? Our excavations yielded a number of tantalizing clues. The cache vessels are of a type known from the city of Oxkintok, 75 miles to the east, but unknown at Yaxuná except in this set of offerings. We know that Oxkintok was an ally of Tikal during its Early Classic expansion into the Maya lowlands based on similarities in ceramic assemblages from the two sites dating to this period.

From inscriptions carved on monuments at Tikal and its northern neighbor, Uaxactún, we know that the king of Tikal, Toh-Chak-I'Chak, and his comrade-in-arms,

K'ak'-Sih, conquered Uaxactún in A.D. 378. Artifacts typical of the central Mexican site of Teotihuacan found at Tikal and images of K'ak'-Sih and Yax-Ain, Toh-Chak-I'Chak's son, dressed as Teotihuacano warrior kings lead us to believe that Tikal defeated its enemies because it was closely allied with Teotihuacan. K'ak'-Sih is portrayed on stela 5 at Uaxactún wearing the animal tails and balloon headdress of the Tlaloc-Venus war cult practiced at Teotihuacan. Atop his headdress is a macaw, a symbol that also occurs on a painted vessel from Yax-Ain's tomb, which shows the ruler as a Teotihuacan war god, Waxaklahun-U-Bah-Kan.

Vessels found in Yaxuná burial 24 include some made in Teotihuacan style. A ceramic plate found atop the king's burnt crown bears the portrait of a lord dressed in a red macaw costume and wearing the animal tails of the Tlaloc-Venus war cult. The goddess effigy cradled by the young woman in the tomb bears the same step-fret facial markings as the Teotihuacan Great Goddess. We suspect that the executioners placed these items in the tomb to show their own sources of authority and affiliation with the Tikal-Teotihuacan alliance.

A defaced and broken monument known as Yaxuná stela 1, found by Brainerd not far from the Early Classic temple, also depicts a lord in Tlaloc-Venus war regalia strikingly similar to the portraits of Yax-Ain on Tikal stela 31. It is possible that stela 1 was commissioned by the man responsible for the deaths of those in burial 24, and that the monument may have stood in front of a vaulted gallery constructed in association with the dance platform and terrace along the western side of the pyramid. Several years ago ceramicist Dave Johnstone of Southern Methodist University found a broken monolith with a k'an glyph carved on it in the ballcourt south of the North Acropolis. The stone was of the same color, dimensions, and finish as monoliths used to construct the staircase built in association with the dance platform, terrace, and gallery. The k'an glyph might have been part of a victory text carved into the staircase risers.

Why should Yaxuná matter to the alliance? Slowly but surely a picture is emerging of a pan-peninsular war in the Maya lowlands of the Classic period, one that pitted two confederacies, one led by Tikal some 220 miles south of Yaxuná and the other by Calakmul 170 miles to the south, against each other. Yaxuná's North Acropolis and Calakmul's main plaza are mirror images of each other, leading us to suspect that these two sites were allies. If that was the case then Yaxuná would have been a prime target for Oxkintok, an ally of Tikal and Teotihuacan.

We do not know how long the conquerors held onto the city, but the dance platform, terrace, and gallery that they built were destroyed during a later conquest, perhaps when Cobá seized the city at the beginning of the seventh century. The gallery vault was brought down, the staircase disassembled, and the stela thrown down and smashed. Whoever did it was careful not to disturb burial 24. We suspect that the conquerors were avengers of the sacrificed king and his entourage.

We know that the warfare did not end with the sacking of the Puuc palace by warriors from Chichén Itzá in the ninth century. Recent excavations in a nearby pyramid have yielded the remains of a middle-aged man who died a violent death. Ceramics found near his grave suggest that he had been sacrificed by warriors from Mayapán sometime in the early thirteenth century, a time when that site was taking control of the northern Yucatán.

In the stratigraphy of the Puuc-style palace and Early Classic temple, long-term patterns of urban warfare are archaeologically visible, and include episodes of deliberate destruction and construction, desecration and dedication. Classic texts tell the story of the winners in these struggles. Evidence such as that gleaned from Yaxuná may yet reveal the story of the losers, giving us a more balanced understanding of Maya history.

Battlers at the Bottom of the World

MAORI WARRIORS BUILT FORTIFICATIONS NOT UNLIKE
THOSE OF THEIR CELTIC COUNTERPARTS.

by BRIAN FAGAN

We were sailing along the coast northward from
Auckland to the Bay of Islands, retracing Captain Cook's epic circumnavigation of New
Zealand in 1769. His charts were so good, we used them to
find our way around. Preoccupied with the problems of
navigation, I was free of archaeology. But a few days later
there we were, standing among the ramparts of an ancient
Maori *pa* (fort), perched high above the Bay of Islands on a
lofty promontory surrounded on three sides by wind-
ruffled water. Below us, white sandy beaches curved around
to other headlands, easy of access and perfect for landing
war canoes. There were no sails on the water, just the sound
of the wind sloughing in the trees. It was easy to imagine
this pa in its heyday, just before the Europeans came, its
ramparts bristling with wooden palisades, and thatch
dwellings huddled inside the fortifications.

In the days that followed, I became intrigued by the pas, remembering my youth, when I lived within easy reach of the great Iron Age hill fort at Maiden Castle in southwestern England. Maiden Castle was investigated by Sir Mortimer Wheeler in one of the classic excavations of all time just before World War II. His description of the Roman attack on the fort in A.D. 43 ranks as one of the most compelling reconstructions of the past ever written. What were the Maori pas like in their heyday? Did they see brutal attacks like Maiden Castle? Were they just forts of permanent settlements? And why did the Maori, a people with no metals, lavish such care on their fortifications?

I started my search with Captain Cook, not only the finest navigator of his day, but a consummate observer of people and places. He had admired the ingenious fortifications of Wharetaewa pa in the Bay of Plenty to the south. He wrote in his journal:

> It is in some places quite inaccessible...and in others very difficult except on that side which fac'd the narrow ridge of the hill on which it stands, here is defended by a double ditch, a bank and two rows of Picketing—the inner row upon the bank but not so near the Crown but what there was good room for men to walk and handle their arms between the Picketing and the inner ditch.

THERE WERE FORMIDABLE defenses with a special staging inside where warriors stood to throw darts at their attackers. The main entrance gate was narrow, only about 12 feet wide, and located right under convenient defensive stages. The houses inside were built on level ground, each fenced and joined to its neighbors by staked paths that made it hard for an attacker to take the entire village. The inhabitants of the pa were prepared for a long siege, having stored an immense quantity of fern roots and many dried fish.

The archaeology of New Zealand encompasses little more than a millennium; it was only settled at the end of the tenth century A.D. The first canoe-loads of Polynesians arrived at the North Island of New Zealand from central or eastern Polynesia, some 3,100 miles to the northeast. These were Neolithic people who brought dogs and only five cultivated plants, among them the *kumara* or sweet potato, taro, and a small species of yam. Judging from excavations on Moturua Island in the Bay of Islands, the earliest Maori relied heavily on fishing and seal hunting for much of their food. Their most famous prey was the flightless moa bird, which became extinct through overhunting within a few centuries. Increasingly, net fishing, fern-root gathering, and agriculture became the basis of the Maori economy. At the same time, Maori society became more complex.

When Europeans arrived in the eighteenth century, Maori groups lived in every part of New Zealand. By this time, warfare was endemic in hierarchical societies ruled by an elite or *ariki* (paramount chiefs), many *rangatira* (warrior chiefs), and *tohunga* (priests). A Maori ariki was sometimes a venerated elder, but usually a warrior of bravery and cunning. He ruled from his pa, occupying his fortified village for at least part of the year, especially during the agricultural season when wars were fought. War itself was surrounded with elaborate rituals that included challenges to single combat and spectacular war dances. Warriors fought naked except for a loincloth, with long wooden spears and *taiaha,* long sticks somewhat resembling quarterstaves.

Traditionally, defensive works were adapted to close-quarters warfare on foot. But they were useless against Europeans armed with muskets. When the French attacked a fortified village at Paeroa in 1772, they simply picked off the defenders on their stages with musket balls, shooting at the Maori through gaps in the wooden palisade. It did not take the Maori long to learn the art of defense against firearms. Some of the fortified positions they erected against British troops during the infamous Maori wars of the 1860s were masterpieces of defensive engineering.

The deserted Maori earthworks on Urupukapuka Island in the heart of the Bay of Islands reminded me of Wheeler's description of the Romans at Maiden's Castle: "In the innermost bay of the entrance, close outside the actual gates, a number of huts had recently been built; there were now set alight, and under the rising clouds of smoke the gates were stormed and the position carried." The Roman attack was efficient and ruthless, a form of utterly professional warfare completely alien to the Celts. Similarly, the Maori's pas were part of an entirely different philosophy of war, one that focused on immediate issues, not long-term imperial gains. *He wahine, he whenua e ngaro ai te tangata,* a Maori proverb explains: "Men die for women and land."

Archaeologist Aileen Fox has dug both pas and Celtic hill forts. She notes that both Celtic and Maori societies were led by war-rior chiefs who went to war to acquire status and prestige, to avenge perceived insults, or simply to attack a weaker neighbor. Like a Celtic chieftain, the prestige of a Maori chief was tied to his ability to defend his people and to lead war parties against near neighbors. All warfare was imbued with deep symbolism. For example, both Celts and Maoris practiced headhunting. The classical author Diodorus described how Celts would cut off the heads of prominent enemies and "embalm [them] in cedar oil and carefully preserve [them] in a cedar chest and these they exhibit to strangers." Likewise the Maori would dry and smoke the tattooed heads of slain chiefs. To both Celts and Maori, the head was a symbol of the whole person, the center of his prowess and bravery. By preserving, or even degrading it by displaying it in public or throwing stones at it, the new owner acquired its good qualities. Fox believes that fortified villages were inevitable in both societies, for both warfare and defense were fundamental social values.

What struck me on that fall day in the Bay of Islands was just how the Celts and the Maori—prehistoric people from entirely different cultural traditions—seem so often to have come up with the same kinds of solutions to problems of daily living and defense. There were times on my brief excursions through the pas when I could imagine the ghost of Sir Mortimer Wheeler by my side conjuring up fierce battles and hard-fought victories from the silent earthworks and hut foundations. Alas, Wheeler has long departed to the world of celestial excavations. The work of studying long-forgotten Maori battles at the bottom of the world has hardly begun.

PART II:
Ancient Warfare

Egypt's New Kingdom Warrior Kings

PHARAOHS TOOK TO THE FIELD TO DEFEND OR EXPAND THEIR EMPIRES.

by MARK ROSE

Throughout much of the New Kingdom (1549–1064 B.C.), Egypt was the greatest military power in the ancient world. It could field an army of 20,000 men, both conscripted native troops and foreign soldiers, such as skilled Nubian archers. But there was more to the army than its large size. One of the Egyptians' strengths was their flexibility in adopting new or improved weapons from outside. In addition to a spear or mace, soldiers might carry a sickle sword, a hacking weapon of Mesopotamian origin. Powerful composite bows and chariots, the pride of the army, were both introduced from the Near East. Late in the New Kingdom, sword began to be used, perhaps coming via Anatolia and among the weapons carried by Sea Peoples who attempted to invade Egypt then.

At the head of the army was the pharaoh. Some pharaohs were content to send generals out to defend frontiers or

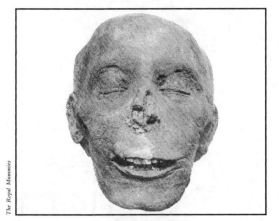

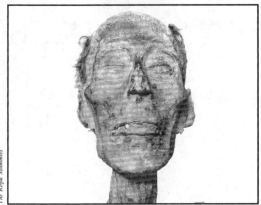

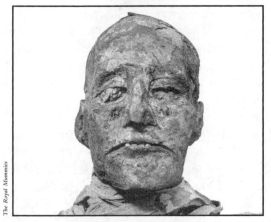

The Royal Mummies

Pharaohs who led Egyptian armies into war included Thutmosis III (top), Ramesses II (middle), and Ramesses III (bottom).

bring rebellious vassals into line, but others took to the field in person and acquitted themselves well. Among the most successful was Thutmosis III (circa 1479–1424 B.C.) of the 18th Dynasty. He began his long string of victories in Syria-Palestine, defeating the king of Qadesh at Megiddo, and capturing the latter city after a seventh-month siege. Later, Thutmosis led an expedition as far as the Euphrates, defeating the king of Mitanni and pushing Egyptian control to the borders of the Babylonian and Hittite empires. Toward the end of his reign, he headed south, campaigning along the Nile into Nubia. Under Thutmosis III, Egypt's power was at its height. But by the end of the Dynasty, around 1298 B.C., the cities of Syria-Palestine were restless, acting independently and even allying themselves with the Hittites. In the 19th Dynasty, Ramesses II (circa 1279–1212 B.C.) attempted to recover lost ground. Taking advantage of Egypt's weakness, the Hittite Empire had extended its influence southward, and Ramesses wanted to counteract that by bringing Qadesh back into the Egyptian fold. Marching in four widely separated divisions, the Egyptians were unaware that the Hittite army was already at Qadesh. Ramesses and the first division set up camp and, as the second division approached, were assaulted by the Hittite chariots. In a close battle, the Egyptians broke at first, then were able to reform and hold the field. On the second day, the entire Egyptian force fought the Hittites to a draw. Egyptians failed to recapture Qadesh, but the Hittites were forced to pull back. Eventually, after several more years of skirmishing, a treaty for mutual nonaggression and defense was signed.

In the early 20th Dynasty, during the reign of Ramesses III (circa 1185–1153 B.C.), Egypt faced one of its gravest military threats, the attempted invasion by a confederacy known as the Sea Peoples. Coming from the central Mediterranean and Aegean, this wave of people included many different groups. Some of them can be recognized from the names by which the Egyptians recorded them: the Peleset (Philistines), Tjeker, Shekelesh (possibly Sikels, the Sicilian natives), Weshesh, Denyen or Dardany (possibly Danoi, the Greeks), and others. The causes of this mass movement are not known. Collapse of regional kingdoms, famine, and regional invasions from farther north are among the possibilities.

Whatever the cause, the Sea Peoples were approaching the border of Egypt and Syria-Palestine in the eighth year of Ramesses III's reign. The story of the ensuing conflict is recorded, both in a long inscription and in battle scenes carved in relief, on the wall of the pharaoh's mortuary temple at Medinet Habu near the Valley of the Kings, the burial place of most New Kingdom rulers. (See page 3 of the photo insert.) The Sea Peoples are described as a formidable force indeed: "no land could stand before their arms: the land of the Hittites, Qode, Carchemesh, Arzawa, and Cyprus were wasted, and they set up a camp in southern Syria. They desolated its people and made its land as if non-existent. They bore fire before them as they came forward toward Egypt."

Ramesses defeated the Sea Peoples in person on land and the Egyptian fleet, supported by archers on the river and canal banks, won in Delta. Ramesses' record of the victory is boastful: "I, king Ramesses III, was made a far-striding hero, conscious of his might, valiant to lead his army in the day of battle. Those who reached my boundary, their seed is not; their heart and their soul are finished forever and ever. As for those who had assembled before them on the sea...they were dragged, overturned, and laid low upon the beach; slain and made heaps from stern to bow of their galleys." Matching the grandiosity of the words, he is depicted at great scale in the battle scenes, mounted on his chariot and firing arrows into the mass of enemy soldiers. Despite the verbal and pictorial bombast, Ramesses III's victory here, and in other campaigns, helped earn him recognition today as Egypt's last great pharaoh.

Was There a Trojan War?

TROY'S CHIEF ARCHAEOLOGIST WEIGHS IN ON THE WESTERN WORLD'S MOST MYTHIC BATTLE.

by Manfred Korfmann

*R*ecorded sometime in the eighth century B.C., the Iliad represents the culmination of several centuries of oral epic poetry that wove a complex story of the relationship between mortals and gods. This narrative takes place against the bloody backdrop of the ten-year-long Greek siege of the city alternatively called Ilios or Troy, a war launched over the abduction of the beautiful Greek queen Helen by the Trojan prince Paris.

The ancient Greeks and Romans generally believed in the historicity of the Trojan War, and even Alexander the Great paid homage at what they believed was the site of the great battle. But eventually Troy was forgotten except for the Iliad, and it wasn't until the late nineteenth century, when Heinrich Schliemann's excavations at the site of Hisarlik in northwestern Turkey raised the possibility that Troy was rediscovered, that scholars would consider the battle between Greeks and Trojans to be more than Homeric fantasy. Some scholars, however, still cast doubt on the notion of a historical Trojan War, stressing that our belief in its existence is based ultimately on the creation of Homer, who was a poet, not a historian.

The late Manfred Korfmann, director of excavations at Hisarlık/Troy beginning 1988, was the first to admit that his team was not at the site to dig for evidence of the fabled event. But evidence in favor of a historical Trojan War appears to grow with each year, and comes not only from archaeologists but from specialists across academia. In an ARCHAEOLOGY exclusive, Troy's chief excavator, with contributions from world-renowned specialists in the fields of Homeric and Hittite studies, explained why it is time for doubters to change their minds about the Western world's most famous—and mythic—battle.

Despite assumptions to the contrary, archaeological work of the new Troy project has not been performed for the purpose of understanding Homer's *Iliad* or the Trojan War. For the past sixteen years, more than 350 scholars, scientists, and technicians from nearly twenty countries have been collaborating on the excavations at the site in northwestern Turkey that began as an Early Bronze Age citadel in the third millennium B.C. and ended as a Byzantine settlement before being abandoned in A.D. 1350. However, as current director of the excavations, I am continually asked if Homer's Trojan War really happened.

The Size of Troy

Troy appears to have been destroyed around 1180 B.C. (this date corresponds to the end of our excavation of levels Troy VIi or VIIa), probably by a war the city lost. (See page 3 of the photo insert.) There is evidence of a conflagration, some skeletons, and heaps of sling bullets. People who have successfully defended their city would have gathered their sling bullets and put them away for another event, but a victorious conqueror would have

done nothing with them. But this does not mean that the conflict was the war—even though ancient tradition usually places it around this time. After a transitional period of a few decades, a new population from the eastern Balkans or the northwestern Black Sea region evidently settled in the ruins of what was probably a much weakened city.

The main argument against associating these ruins with the great city described in the *Iliad* has been that Troy in the Late Bronze Age was a wholly insignificant town and not a place worth fighting over. Our new excavations and the progress of research in southeastern Europe have changed such views regarding Troy considerably.

It appears that this city was, by the standards of this region at that time, very large indeed, and most certainly of supraregional importance in controlling access from the Mediterranean to the Black Sea and from Asia Minor to southeast Europe and vice versa. Its citadel was unparalleled in the wider region and, as far as hitherto known, unmatched anywhere in southeastern Europe. Troy was also evidently attacked repeatedly and had to defend itself again and again, as indicated by repairs undertaken to the citadel's fortifications and efforts to enlarge and strengthen them.

A spectacular result of the new excavations has been the verification of the existence of a lower settlement from the seventeenth to the early twelfth centuries B.C. (Troy levels VI/VIIa) outside and south and east of the citadel. As magnetometer surveys and seven excavations undertaken since 1993 have shown, this lower city was surrounded at least in the thirteenth century by an impres-

Evidence from Hittite Records

The Hittites were a powerful civilization that controlled most of Anatolia in the second millennium B.C. Their language, written in cuneiform script on clay tablets, was recovered and deciphered in the first decades of the twentieth century, but scholars are still wrestling with the problem of placing the cities and countries named in their ancient texts onto modern maps. The kingdom of Arzawa, located roughly in western Anatolia, was a threat to the Hittites throughout most of the fourteenth century B.C. but toward the end of that period was decisively defeated and broken up into provinces. The treaties concluded with the vassal rulers of these provinces are known among the Hittite texts.

Recent inscription readings have allowed scholars to locate the two main Arzawa lands in the central-west part of Turkey, extending from the inland plateau to the coast. The recent recognition that another kingdom, which the Hittites referred to as the Lukka lands, occupied what is now southwest Turkey thus leaves only northwest Anatolia as yet-to-be-filled space on the Hittite map.

One Arzawa land, Wilusa, is known principally from the treaty between its ruler Alaksandu and the Hittite king Mutawalli II (who ruled circa 1295–1272 B.C.). Sparse references in other texts of the fourteenth and thirteenth centuries B.C. imply that Wilusa was the remotest Arzawa land and lay on the coast, and this may be combined with that rare item, a Late Bronze Age city in northwestern Turkey. The evidence of its citadel and lower city is sufficient to suggest the seat of a local ruler of the period; and while the textual evidence points to Wilusa as a land, it would be usual for its capital city to have the same name.

A long letter from a Hittite king, probably Hattusili III (who ruled circa 1267–1237 B.C.), to the king of Ahhiyawa mentions that Wilusa was once a bone of contention between the two. The location of Ahhiyawa has been controversial since its earliest recognition in the Hittite texts in the 1920s. The scattered references to it suggested that it lay across the sea and that its interests often conflicted with those of the Hittites. What is now known of the geography of western Anatolia makes it clear that there could be no room on the mainland for the kingdom of Ahhiyawa. Furthermore, the references to the political interests of Ahhiyawa on the west coast mesh well with increasing archaeological evidence for Mycenaean Greeks in the area, so that it is now widely accepted that "Ahhiyawa" is indeed the Hittite designation for this culture.

From what we now can understand from the Hittite sources, the Arzawa land Wilusa, identified with the archaeological site of Troy, was a point of conflict between the Hittites and the Ahhiyawa. This provides a striking background for Homeric scholars researching the origin of the tradition of the Achaean attack on Ilios. There is every likelihood that the Iliad and the traditions of the Trojan War, however immortalized in epic narrative, do indeed preserve a memory of actual events of the Late Bronze Age.

by J.D. HAWKINS

sive U-shaped fortification ditch, approximately eleven and a half feet wide and six and a half feet deep, hewn into the limestone bedrock. Conclusions about the existence and quality of buildings within the confines of the ditch have been drawn on the basis of several trial trenches and excavations, some of them covering a very large surface area. The layout of the city was confirmed by an intensive and systematic pottery survey in 2003. We have also discovered a cemetery outside the ditch to the south. The most recent excavations have determined that Troy, which now covers about seventy-five acres, is about fifteen times larger than previously thought.

The Setting of the *Iliad*

Homer took for granted that his audience knew a war had been fought for what was alternately called Ilios or Troy (see "Evidence from Homer," page 36). The bard was mainly concerned with describing the wrath of Achilles and its consequences. He used Troy and the war as a poetic setting for a conflict between men and gods. From the archaeologist's point of view, however, the *Iliad* can be interpreted as a "setting" in an entirely different sense. One may see Homer or his informants as eyewitnesses to Troy and the landscape of Troy at the close of the eighth century B.C., the period when scholars generally agree Homer composed his epic.

Troy was largely a ruined site in Homer's day, but the remains of Troy VI/VIIa, both the citadel and the lower city, were still impressive. Contemporary audiences and later ones from the area around the city were supposed to be able to recognize the general outlines of places where the action happened from descriptive

Blegen interpreted the numerous pithoi buried beneath the floors of the houses in Troy's Stratum VIIa as evidence of preparations for a siege.

references in the *Iliad*. They could visualize it, for instance, whenever they climbed up a slope to a sanctuary in "holy Ilios." "Holy Ilios" is the most frequently repeated epithet in the *Iliad,* and one would expect to see a sacred building in such a place. We can make a convincing case for a sanctuary or sanctuaries, maybe in the form of a wooden building, from the early seventh century B.C. at the latest—roughly contemporary with Homer— on this site, which subsequently served as a cult center into the late Roman Empire. There is nothing in the archaeological record to contradict the assertion that Troy and the surrounding countryside formed the setting for Homer's *Iliad* in 700 B.C.

The Hittite Connection

Although Troy is in Anatolia, Carl Blegen, who directed excavations at the site in the

Evidence from Homer

Recent Homeric scholarship has shown that the Iliad *is the culmination of a protracted oral transmission of past events, transmitted by epic poetry improvised and performed by singers. Comparative historical linguistics has shown that the poetic medium in which the* Iliad *was passed on through the ages, the hexameter, in all probability was in use in Greece at the latest by the fifteenth century* B.C., *so that kernels of information transmitted via hexametric formulas from that time on could have been conveyed in Greek epic poetry. Here are a few examples of critical information transmitted in the* Iliad *from the Late Bronze Age to the period of Homer in the eighth century* B.C.:

The city called "Ilios" that sustained the attack in the *Iliad* must still have been known as "Wilios" in Bronze Age Greece. The sound /w/, spoken and written in Greek until at least 1200 B.C., was increasingly slurred in the dialect that Homer used around 450 years later until it was finally left off altogether. Consequently, the "Ilios" of the *Iliad* must have been the "Wilios" of the Late Bronze Age and in this way identical with "Wilusa," as Troy was known by the Hittite rulers of Anatolia at that time and in all probability by its inhabitants themselves.

The Greek aggressors who attack Troy in the *Iliad* are called consistently "Achaiói" (which was in the Late Bronze Age "Achaiwói") or "Danaói," but at the time the *Iliad* was composed in the eighth century B.C., there were no such names for the Greek people.

The "Achaiwói" of the *Iliad* must, therefore, be identical with the inhabitants of Ahhiyawa, a western kingdom implicated in Hittite documents of the fourteenth and thirteenth centuries B.C. in attacks on the western Anatolian coast. (The "Danaói" of the *Iliad*, on the other hand, must be identical with the inhabitants of "Danaya," a northern kingdom described in Egyptian documents of the fourteenth century B.C.)

From this, Homeric scholars can conclude that remnants of the memory of, among other things, one or several acts of aggression against the western Anatolian coast could have been transported via the hexameters of Ahhiyawan poetry down through the centuries between about 1200 and 800 B.C. Furthermore, Homer's Iliad *has in all probability preserved remnants of the memory of one or more acts of aggression perpetrated by the Ahhiyawans against Wilusa in the thirteenth century B.C.*

So did a "Trojan War" take place? Even with qualifications and certain reservations, I can give a basically positive answer. We still cannot prove that the Trojan War took place. However, all circumstantial evidence points to armed conflicts around 1200 B.C. between the area we now call Greece and the area that was called Wilusa at the time of the Hittite kingdom. The historical event or events left a mark in Greek poetry of that time, and because of the distinctive nature of the orally improvised Greek epic poetry of the Dark Ages, traces of this were preserved down to the time of Homer.

by JOACHIM LATAC

1930s, regarded Troy VI/VIIa as a Greek settlement. The idea of a Greek Troy, one that had also been entertained by Schliemann, became firmly established. These excavators had come from Greece to Troy, both literally and figuratively, and later returned to Greece, and were biased, most likely unconsciously, in their outlook. However, until the 1930s there was very little archaeologically within Anatolia that might have been compared with Troy, and certainly not in western Anatolia.

We know today, from our own excavations and even from earlier ones, that in all main respects, Bronze Age Troy had stronger ties with Anatolia than with the Aegean. We've learned this from the tons of local pottery and small finds, such as a seal with a local hieroglyphic inscription, as well as the overall settlement picture, mud-brick architecture, and cremation burials.

Research by Anatolian specialists (see "Evidence from Hittite Records," page 34) has shown that what we today call Troy was in the Late Bronze Age the kingdom of Wilusa, powerful enough to conclude treaties with the Hittite Empire; even the Egyptians seem to have been familiar with the city. Furthermore, according to Hittite records, there were political and military tensions around Troy precisely during the thirteenth and early twelfth centuries B.C.—the supposed time of Homer's Trojan War.

The Question Remains:
Was There a Trojan War?

On the basis of my years of experience and knowledge of Troy, I feel the question ought to be: "Why should the scholars who won't rule out a possible degree of historicity in the basic events in the *Iliad* have to defend their position?" In light of the remarkable amount of discoverthat has taken place over the last ten to fifteen years, the onus to defend positions should now be on those who believe there is absolutely no historical association between what happened at Late Bronze Age Troy and the events in the *Iliad*. On what basis, for instance, are claims made that Troy in the thirteenth and twelfth centuries B.C. was a third-class city, unworthy of foreign invasion and ultimately of Homer's attention? We expect that doubters will finally take note of the new archaeological facts of the case and the findings of a really interdisciplinary approach to Troy research.

According to the archaeological and historical findings of the past decade especially, it is now more likely than not that there were several armed conflicts in and around Troy at the end of the Late Bronze Age. At present we do not know whether all or some of these conflicts were distilled in later memory into the "Trojan War" or whether among them there was an especially memorable, single "Trojan War." However, everything currently suggests that Homer should be taken seriously, that his story of a military conflict between Greeks and the inhabitants of Troy is based on a memory of historical events—whatever these may have been. If someone came up to me at the excavation one day and expressed his or her belief that the Trojan War did indeed happen here, my response as an archaeologist working at Troy would be: Why not?

Warriors of Paros

SOLDIERS' BURIALS OFFER CLUES TO THE RISE OF CLASSICAL GREEK CITY-STATES.

by FOTEINI ZAFEIROPOULOU *and* ANAGNOSTIS AGELARAKIS

S oldiers' bones in urns—evidence of a forgotten battle fought around 730 B.C.—prompts the question: Did these men perish on their island home of Paros, at the center of the Aegean Sea, or in some distant land? The loss of so many, at least 120 men, was certainly a catastrophe for the community, but their families and compatriots honored them, putting their cremated remains into large vases, two of which were decorated with scenes of mourning and war. Grief-stricken relatives then carried the urns to the cemetery in Paroikia, the island's chief city, and placed them in two monumental tombs.

Excavation of the ancient cemetery began after its discovery during construction of a cultural center in the mid-1980s. It proved to be a veritable guidebook to changing funeral practices, yielding seventh- and sixth-century B.C. burials in large jars, fifth-century marble urns and grave stelae, and

Hellenistic and Roman marble sarcophagi on elaborate pedestals. But the two collective burials of soldiers from the late eighth century are the most important of the finds. As the earliest such burials ever found in Greece, their very existence offers evidence for the development of city-states at this time.

By about 1050 B.C., the Late Bronze Age civilization of Greece had collapsed, its great palace sites destroyed or abandoned. None of the many proposed explanations for this—invasion, internecine war, earthquake, drought, economic disruption—can be proved. Regardless, the old social system was gone. Kings, supported by a warrior caste and administrative officials, had ruled over a larger class of serfs. Now that was all swept aside.

The Late Bronze Age center on a hilltop near the shore at Paroikia was destroyed and then reoccupied in the tenth century, but it was soon surpassed by the growing town around the harbor. The people prospered, for Paros is ringed with fertile coastal plains, and its marble, of the highest quality, was famed throughout antiquity. But its real wealth came after Paros colonized the northern Aegean island of Thasos (circa 680 B.C.), seizing its abundant timber and productive gold mines.

What sort of society did the late eighth- and early seventh-century inhabitants of Paros and contemporary Greek cities have? The soldiers' burials in Paroikia offer some clues. Two out of the 140 vases, most of which can be dated to circa 730 B.C., show scenes with people. The rest of the vases are like ones decorated with geometric motifs found in individual graves in the Kerameikos, Athens' early cemetery.

One of the two vases depicting people is dated to approximately 750 B.C. (perhaps it was an heirloom). It shows a skirmish, with a warrior fighting from a chariot with dead combatants lying next to him, cavalrymen in action (one of whom holds a small round shield), and foot warriors with swords. One carries a large figure-eight–shaped shield, a type used in the Late Bronze Age, but another carries a large round shield. Called the *hoplon,* it is the same basic shield type that would be used throughout the Classical period and would give its name to the citizen soldier, the hoplite.

The other vase with people, which dates to approximately 730 B.C., shows war and mourning, following in a continuous narration the killing of a warrior in battle, fellow soldiers fighting for his body, and the laying out of the corpse before cremation.

The body is placed on a high bed or bier. Mourners stand alongside, women with both hands raised (perhaps tearing their hair) and men with one hand uplifted (possibly in grief or as a salute to the dead). The battle scene depicts the fight for the body of a fallen warrior. On one side of the corpse are cavalrymen with helmets, shields, and spears, supported by archers whose arrows fly toward the enemy. Facing them are lightly armed slingers, loading and throwing their stones (the earliest known instance of such soldiers depicted in Greek vase paintings), followed by a formation of heavily armed foot warriors, each carrying two spears and a hoplon.

In the Late Bronze Age, elite members of society fought on foot or from a chariot, using a throwing spear, sword, and large figure-eight or rectangular "tower" shields.

Hoplites, by contrast, were heavily armed infantry, equipped with a thrusting spear and sword, breastplate, greaves, closed helmet, and hoplon. But the difference was in more than just their equipment. It was also how they fought. War in the Late Bronze Age Aegean was carried out as individual duels rather than combat in organized formations; with hoplites came the tactic of fighting pitched battles in close-packed lines several men deep, known as the phalanx. The two vases from the Paroikia tombs show both older and newer fighting methods, recording an important change in society.

Scholars have long debated the role hoplite warfare played in the rise of social institutions that supported Classical city-states. It was thought that hoplite gear and phalanx were adopted around 700 B.C. The new style of warfare, the argument went, involved farmers, tradesmen, and other common people rather than an elite warrior class. Subsequently these new soldiers claimed a voice in the affairs of their cities, diluting the power of the aristocracy and laying the ground for citizen assemblies—in effect, a social revolution.

This interpretation, however, was criticized as being far too simplistic. Moreover, close study of depictions on vases from ancient Greece suggested that hoplite gear was introduced piecemeal between 750 and 700, and the phalanx came shortly afterward, which further discredits the idea of a quick, revolutionary change. But now, the two vases from the Paros tombs offer evidence that hoplite warfare was established by about 730, possibly supporting the earlier explanation.

The most celebrated of the ancient inhabitants of Paros is the early seventh-century B.C. soldier-poet Archilochus, who took part in the colonization of Thasos. Many of his lyric poems and epigrams deal with his experiences as a soldier. Some provide eyewitness testimony of tactics of his day, including one alluding to battle in a phalanx formation, which we now know was pioneered by his forebears:

> Psyche, my psyche, perplexed with the immeasurable troubles that have found you, stand up. Ward off the dreadful assaults that lie in wait, aiming toward your chest, by standing resolute close to the face of the enemies.

We will likely never know what battle claimed the lives of these Parian citizen soldiers. There were conflicts between Paros and the nearby island of Naxos. Archilochus fought in these, but we know little about them. Ancient authors also speak of a long-running war between Chalkis and Eretria, the two largest cities on the island of Euboia, between the mid-eighth and mid-seventh centuries B.C. It was known as the Lelantine War, after the name of a plain that both cities claimed. "On this occasion the rest of the Hellenic world did join in with one side or the other," wrote Thucydides in the fifth century. Much later, in the first century A.D., Strabo recorded an inscription that told of an agreement between the belligerents to ban missile weapons such as sling stones, arrows, and throwing spears. These were considered inferior and less courageous ways of fighting compared to the phalanx, with its discipline and organization.

Archilochus' verses about the war suggest Paros was involved in it:

Not even the bows will be repeatedly stretched, not even the teeming slings when Ares gathers the toil and moil of war in the plain, there grievous swords will start the job of causing many sighs, for the lords of Euboia are the demons of this battle, famed for their spears.

Do the bones from the Paroikia tombs reflect such savage warfare? Study of the cremated bones is only beginning, but some preliminary observations can be made. The remains of the majority of the 120 individuals were deposited as multiple interments in the funerary vases. They are all males and, of those for whom we could determine an approximate age at death, most were between 18 and 45 years. Some of the remains do show trauma from battle, such as cut marks on fragments of cranial bones, limb bones, and breastbone. More dramatic is a fragment of an iron spear point to which bone still adheres.

This grim evidence brings to mind the words of Aeschylus, the fifth-century B.C. playwright, who wrote, "Men go to war and in their place urns and ashes return to their home." Archilochus was probably speaking for many of his fellow soldiers when he mocked in the following verses the do-or-die approach espoused by the Spartans, who admonished their men to bring back their shields or be carried home dead on them:

One of the Saians [Thracians] is thrilled with that unblemished shield I left unwillingly behind in the bushes. But I saved myself, so what do I care about the shield, the hell with it; I'll obtain an equally good one.

That the dead were interred as a group rather than in individual family graves suggests a state-supported funeral of the sort described by Thucydides in Athens 300 years later. Such a burial indicates their status as citizens and inclusion in the workings of the city. Clearly, the people of Paros were acting as an organized state by 730 B.C. And this may explain their ability to colonize Thasos a few decades later, overpowering the local Thracian tribes after many battles. The community identity and centralized decision-making processes necessary to undertake such an ambitious expedition already existed.

Today, the cemetery is both an ongoing excavation and an archaeological park, with interpretive panels overlooking the site, which is visited day and night by large numbers of people. Contemplating the lives of those memorialized here, we may be reminded of Archilochus' bitter comment:

Once dead, one has no more claim to respect and fame among the people of the city, whereas we that are alive rather seek grace and kind feelings from the living, therefore it will forever be the worst for the dead.

Although we will never know the names of those whose bones we have the privilege of studying, through our work we are trying to learn about their lives and heroic deeds.

Fallen Heroes

BONES OF PERICLES' SOLDIERS COME TO NEW YORK FOR ANALYSIS.

by MARK ROSE

"It is for such a city, then, that these men nobly died in battle, thinking it right not to be deprived of her, just as each of their survivors should be willing to toil for her sake."
—*Funeral Oration of Pericles*

In 1997, construction of a theater at 35 Salaminos Street in downtown Athens was halted when four polyandreia (communal burials) were discovered. Subsequent excavations, directed by Charalambia Stoupa of the Third Ephoreia (Department) of Classical Antiquities, yielded ashes and burned human bones, along with pottery that was initially dated to circa 430 B.C. A fifth polyandreion, found under a building adjacent to the site, has not been excavated. The bones, which may represent as many as 250 individuals, are now in the forensic lab at Adelphi University in Garden City, New York, where anthropologist Anagnosti Agelarakis has begun to analyze them. One question is simply, to whom do they belong?

The location of the tombs and the date of the pottery found in them provide tantalizing evidence about the identity of the remains. The road leading out of Athens' main west gate passed through the Academy, the olive grove sacred to Athena where Plato taught. On either side of the road was the Dêmosion Sêma (People's Grave), a state burial ground for notable statesmen, generals, cultural figures, and Athenian citizen-soldiers who died in battle. In his *Guide to Greece,* the first-century A.D. traveler Pausanias described the Dêmosion Sêma:

> *Outside the city of Athens in the country districts and beside the roads there are sanctuaries of gods and of heroes and the tombs of men. . . .There is a memorial to all the Athenians who died in battles at sea or on the land except for those who fought at Marathon. Their tomb is in that place, in honor of their courage, but the rest lie beside the road to the Academy; tombstones stand on the graves to tell you each man's name and district.*

Pausanias then lists more than 40 monuments he saw between the city wall and the Academy, ranging from the tombs of the tyrant slayers, Harmodios and Aristogeiton (514 B.C.), to the great statesman Pericles (429 B.C.), other leaders such as Conon (392 B.C.) and Thrasyboulos (388 B.C.), and later cultural figures such as the fourth-century painter Nicias and the philosophers Zeno (263 B.C.) and Chrysippos (207 B.C.). The

Academy Road, now beneath modern buildings, follows the route of Plataion and Salaminos streets, and during the recent excavations its retaining wall was discovered near the polyandreia. From their location, it is probable that the polyandreia found beneath Salaminos Street are state burials.

The initial dating of the pottery, around 430 B.C., corresponds to the beginning of the Peloponnesian War, a protracted struggle from 431 to 404 B.C. between Athens and her allies and a coalition whose chief members were Sparta, Thebes, and Corinth. The war had several causes: the Athenian leader Pericles' use of funds intended for the general defense of Greece against the Persians for the Parthenon and other public buildings in Athens; intervention by Athens on behalf of Kerkyra (Corfu) in a dispute with Corinth in 433; and Athens' attack on the Corinthian colony of Potidaea in 432. After futile attempts at negotiating a settlement, Sparta and her allies declared war. Sparta invaded Athenian territory the following year. The "truest cause" of the war, wrote the historian Thucydides, was Sparta's anxiety about the growing power of Athens. Despite the plague, which broke out in 430 and lasted several years, Athens continued the struggle, fortune favoring one side then another, until the disastrous Sicilian expedition of 415–413, in which an Athenian fleet and army besieging Syracuse were destroyed, and the Spartan naval victory at Aegospotami in 404. Athens was forced to surrender. The initial dating of the pottery found in the polyandreia beneath Salaminos Street suggests the bones were interred near the beginning of this war.

In late December 1998, Anagnosti Age-larakis, who has worked in Greece since 1978 on anthropological archaeology and has considerable experience with crema-tions, was notified by Greek authorities that he had been chosen to study the remains. He went to Greece the following summer to supervise the packing of the bones, which were wrapped in acid-free paper and placed in plastic bags according to excavation unit. Cushioned with styrofoam, the bags were placed in a custom-made fire-retardant packing crate that was flown to New York under his care.

Most of the bones came from three of the polyandreia. The remains are not mere ashes but recognizable pieces of arm and leg bones; jaw, skull, vertebra, and pelvis frag-ments; and whole ankle and wrist bones. The polyandreia had been looted in antiquity, further fragmenting the bones and displacing them from their original positions. As a pre-liminary estimate, based on the average weight of bone for cremated individuals, Agelarakis says the remains may represent 200 to 250 people. A quick look at the bones from ten excavation units, randomly chosen from all four polyandreia, revealed that all diagnostic bones were from males.

That the bodies were cremated poses great difficulties for forensic analysis. The chalky, white appearance of the bones indicates they were exposed to temperatures of around 800 degrees Celsius. At such temperatures bones warp and shrink up to one-third, enamel layers on teeth explode, and the organic component of the bone, including DNA, is destroyed. If there is an upside to this, it is that any pathogens from the plague that

swept through Athens—Agelarakis suspects it was typhus or typhoid—would have been destroyed as well.

Nonetheless, it should be possible to gather some information from the bones about the people buried in the polyandreia: the number of individuals present, age range and sex (from morphology and metrical analysis), health (as reflected in pathologies, trauma, and growth checks, known as Harris lines, on long bones), and diet (through trace-chemical analysis). Indications of occupational activities, such as bony modifi-cation of the calcaneus (heel bone) that might reflect constant mounting and dis-mounting of horses, will be of particular importance in identifying the remains. Crosschecking the remains from each polyandreion will reveal any differences, or uniformity, in such characteristics. Age-larakis, now on leave from his teaching duties, hopes to complete an initial exami-nation by the end of the spring of 2000.

EVIDENCE THAT MIGHT HELP pinpoint the identity of the dead will come not just from the bones, but also from the artifacts found with the bones, the Athenian historian Thucydides' description of the war, and our knowledge of the state burial ground from Pausanias' description of it along with archaeological finds related to it.

According to the site's excavator, Char-alambia Stoupa, the pottery from the polyandreia includes red-figure vases and white-ground *lekythoi* (oil vessels) with bat-tle and funerary scenes. The pottery, she says, dates the complex to between 430 and 420 B.C. Stoupa notes that the pottery from the polyandreia is unburnt, though the bodies were cremated. This might reflect, she says, the Athenian custom of cremating soldiers killed abroad and bringing their ashes home for burial.

Thucydides is our chief source for this period. A young man at the outset of the war, he survived the plague and eventually was made a general and served in the northern Aegean. In 424 he was exiled for not getting his ships to Amphipolis in time to save it from the besieging Spartans. He returned to Athens at the end of the war and died soon afterward. Thucydides' account of the war provides details of battles on land and sea, often giving information about the numbers of soldiers involved, whether infantry or cavalry, their leaders, and casualties.

Thucydides recorded, for example, the following battles in the first year of the war: an unsuccessful Spartan attack on Oenoe, a fortified border post; defeat of an Athenian cavalry detachment at Rheiti, near Eleusis; a minor cavalry engagement at Phrygia between the Athenians, with Thessalian support, and Boeotians; fighting by the Athenian fleet at Methone, Pheia, Thronium, Alope, Sollium, and Astacus; actions against the Chalcidians and Potidaeans in the north; and an expedition Pericles led against Megara. It might just be possible to match the Dêmosion Sêma remains with casualties from one or more of these battles.

Pausanias noted monuments in the Dêmosion Sêma to Thessalian cavalrymen who died fighting with their Athenian allies (431 B.C.); Athenian cavalrymen who perished with the Thessalians (431 B.C.); Melasandros, killed fighting in Lycia (430

B.C.); and Athenians killed fighting at Tanagra (424 B.C.) and Amphipolis (422 B.C.). It might be tempting to try to match the remains excavated in 1998 with one or more of these monuments, but there is good reason to be cautious. Soon after the Peloponnesian War the Academy Road was rebuilt in the form of a 121-foot-wide ceremonial avenue. After the Greek defeat by the Macedonians at Chaironea in 338, when Athens expected attack, grave monuments were used to reinforce the city walls. Furthermore, Hellenistic graves were later built among the state monuments. Finally, the area was doubtless altered more when first Philip V of Macedon, in 200 B.C., and then the Roman general Sulla, in 86 B.C., attacked Athens at the western (Dipylon) gate. Thus the Dêmosion Sêma of Pericles' day had been considerably transformed by the time Pausanias saw it in the first century A.D.

We have some additional knowledge of Dêmosion Sêma monuments from excavations and chance finds. Early state tombs dating to 479 B.C., the time the city wall was built, have been found flanking the gate and oriented parallel to the wall rather than the Academy Road. For whom the tombs were built is unknown, but by the end of the Peloponnesian War they were covered over. A nearby polyandreion on the south side of the Academy Road has been excavated. An inscription on a cornice block identifies it as the burial place of members of the Spartan garrison killed in 403 B.C. After their victory, the Spartans helped to establish an oligarchical government in Athens. The so-called "Thirty Tyrants" ruled for several months in early 403, until democratic forces were strong enough to mount a series of attacks that led to full-scale civil war. Spartan troops fought on the oligarchical side, but the opposition won and democracy was restored. The tomb, a 34-foot-long ashlar masonry structure divided into three chambers, held the remains of 13 men. Just west of the Spartans' tomb were other burials of warriors, unidentified, that shared a common facade on the Academy Road.

Also on the south side of the Academy Road is an elaborate mid-fourth-century tomb, a 49-foot-long rectangular enclosure, built of ashlar masonry and with guardian dog sculptures on the corners, around a circular structure that was topped off by a six-foot-high marble vase. It has been called the tomb of Chabrias, an Athenian general who died in 357 B.C., but only because Pausanias mentions that Chabrias' tomb was along the Academy Road. The date is appropriate, but there is no proof of the identification.

What Pausanias does, or does not mention, when checked against archaeological evidence underscores the need for caution in using his information in identifying the polyandreia. Fragments of the monuments to those killed at Corinth and Koroneia in 394/93 B.C. and an inscription relating to the dead in fighting at the Hellespont have been found, and both are noted by Pausanias. On the other hand, an inscription for Athenians killed at Potidaea (perhaps in 432 B.C. or during the siege of 430/29) has been found, but Pausanias lists no such monument. He does not mention the early state graves flanking the gate or the polyandreion of the Spartans from 403 B.C., nor does he mention a monument for those killed at

Samos in 440/39, though we know from the biographer Plutarch (circa 50–120 A.D.) that Pericles gave their funeral oration.

ATHENS HONORED ITS WAR dead with a public procession and funeral and an annual celebration. The state funeral for those who died in the war's first year is described by Thucydides:

> In this winter, following their traditional custom, the Athenians held burial rites at public expense for the first to die in this war, in the following manner. They lay out the bones of the dead two days beforehand, after setting up a tent, and each person brings whatever offerings he wishes to his own relatives. When the procession takes place, wagons carry cypress coffins, one for each tribe, and within are the bones of each man, according to tribe. One empty bier, fully decorated, is brought for the missing, all who were not found and recovered. Anyone who wishes, citizen or foreigner, joins the procession, and female relatives are present at the grave as mourners. They bury them in the public tomb, which is in the most beautiful suburb of the city and in which they always bury those killed in war. ...After they cover them with earth, a man chosen by the state, known for his wise judgement and of high reputation, makes an appropriate speech of praise, and after this they depart. This is their burial practice, and throughout the whole war, whenever there was occasion, they followed the custom.

Nobody is claiming that these are the bones of Pericles. It seems possible, however, that they belong to citizen-soldiers who fought under his orders, perhaps even those who perished in the first year of the war and were commemorated in Pericles' funeral oration, one of the greatest speeches of all time. Thucydides, who was probably present, recorded the speech and is believed to have captured the spirit of Pericles' message if not the exact words. Speaking from a high platform so that as many could hear as possible, Pericles described the greatness of Athens at length, then shifted to the greatness of those who had fallen to preserve the city:

> It is for such a city, then, that these men nobly died in battle, thinking it right not to be deprived of her, just as each of their survivors should be willing to toil for her sake.... For it is their virtues, and those of men like them, that have given honor to the qualities I have praised in the city, and for few other Hellenes [Greeks] would it be manifest, as it is for them, that reputation is equal to the deeds.... None of these men turned coward from preferring further enjoyment of wealth, nor did any, from the poor man's hope that he might still escape poverty and grow rich, contrive a way to postpone the danger. Thinking defeat of the enemy more desirable than prosperity, just as they considered this the fairest of risks, they were willing to vanquish him at that risk and long for the rest, leaving to hope the uncertainty of prospering in the future but resolving to rely on their own actions in what confronted them now, and recognizing that it meant resisting and dying rather than surviving by submission, they fled disgrace in word but stood up to the deed with their lives and through the fortune of the briefest critical moment, at the height of glory rather than fear, departed.
>
> So fared these men, worthy of their city; you survivors must pray to meet the enemy at lesser cost but resolve to do so just as unflinchingly.

We glorify Periclean Athens for the great monuments of the Acropolis and as the birthplace of democracy, but to Pausanias the leaders on both sides during the Peloponnesian War were "the assassins and almost the wreckers of Greece" and he excludes them from his list of the greatest Greek patriots. Thucydides recorded atrocities on both sides: after capturing Scione and Melos, the Athenians put to death all adult males and sold the rest of the population into slavery; the Spartans slaughtered 3,000 Athenians captured at Aegospotami. Agelarakis shares Pausanias' view, but also acknowledges the noble qualities Pericles espoused. "This was the longest, most vicious and destructive war ever fought among Greeks," he says, "gilded with so many aspects of the human condition that we all recognize even today: the struggle fueled by differences in ideals and in the hunger for power and resources; the maliciousness of warfare and the suffering and loss of countless lives resulting not only from armed conflict, but also from disease; and the desperate strategies for survival and the hope for peace and salvation."

Today, forensic anthropology is ever more the final act to conflict. We in the United States try to identify our dead and account for each and every one of them from recent and past wars. The ancient Athenians would appreciate this attitude, because, unlike other classical Greek city-states, Athens brought home her dead. They would also understand Anagnosti Agelarakis' efforts to identify some of those killed at the outset of the Peloponnesian War. For his part, Agelarakis, while maintaining scientific objectivity, sees his work on the bones as a sacred trust. "Discovery of the remains of the ancient Athenian warriors who offered their lives fighting for the ideals, values, and traditions of their city during the first years of the Peloponnesian War presents a time capsule of singular importance," he says. "One cannot evade feelings of tremendous responsibility to both past and future generations. This is a rendezvous with history."

◉ EYEWITNESS: Alexander at Granicus

compiled by MARK ROSE

No firsthand accounts of Alexander exist, but we have several histories—by Arrian, Curtius, Diodorus, and Plutarch—based on the writings of those who took part in the expedition into Persia. These primary sources included writings of Callisthenes, a nephew of Aristotle and author of an official account (until found guilty of conspiring against Alexander); Ptolemy, a Macedonian officer, later general and founder of the dynasty that ruled Egypt after Alexander's death; and Aristobulus, an engineer in the army.

Alexander's first major battle against the Persians was at the Granicus River in northwestern Anatolia, now Turkey, in 334 B.C. The following narrative, based on Diodorus and taken from *Diodorus Siculus,* based on a translation by G. Booth, reflects both Alexander's willingness to throw himself into the fray, regardless of danger, and his great personal

Alexander was depicted as youthful and vital in official portraits and later copies of them.

Courtesy Mark Rose

good fortune, which preserved him in spite of his impetuosity. Alexander put himself in command of his right wing, with the elite companion cavalry made of young Macedonian nobles:

> *Alexander, with the choicest of the body of horse in the right wing, was the first that charged, and rushing into the thickest of his enemies, made great slaughter among them. The Persians fought valiantly, striving to outdo the Macedonians. Spithridates, the satrap [governor] of the province of Ionia and a son-in-law to Darius [the Persian king], a very valiant man, charged the Macedonians with a great body of horse, seconded by*

> *40 of his guard, all noblemen, and inferior to none for valor and courage. With these he put the enemy hard to it, laying about him and killing some and wounding others. When none were able to deal with him, Alexander rode up to the Persian and fought with him hand to hand.... The Persian cast his spear at Alexander with such force that it pierced his shield and breastplate into his right shoulderpiece. The king, Alexander, plucked out the spear, threw it away, and flew upon the Persian with such fierceness and violence that he fixed his spear in the middle of his breast. But the point broke in the breastplate, and the spear pierced no farther. The Persian made at Alexander with his drawn sword when Alexander threw a second spear at his face that went right through his head. At this instant, Rhosaces, a brother of Spithridates, rode at Alexander and struck him such a blow with his sword that it cut through Alexander's helmet and wounded him on the head. As he raised his sword to strike again, Cleitus Niger charged in and cut off his arm.*

Arrian gives a different account in which Alexander spears Mithridates, a son-in-law of Darius, and is then struck in the helmet by Rhosaces, but counterattacks and spears him through chest. According to Arrian it is Spithridates who nearly killed Alexander, raising his sword to strike his head from behind when Cleitus came to the rescue (see Arrian's *The Campaigns of Alexander,* translated by A. de Sélincourt, 1971).

The Spoils of Actium

AN ANCIENT WAR MEMORIAL PROVIDES STARTLING DETAILS ABOUT THE SHIPS IN ANTONY AND CLEOPATRA'S FLEET DURING ONE OF HISTORY'S MIGHTIEST NAVAL ENGAGEMENTS.

by WILLIAM M. MURRAY *and* PHOTIOS M. PETSAS

Near the bustling harbor town of Preveza on the western coast of Greece, a long-forgotten war memorial lies open to the wind and rain. Though today it is choked with weeds and in places broken apart, it still preserves important details from a war that redirected the course of Western history. The man who emerged victorious spent the succeeding years rejuvenating and reforming the Roman State. His success earned him the name Augustus ("revered one"), the praise of his contemporaries, and the admiration of future generations for whom he was the first in a long line of Roman emperors.

The final sea battle which set all this in motion was fought near Preveza, off Cape Actium. Though it ranks among the most significant conflicts of all time, we know little of its course or character and even less about the warships that determined its outcome. A review of the events that led to this epoch-making clash is in order.

Throughout the first century B.C., powerful generals, backed by armies more loyal to themselves than to the State, dominated Roman politics. Julius Caesar was one of these men—able and influential, a general with many soldiers. Although he controlled the government for a brief time, he seriously underestimated his opposition, which struck him down on the Ides of March in 44 B.C. Caesar's will provided for the adoption of his grandnephew, Gaius Octavius, the future victor at Actium.

From the start, Octavian (as historians refer to him after the adoption) sought to avenge the assassination and to gain power for himself. At first he maneuvered Caesar's most powerful lieutenants, Mark Antony and Lepidus, into helping him punish the murderers. Then he removed Lepidus from power and consolidated his control of the empire's western provinces, thus countering Antony's tight grip on the East. The uneasy alliance that bought these two dissolved when Antony—by choosing to live with his ally Cleopatra, the Queen of Egypt—publicly insulted Octavian, whose sister was Antony's Roman wife.

From 34 B.C. onward, both sides steadily drifted toward war. The conflict was resolved by the mighty naval battle, involving hundreds of warships on both sides, that took place on September 2, 31 B.C., off Cape Actium.

A word about the nature of naval warfare at this time: we must dismiss the Hollywood image of Ben Hur chained to his bench on a slave galley. In reality, Greek and Roman fleets were normally manned by free men who rowed vessels of different sizes built for different purposes (see "Rating Ancient Warships," page 54).

Small- and medium-sized ships were quicker and more maneuverable than the larger classes and were used in squadrons, much like modern-day fighter planes. All ships, both large and small, were equipped with a ram, a heavy bronze sheathing fitted over the bow. Each crew tried to drive its ram into the side of an enemy vessel, splitting apart the seams of its hull and sinking it. The larger galleys in the fleet were also used as floating platforms for marines and for catapults. These ships lobbed stones at their foes, or shot grappling devices to ensnare their prey. Once an enemy was dragged alongside, the marines swarmed aboard to capture the ship in a hand-to-hand struggle.

At Actium all of these tactics were used. According to the most detailed accounts, Antony tried to crush his rival by using gigantic warships. During the battle, however, the great size and weight of his ships actually brought about Antony's defeat. Octavian's smaller vessels proved more maneuverable and faster, and his crews more skilled and courageous. By darting quickly in and out among the sluggish enemy vessels, they delivered their deadly blows and sank many ships.

At the height of the battle, Cleopatra took fright and fled from the scene with her squadron. Antony, misguided by his passionate love for the queen, broke off his attacks and fled after her. Though the fight continued for some time, Octavian's smaller ships eventually proved superior, and either destroyed or forced the remainder of Antony's fleet to surrender. Such, at least, is the account that has survived, reflecting, as we would expect, the winner's view of the action.

Octavian led his army to Egypt in pursuit of his rival. Shakespeare and Hollywood dramatized the finale that most people remember. Tragic lovers to the end, Antony fell on his own sword while Cleopatra chose to die as Egypt's queen—by the venom of a sacred snake. They were buried together in her mausoleum.

During the decade that followed, Augustus (as he is called after 27 B.C.) proclaimed his victory at Actium, the decisive event in his rise to power, and the battle's importance increased in retrospect as Augustus steadily extended his rule. He himself spread an "official" version in two ways: through the publication of his own personal account, and through the erection of public memorials celebrating the victory.

In early August of 29 B.C., as Octavian made his way triumphantly back to Rome from the East, he stopped off at the site of his old army camp near Actium to dedicate a new city and war memorial. He called the city Nikopolis ("Victory City") and hoped it would serve as both a living war memorial and a regional center to revitalize an area depressed by years of war. His hopes were not in vain; the city prospered for centuries.

The showpiece of this new city was its official war memorial, built on the site of Augustus' own former command post. Consecrated to the gods in 29 B.C., the memorial was among the city's first public and sacred buildings. In the words of the historian Dio Cassius, who in the third century A.D. wrote the most detailed account of Augustus' reign: "On the spot where he had pitched his tent, he laid a foundation of square stones, adorned it with the captured ships' beaks, and erected on it, open to the sky, a shrine of Apollo." Although Dio was wrong on this last detail (an inscription found at the site makes it clear that Neptune and Mars were the gods honored there), he was accurate concerning the rest of the monument. In fact, every ancient author who describes the monument mentions its array of warship rams—this hillside display must have been an impressive sight. The rams are, of course, long gone. They were melted down centuries ago for their tons of precious bronze. The memorial's remains were first located and explored by Alexander Philadelpheus in 1913, when this area became part of modern Greece. Subsequently, a series of excavations uncovered a hillside terrace supported by a U-shaped retaining wall, the north foundation of a long building atop the terrace, fragments of Corinthian columns, small bits of marble decoration, and pieces from the building's roof.

The most important feature of the monument went unrecognized for years. A series of complex sockets of different sizes pocks the face of the southern retaining wall. It was impossible to know for certain what these sockets had held since nothing like them had ever been seen before.

The key to solving the problem appeared in 1980 when Haifa University's Center for Maritime Studies recovered a warship's ram intact from the sea floor of Athlit, Israel. Made of high-grade bronze

Rating Ancient Warships

Ancient navies, like their modern counterparts, were composed of different classes or ratings of ships introduced at various times for various purposes. Although the names and partial descriptions for some of these classes exist in accounts by ancient authors, no complete warship of known class has yet been located on the sea floor. The one about which we know the most, the "three" or trieres, was the most popular class in the ancient navies of the Mediterranean.

The fourth century B.C. saw the introduction of larger classes designed to withstand and deliver stronger blows and with greater deck space to carry marines and catapults. Early in the century, the Carthaginians invented the "four" and soon thereafter Dionysius of Syracuse added both "fours" and "fives" to his fleet. After the death of Alexander the Great (323 B.C.), a naval arms race erupted between his successors which produced ships of gigantic proportions. The fleet of Demetrius "the City Besieger" (circa 300 B.C.) included "sevens," "eights," "nines," "tens," "elevens," "thirteens," "fifteens," and "sixteens." And at the height of his power, the fleet of Ptolemy II (285–246 B.C.) contained one "twenty" and two "thirties."

The largest ship produced at this time was a "forty" launched during the late third century by Ptolemy IV Philopator (221–203 B.C.). Primarily because of the "forty's" incredible size, someone wrote down its dimensions to amaze succeeding generations. It was 420 feet (128 meters) long, 57 feet (17.4 meters) wide, its stern towered 79.5 feet (24.2 meters) above the water, and its bow stood 72 feet (21.9 meters) above the sea. On its maiden voyage, the vessel had 4,000 oarsmen, 2,850 marines, and 400 men who served as officers, ratings, and deckhands. As you might expect, it moved only with difficulty and was intended solely as a showpiece.

But even if we dismiss the "forty" as an extraordinary freak, we are still left with a large number of different classes which worked quite well and for which we have very little evidence.

It is now thought that the names of each class derive in some way from the total number of oarsmen per "rowing unit." We know we that this unit on a "three" has three oarsmen, each pulling his own oar, arranged in three superimposed banks. Since none of the "polyremes"— classes larger than the "three"—were built with more than three superimposed banks of oars, their names must be explained by assigning more than one man to each oar.

On this analogy, the "four" might be rowed by two men per oar arranged in two superimposed banks; a "five" could be rowed by two banks of oars, one with three men per oar, the other with two. One ingenious theory explains the classes above the "sixteen" as large catamarans with expansive decks bridging two parallel hulls.

Like our own "Stealth Bomber" and laser-guided missiles, these large polyremes stood at the cutting edge of contemporary technology. But like so much else from the ancient world, they have passed from the historical record leaving little more than their names. Octavian's campsite memorial amazingly preserves our first tangible evidence of these complex war machines that determined the conduct of battle in a bygone age.

by WILLIAM M. MURRAY

and weighing one-half ton, the ram seems to have come from a warship of King Ptolemy V or VI of Egypt (symbols on the weapon imply a date between 204 and 167 B.C.). And its shape corresponded exactly with the shape of the sockets. What these had held was now clear—"the captured ships' beaks" with which Augustus adorned his victory monument.

With permission from the Greek Archaeological Service and the Athenian Archaeological Society, we developed a cooperative project to photograph and measure the Nikopolis sockets. Our team arrived in Preveza in early May 1986, just after the Chernobyl nuclear accident, and much to our dismay we found the site to be slightly radioactive. Both soil and weeds had been contaminated by recent spring rains carrying the accident's fallout. In Athens, people panicked; but as calm prevailed in Preveza, we mimicked the blasé attitude of local shepherds and quickly cut back the "glowing" weeds from the monument's face.

To our delight, 23 carefully cut sockets emerged from the undergrowth. They ranged in size from large to small in a generally decreasing progression from west to east. Two additional sockets once filled a gap in the middle stretch of the wall, and at its unexcavated eastern end there is room for eight to ten more. The original total, therefore, must have been roughly 33 to 35. This amount certainly represents a tithe, an offering of ten percent—standard practice when dedicating spoils to the gods in thanksgiving for victory. Octavian wrote in his own account (an ancient writer who read the now lost account quotes Octavian on this detail) that

the total number of ships captured was 300, but this suspiciously "round" number must exclude ships from classes smaller than "threes" (called *triereis* or triremes). It now seems that Octavian's generals captured closer to 350 of Antony's 500-ship fleet during the course of the summer campaign.

Other new details can be recovered from the sockets themselves—in particular from their shapes and relative sizes—because of the similarity in shape between a cross-section of a ram and the shape of a socket cutting. The reason for this similarity is simple. Since the ground supported the immense weight of the weapon, the monument's designers needed only to ensure a tight fit between the ram and the wall. To accomplish this, they carefully cut back the timbers inside each ram to create a hollow. When they carved the socket for each ram, a central, uncut section or "core" was left, which corresponded in shape to the ram's hollowed interior. Then, as they jockeyed the ram into its socket, the core of each cutting slid into the cavity created by the removal of the ram's timbers.

This "hand-in-glove" fit explains why no clamps held the rams in place on most of the cuttings. It also explains why the core of each cutting corresponds so closely in shape to the wooden timbers found inside the Athlit ram. The dimensions of the sockets and their cores, therefore, preserve the precise dimensions of the bow timbers of Antony's largest ships.

There is more. Because the sockets were carved to receive the back side of each ram (or more precisely its after-end), they preserve the after-cowl curvature and rear contours of each ram's trough ear and bottom plate. By carefully recording each socket's varying depths with a large measuring device, we managed to recover the actual three-dimensional shape of each ram's back end to a depth of about 18 inches (0.45 meters).

As we laboriously recorded hundreds of measurements from each socket on paper, the bows of Antony's largest ships took shape, like ghosts from the past. Incredibly preserved in stone for two millennia, the massive dimensions of these giants once again amaze the beholder, and once again they glorify the victor of Actium. Augustus would be pleased.

Our work at the site also resolved some old problems concerning the memorial's inscription. The 165-foot length (55 meters) of the text, and the sizes and shapes of the inscribed blocks, prove that the inscription was carved on the retaining wall above the ram display. We also found new evidence for the word order of the text and discovered some new letters which changed the dedication's concluding verb.

For example, Octavian's name, "Imperator Caesar," was cut above the biggest ram at the dedication's beginning. At the other end, above the last ram, appeared the final verb "consecrated." And in the middle, near where the fallen inscribed blocks still lie, the words "to Neptune and Mars" indicate the gods who were honored here. An important aspect of the discovery concerns the memorial's value as an historical source, for we can clearly see the workings of Octavian's mind before he was comfortably established in power. The clues are provided by the sizes of the rams he chose to display.

Ancient accounts make it certain that ships from "ones" to "tens" must represent the limits for the sockets on the campsite memorial. The smallest sockets are clearly larger than a "one," a "two," or a "three" (the size of the ram on the recently reconstructed trireme Olympias). They are also larger than the half-ton Athlit ram, which may come from a "four" or perhaps a "five." And the largest sockets presumably held rams from "tens," immense castings that must have weighed two tons or more. Until now, we had no idea that these warships carried so mighty a weapon, no idea that the Greeks or Romans were capable of turning out such huge castings.

Octavian's intention emerges from this comparison and it is simple and clear: the magnitude of the dedication must match the magnitude of the victory. Unless some smaller-sized sockets lie buried at the unexcavated eastern end of the wall, Octavian has deliberately omitted examples from moderate- and smaller-sized ships. The monument's 23 sockets roughly divide into five or six groups of similar sizes. The irregular number of sockets in each group implies that Octavian simply mounted every large example that fell into his hands. He clearly realized that the more he stressed the giant sizes of the ships vanquished, the more glory would be reaped by himself and his men for emerging victorious.

The finished monument must have been indeed impressive. As you approached from Apollo's sacred grove at the base of the hill, your first sight was the long retaining wall fronted by a stepped terrace some 15 to 18 feet wide. Like the Rostra in the Roman Forum, this wall was studded with bronze rams. By comparison, however, the examples here were gigantic. Arrayed in a line of generally decreasing sizes, the weapons led your attention to the west end of the wall where the inscription began above the first trophy—a monstrous ram weighing two tons or more.

The sight was designed to take your breath away—and it did, to judge from the brief accounts describing the place. Each one mentions this display as the basic feature of the sacred precinct.

To remind the awed visitor of the important facts, the inscription paraded them in foot-high letters across the full length of the wall:

IMPERATOR CAESAR, SON OF THE DIVINE JULIUS, FOLLOWING THE VICTORY IN THE WAR WHICH HE WAGED ON BEHALF OF THIS REPUBLIC IN THIS REGION, WHEN HE WAS CONSUL FOR THE FIFTH TIME AND COMMANDER-IN-CHIEF FOR THE SEVENTH TIME, AFTER PEACE HAD BEEN SECURED ON LAND AND SEA, CONSECRETED TO NEPTUNE AND MARS THE CAMP FROM WHICH HE SET FORTH TO ATTACK THE ENEMY NOW ORNAMENTED WITH NAVAL SPOILS.

In the years that followed, visitors flocked to Nikopolis every fourth year to attend the *Aktia,* a festival to honor the victory that secured the Augustan Peace. Equal in stature to the Olympics, the Atkia were celebrated downhill from the monument in Apollo's sacred grove at the base of the hill. An overgrown stadium and crumbling theater still mark the famous site.

The spot was carefully chosen. From the city, from the surrounding plain, from the stadium and from the upper rows of the theater, you could easily make out the monumental display. To an empire thankful for renewed peace and prosperity, Octavian's campsite memorial marked the sacred spot that witnessed the birth of the "New Age."

Today, though unprotected, neglected, and overgrown with weeds, the site still preserves its beauty and its quiet sanctity at the edge of the modern village called Smyrtoula. Occasionally a few tourists see an old sign at the base of the hill and come here to look for a temple of Apollo. Such was the flawed interpretation of the monument by its first excavator, and the locals still believe it to be true.

The visitors gaze in confusion at the tumbled blocks, the large inscribed letters and the curious sockets behind the thistles. And few, if any, know what priceless details from the battle of Actium still survive beneath the weeds.

This is an amazingly important site, and one that cries out for protection and for further investigation. Now that we have begun to understand the secrets of this monument, we hope to return to consolidate its remains and, for their protection, to collect the inscription blocks scattered over the hillside (28 have been spotted over the years, but we saw only 13). Eventually, we hope to excavate the terrace above the ram display to learn the function of the long colonnaded building, which once crowned the memorial. Might it be possible that Octavian displayed here, as trophies of battle, additional equipment from the enemy fleet?

Monuments to War

Titus appears in his chariot, followed by a winged goddess of victory, on the arch commemorating his capture of Jerusalem.

The Jewish revolt against Roman rule in A.D. 66 was a bitter struggle. Nero sent the veteran general—and future emperor—Vespasian and his son Titus to crush the uprising. After Nero's death and Vespasian's march on Rome, Titus assumed control over the Roman legions, besieging and sacking Jerusalem in A.D. 70. By the end of the revolt, tens of thousands perished—combatants and civilians—at the hands of the Romans and the various rebel factions.

In A.D. 71, Titus' victory over Jerusalem was commemorated in Rome by a triumph. A decade later, the success of Titus was immortalized by an arch near the Temple of Roma and Venus depicting various scenes from the campaign. Though much of the original Arch of

Vespasian and Titus built the Colosseum with spoils and slaves taken in the Jewish War.

Titus was damaged or destroyed in the Middle Ages when it was incorporated into fortifications around the city, two original friezes on it are almost entirely preserved. This panel from the interior of the arch depicts the triumphal parading of the spoils seized from the Second Temple of Jerusalem into Rome. The Roman legionaries hoist a large menorah on their shoulders, along with Jewish shewbread. (See page 3 of the photo insert.) Silver trumpets are crossed at the head of the procession, heralding the procession as it approaches the city of Rome.

In 1995, Géza Alföldy of the University of Heidelberg discovered new significance to the Arch of Titus, linking it to one of its closest neighbors—the Colosseum. Roman inscriptions made of bronze letters sometimes leave a "ghost" in the form of a pattern of holes from which the letters once hung. Alföldy found a "ghost" inscription on the Colosseum that had been overlooked for centuries. It indicates that the Colosseum, begun by Vespasian and dedicated by Titus in A.D. 80, was funded by the spoils of war. This didn't just mean selling of sacred objects but also probably referred to the use of Jewish slaves as construction workers.

Though historians had long suspected such a connection between great Roman public works and revenue from wars, Alföldy's discovery offers the first such link between these two specific imperial monuments. The Arch's frieze and the reconstructed Colosseum inscription are vivid reminders that the Roman Imperial war machine was as much a tool for generating revenue and labor as it was for military and political conquest.

by ALEXANDER BENENSON

A hillside is an odd place to look for ancient warships, but here they are, nevertheless. When you know what to look for, you can sit on the terrace as the sun sets and bathes the empty sockets in gold, and let go the reins of your imagination. Alone on the hillside, far from the distractions of the modern age, you can restore in your mind's eyes the massive timbers and tons of bronze, and envision the gigantic ships from Antony and Cleopatra's fleet. For naval historians and for those who study Augustus, this discovery is worth more than a treasure ship laden with gold and silver.

Rescuing an Old Dig

WOMEN WARRIORS FROM BEYOND THE DANUBE
AND COMPLEX BURIAL RITUALS ARE AMONG THE
UNEXPECTED FINDS AT A ROMAN MILITARY CEMETERY.

by HILARY COOL

The existence of a cemetery outside the Roman fort at Brougham, some 20 miles south of the western end of Hadrian's Wall, had long been known from finds of tombstones. So when it was announced that the modern highway that ran through it was to be straightened, excavations were planned. But this was in 1966, a time when archaeological concerns were of little importance to road builders and archaeologists were poorly funded. Work started unexpectedly in early 1967, before it was scheduled to begin, and under very difficult circumstances a small team of government-sponsored excavators saved what they could—digging more than 300 deposits, including cremation burials, the foundations of at least two large monumental tombs, and a number of what they thought were robbed graves. Detailed recording had to be sacrificed for speed, and some burials were destroyed before they could be recorded fully; part of the adjacent settlement was lost because, as one archaeologist noted at the time, "the machines were working vigorously at this stage."

Study of the discoveries began immediately, but the scholar in charge died before finishing her analysis. Incomplete records and lack of funding brought efforts to finish the work in the 1980s to a halt. What was accomplished did, however, reveal the importance of the artifacts—which include Britain's best collection of third-century A.D. glass vessels, an unrivaled group of glossy, bright-red pottery (known as Samian ware), and thousands of burnt scraps from objects placed on funeral pyres.

Our company, Barbican Research Associates, specializes in analyzing old sites, looking at the excavation notebooks, plans, and objects with fresh eyes. We knew from what work had been done that it was important to publish this cemetery, and in 2000, we persuaded the government agency English Heritage to fund a reexamination of all the evidence from the Brougham excavation, including the finds from the site, donated by the landowner to the Tullie House Museum in nearby Carlisle, and the hastily written field notes, some photos from the dig, and various bits of reports that had been written over the years. We felt we could use new information from other cemeteries to help us understand the site. For example, we now know that in cremation cemeteries like this, you don't just get formal burials with the bones placed in urns and deposited with other goods. You also get disposal of debris from pyres in pits. (It was these pits that the excavators had thought were robbed graves.) Other advances in the intervening years included great improvements in the ability of experts to determine the age and sex of cremated bone, a highly skilled job. We also knew far more about the types of pottery recovered, and could date them more closely.

In short, archaeological thought and expertise had finally caught up with what had been found at the site in the 1960s.

WE NEVER DREAMED, however, of the remarkable story that would emerge. While the Roman army has long been thought of as a very masculine institution where women and children were virtually invisible, the evidence from Brougham shows that may be very far from the truth. Women and children—the soldiers' families—buried in the cemetery there were treated with just as much care and attention as the men. And, remarkably, some of the women might have served in the forces guarding Rome's northwest frontier.

Roman Brougham—then known as Brocavum—was at the intersection of a main north-south route and branch roads to the east and west. The fort, now partially covered by the ruins of a thirteenth-century castle, was built in the last decades of the first century. On its east was the *vicus,* the settlement of civilians, families, and others who were linked to the fort. Beyond it was the cemetery. The modern highway had cut through part of the cemetery in use in the third century, when the fort was the base for a cavalry unit.

By that time, Britain had been part of the empire for 150 years. Though generally peaceful, it was still regarded as a frontier province, a good place to send unruly groups to get them out of the way—which is what Marcus Aurelius did in 175. Defeated by Roman forces on the Danube, the troublesome Sarmatian tribes had to provide 8,000 cavalry under a peace settlement. Aurelius promptly dispatched many of them to Britain. It was also the place Septimius Severus brought his troublesome sons in 208 in the vain hope that campaigning against the barbarians to the north might distract them from Rome's temptations.

The excavated part of the cemetery was used circa 220–300, and the whole community was buried there, from babies to old people, women as well as men. As we looked at what had been placed on the pyre of each individual, and then at what had been placed with them in their graves, we discovered that each funeral was governed by the age and sex of the deceased. Many items, not just obvious ones like jewelry, were regarded as age and gender specific. In fact, the Brougham cemetery, which is among the largest excavated from this period, has given us an unprecedented look at surprisingly complex burial rituals, producing rare items and many unexpected ways of using common things. But it simply is not known to what extent such complexity was typical of the period elsewhere in Britain.

The dead went to their pyres dressed in clothes. Women and children regularly wore glass-bead necklaces, with some women having gold earrings. Adults had hobnailed shoes, while children were barefoot or wore shoes without nails. Among the remains were thousands of fragments of burnt decorated bone plaques. From a discovery at another site we were fairly sure that these would have decorated biers. Such fragments were only found with remains of adults, not with children or adolescents, so the funeral processions of the young and the old would have been very different.

The young were clearly treated in special ways. Among the earliest burials, color-coated pottery beakers were only placed with young people, while at all times small Samian cups were placed only with children younger than eight. Special treatment can also be seen in the location of babies' and toddlers' graves. They are first scattered throughout the cemetery, then cluster around one of the monumental tombs, and finally disappear from the cemetery completely. Possibly by then another location outside the excavated area was thought more appropriate for them.

Adults had their own specific offerings. Though shallow Samian dishes accompanied people of all ages, deep ones were found only with adults. Animal offerings on the pyre again occurred only with adults. These included not only the normal range of meat joints and poultry, but also whole cattle and sheep. But we found differences among the adults as well. Only adult men, and possibly only those of high status, were ever accompanied by glass drinking cups. Bronze buckets, on the other hand, seemed especially associated with women.

One of the curious aspects was the age of the decorated bowls when they were placed in the graves. They ranged from perhaps 20 to 30 years old to more than 70. Other antiques included an enameled *patera,* or handled bowl, that might have been anywhere between 100 and 150 years old when it was deposited, and glass vessels that had seen long use. In cases when it was possible to determine their age, the adults buried with antiques were among the oldest. So not only were there differences in the items thought appropriate for children and adults, there were also differences between young adults and the elderly.

Much wealth literally went up in smoke. The remains of ivories, metal vessels inlaid with silver, and gold and silver jewelry were regularly recovered. So many items were placed on some pyres that they must have been very large. Perhaps they were tiered like the depictions of imperial funerals seen on coins of Septimius Severus and others. In comparison to the pyres of adults, those of children and young people appear curiously bare, with few remains found. One explanation for this may relate to the time the Brougham excavations took place. Today, remains of fruit and grain are often found when cremation burials are excavated. The pyres of the young may have been covered with flowers and fruits, but in the 1960s such remains would not have been retrieved.

Not surprisingly, objects placed on the pyre included military gear such as belt and scabbard fittings. A most remarkable feature at Brougham is that horses were occasionally burnt on the pyre. This has never been observed in a Romano-British cemetery before, and only very rarely elsewhere in the empire. While burning horses alongside their riders is not a "Roman" way of doing things, the fort was garrisoned by cavalry, so the combination of military equipment and horses provided good evidence that soldiers from the unit were buried there.

AGAINST THIS BACKGROUND, two of the burials proved to be of great interest and, indeed, may necessitate a rethinking of Rome's frontier forces. Both individuals had been burned on the pyre with horses and fittings from sword scabbards. Both were generously provided with other goods, in one case including a silver bowl and an ivory object. One had been placed in the grave with a glass vessel, a

joint of meat on a pottery dish, and a pottery jug with an engraved good-luck motto. All this marks the grave as belonging to one of the highest-ranking members of the community. The combination of horses, military equipment, and expensive pyre and grave goods naturally suggested we were dealing with cavalry officers. Then our human-bone expert told us these individuals were most probably females in their 20s or 30s.

To a professional archaeologist, this is an "oh dear" moment. You know what is going to happen. Some of your fellow professionals will say, "Don't be stupid, the Roman army didn't recruit women," and mark you down as publicity hungry. And indeed, this is precisely what has happened.

So what are the options when faced with evidence like this? We could say the sex identifications are just wrong, but our specialist is the acknowledged expert in her field. We could say they are female, and they had military items because they were actually marking the status of a male family member who was a soldier. At Brougham, however, we do not see this transfer of objects anywhere else. No much-loved young sons, for example, went to their pyres with one of their fathers' horses. Or we could say, they are female, and they have the attributes of being cavalry officers, so maybe they had a military role. If we are prepared to contemplate this, then the origins of the unit stationed at Brougham may provide some help. So what are the options when faced with evidence like this? We could say the sex identifications are just wrong, but our specialist is the acknowledged expert in her field. We could say they are female, and they had military items because they were actually

Were Sarmatians the Source of Arthurian Legend?

In A.D. 175 the Roman emperor Marcus Aurelius dispatched some 5,500 Sarmatian cavalry of the Iazyges tribe from the Danube region to northern Britain. After their terms of service were up, many of them settled in a vicus, or veterans' community, at Bremetennacum Veteranorum on the Ribble River in Lancashire, near what later became the village of Ribchester (Latin for "Ribble Camp"). Evidence of Sarmatians found there and nearby includes an inscription of circa 238–244 A.D. mentioning a "troop of Sarmatian cavalrymen [stationed at] Bremetennacum"; a grave stela from Chester depicting a Sarmatian warrior; and an image, probably of a Sarmatian cavalryman, known as the "Naked Horseman" of Ribchester, first described by the English antiquarian Thomas Braithwaite in 1604 and now lost.

The Sarmatians' first commander in Britain was Lucius Artorius Castus, who, according to his grave stela, took his troops to Gaul to put down a rebellion in 184 A.D. Like the legendary King Arthur, he led mounted warriors into battle on the continent. Later Sarmatian leaders may have adopted the title artorius, borrowing it from Lucius Artorius Castus' name. One such leader (or a series of leaders) may have served as the prototype of the "King Arthur," that is, the "Artorius, dux bellorum [war leader]" who, according to some early accounts, saved Britain by defeating the Saxons at Badon Hill ca. 510 A.D.

The Sarmations spoke a Northeast Iranian dialect and shared many traits with other ancient Northeast Iranians, including the Scythians and Alans. There are many parallels between Arthurian legend and the folklore of the modern Ossetians, descendants of the Alans who live in the Caucasus. A conflict over who shall be the guardian of a magical cup or cauldron parallels the Arthurian quest for the Holy Grail, and the Alans, who invaded western Europe in the fifth century A.D., brought legends of a figure we know as Lancelot.

Ossetic folklore centers on the Narts, a band of heroes whose chief is named Batraz. On his deathbed, Batraz orders the Narts to consign his magical sword to the sea. They are, however, loath to do so and attempt to deceive Batraz into thinking his order has been carried out. In the end the sword is finally thrown into the sea; as the blade enters the water, the sea turns blood red and becomes extremely turbulent. Afterwards, Batraz ascends to Heaven.

When this legend is juxtaposed with that of Arthur's death, the Sarmation connection becomes clear. Dying, King Arthur asks Sir Bedivere to throw his sword, Excalibur, into a lake, but the knight does not want to and tries to trick Arthur into thinking his request has been honored. When Excalibur finally is thrown into the water, a parallel extraordinary event occurs: a hand rises from the lake, grasps the sword, and pulls it beneath the surface. Then, like Batraz, Arthur departs for the land of the dead, in this case called Avalon.

by C. SCOTT LITTLETON

marking the status of a male family member who was a soldier. At Brougham, however, we do not see this transfer of objects anywhere else. No much-loved young sons, for example, went to their pyres with one of their fathers' horses. Or we could say, they are female, and they have the attributes of being cavalry officers, so maybe they had a military role. If we are prepared to contemplate this, then the origins of the unit stationed at Brougham may provide some help.

From inscriptions we know the garrison at this time was the *Numerus equitum Stratonicianorum*. The name is not much help. We know of places or towns named Stratonica in Greece, Turkey, and Iraq, and there were likely others. Little is known about the numerus, but it was a type of cavalry unit thought to have been recruited from the tribes on the empire's border. The evidence from the cemetery suggests this one came from Central Europe. We regularly found items, such as gold-in-glass beads and small beads with distinctive colored chevrons, that we would expect to have come from the Danube frontier provinces of Noricum, Pannonia, and Ilyria (including parts of Austria, Hungary, and the former Yugoslavia). Four deposits had small iron bucket pendants. These have never been found in Roman Britain before, but were common then in what is now Hungary, the Czech Republic, Slovakia, and into Poland. There are hints in the records that some of the grave pits may have been purified by fire prior to use, a common practice in the Danubian provinces. There is even a certain amount of evidence from inscriptions. One tombstone records the burial of a 70-year-old man from Pannonia. A 10-to-12-year-old girl was buried in an urn with the grafitto "Bata," an Illyrian name.

So it seems highly probable that what we have here is a unit raised in the Danubian lands and transferred to Britain. Our first impulse was to think we had found a unit of the Sarmatians sent by Marcus Aurelius. In their homelands, however, the Sarmatians buried their dead without cremating them, so this seems unlikely. Despite this, the geographical origins of our tribe are clear and perhaps explain our cavalrywomen.

The ancestors of the Sarmatians, when they lived in steppes, are thought to have given rise to the Greek legends of the Amazons, a female warrior tribe ("Warrior Women of Eurasia," ARCHAEOLOGY, January/February 1997). Certainly women did play a military role then, but we don't know what role they played by the third century among the Sarmatians and similar tribes. It is very likely that a numerus would have had an organization that reflected its tribal origin, rather than the usual hierarchy of a Roman cavalry unit. If women played a military role in their tribe, they could be expected to do so here at Brougham. In these circumstances, cavalrywomen are not an unthinkable concept.

Archaeology can prove nothing incontrovertibly, but Brougham does open up the possibility that we don't know as much about the Roman army as we thought. It has also shown the value of going back to old digs and studying them afresh.

Chinese Chimes and Chariots

CAVALRY IN THE AFTERLIFE?
YOU *CAN* TAKE IT WITH YOU.

by Jarrett A. Lobell

A wealth of musical instruments, historical documents written on bamboo slips, and a pit filled with thirty-three bronze battle chariots are among the astonishing finds recently recovered from two Warring States Period (475–221 B.C.) tombs in central China. The more than two thousand objects comprise the largest and best preserved collection of artifacts from the Chu state, one of the strongest of the seven Warring States, which at its peak ruled all of southern China.

Ongoing excavations have revealed a three-foot-tall elevated drum on a bronze support of phoenixes standing atop tigers, one of the largest drums ever found; a *se*, a twenty-five-string plucked instrument, the first of its kind; and dozens of chimes, including a set of Bianzhong bronze chimes, which were symbols of high status, wealth, and power. Li Youping of the Wuhan Conservatory of Music says the chimes are "of such variety and so well-preserved that they could still be used to give a concert."

Ancient Chinese musical instruments have seen a surge of interest since the 1977 discovery of sixty-four bronze bells from the Warring States Period tomb of the Marquis Yi of Zeng ("Bells of Bronze Age China," ARCHAEOLOGY, January/ February 1994).

In addition to the musical instruments, the tombs' excavation has also yielded bronze cauldrons and other vessels, and a rare bronze lamp decorated with a scene of a man holding a lamp and a bird.

Thirty-three bronze battle chariots and the bones of 72 horses are also buried at the site, in what is the largest chariot pit ever found in China. One of the chariots is a rare six-horse type that until now was thought only to have belonged to emperors of the earlier Eastern Zhou Dynasty (770–221 B.C.).

A thousand three-foot-long bamboo slips found in a tomb may have recorded writings on astronomy, music, and divination, as well as information on politics, economics, art, and religion. Along with inscriptions on bronze vessels and swords found at this and other Chu period sites, bamboo slips from the Chu state represent the only Chinese historical documents that predate the Qin Dynasty (221–206 B.C.), during which the historical documents of all previous states were destroyed.

Unfortunately, like other recent excavations of wealthy Chinese tombs, the tombs' owners remain a mystery. The opening of a bright-red coffin found in one of the two tombs was broadcast live on state-run television, but viewers were disappointed when the male skeletal remains inside offered no obvious indicators of identity. A bronze sword with a possible inscription, found by the skeleton's side, might provide some clues. Experts note that the body was buried facing east to allow the occupant to inspect the chariots and horses buried in front of him when he sat up. They believe the tomb may belong to a senior official or general of the Chu state.

Archaeologists now face the enormous task of recording and conserving the thousands of artifacts from the ongoing excavations. "Archaeology is a science that demands boring research," concedes head excavator Wang Hongxing of the Hubei Provincial Archaeological Institute. "It's not an Aladdin story of treasure-seeking."

PART III:

From the Middle Ages to the Age of Exploration and Conquest

A Day of Much Slaying

A MASS GRAVE OF SLAUGHTERED SOLDIERS REVEALS THE BRUTALITY OF LATE MEDIEVAL WARFARE.

by MARK ROSE

On Palm Sunday, March 29, 1461, the forces of Henry VI were crushed near the village of Towton in Yorkshire by the army of his rival, Edward IV. A contemporary chronicler, Jean de Waurin, wrote of the battle, "So followed a day of much slaying between the two sides, and for a long time no one knew to which side to give the victory so furious was the battle and so great the killing: father did not spare son, nor son his father."

Towton was a pivotal battle in the Wars of the Roses, the protracted struggle between two lines of Edward III's descendants, that of his third son, John of Gaunt, the Duke of Lancaster, and that of his fourth son, Edmund, Duke of York. The House of Lancaster, to which Henry VI belonged, used as its emblem a red rose, while York, the family of Edward IV, used a white rose. From 1460 to 1487, the crown would change hands six times and three of five kings would die violently as the two houses fought for the throne.

Popular books about the Wars of the Roses and general histories focus on the members of the York and Lancaster dynasties and their noble allies, raising questions about Henry VI's mental competency (he suffered a prolonged nervous breakdown in 1453), or the Earl of Warwick's decision to change sides. Left out of the discussion has been the common people drafted into the armies of their royal and noble lords. That is now addressed with the publication of *Blood Red Roses: The Archaeology of a Mass Grave from the Battle of Towton A.D. 1461* (Oxbow Books Limited, 2000).

Towton differed from earlier battles in scale—more than 50,000 took part—and viciousness, historical sources suggesting that both sides ordered that no quarter would be given. The resulting carnage was described in a letter from the Bishop of Exeter to the Papal Legate: "there was a great conflict, which began with the rising of the sun, and lasted until the tenth hour of the night, so great was the boldness of the men, who never heeded the possibility of a miserable death. ...from what we hear of persons worthy of confidence, some 28,000 persons perished on one side and the other."

Most of the slain, because of their sheer numbers, were buried near the battlefield, and in 1996 construction workers at Towton discovered a mass burial. The skeletal remains of 23 people were removed and reinterred without study, following the laws governing such finds. Alerted by this initial find, researchers from

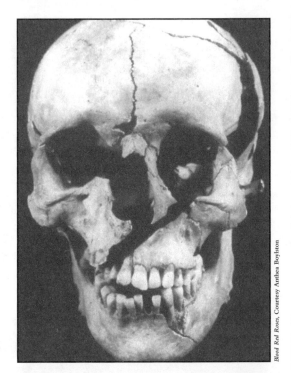

Blood Red Roses, Courtesy Anthea Boylston

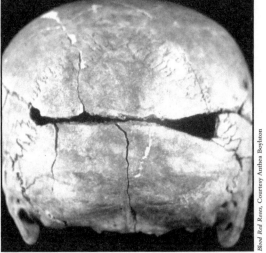

Blood Red Roses, Courtesy Anthea Boylston

No fewer than eight blade-caused wounds are apparent on this single skull from Towton including a large one on the back, likely lethal and certainly disabling, followed by a sweeping blow diagonally across the face.

Lancaster vs. York

Henry VI's abilities as a king were negligible. Historian K.B. McFarlane wrote of him, "Henry VI's head was too small for his father's crown." In 1460, Pope Pius II labeled him "utterly devoid of wit or spirit." The real powers behind Henry were Margaret of Anjou, his wife and mother of Edward, Prince of Wales, and the Beaufort family, headed by the Duke of Somerset. Manipulation of Henry was the key to power, and, during the wars, those who controlled him could claim to rule in his name. Little wonder historian Charles Ross referred to Henry as "that useful political vegetable."

Watching his incompetent cousin's rule and coveting the throne was Richard, Duke of York. In 1453, Henry suffered a nervous breakdown and, over the queen's objections, York was named protector. With Henry's recovery in February 1455, the Lancastrian party of Margaret tried to clip York's wings, but he and his followers took up arms. At St. Albans on May 22, they captured Henry and left the chief Lancastrians dead on the battlefield. With Henry in his vest pocket, York ruled until 1459. But the queen and the sons of the Lancastrian leaders killed at St. Albans regrouped. When the two sides met at Ludford, in October 1459, the Yorkist soldiery deserted and their leaders fled: York to Ireland and his eldest son, Edward, Earl of March, and powerful Neville family backers—the Earl of Salisbury, the Earl of Warwick, and Lord Fauconberg—to Calais. Henry was freed and his queen and followers ruled.

The Yorkist earls returned in June 1460. When they met Henry's army at Northampton, another batch of Lancastrian leaders was left dead on the field and Henry, captured again, was taken to London to serve as their figurehead. In early September, York returned from Ireland intent on deposing Henry VI and having himself crowned. But the nobility would not sanction his usurping the throne, though they agreed to an accord stipulating that it would pass to the York line on Henry's demise.

This pact disinherited the Prince of Wales and was anathema to Margaret. The Lancastrians gathered at Hull, while York, with his second son, Edmund, and the Earl of Salisbury went in pursuit. They met at Wakefield on December 30. York died in the fighting, Edmund was stabbed to death, and Salisbury was captured and beheaded. Elsewhere, Edward, York's oldest son, defeated the Welsh Lancastrians at Mortimer's Cross on February 2–3, 1461. But two weeks later, Queen Margaret defeated the Earl of Warwick at a second battle at St. Albans, freeing Henry once more.

The Lancastrian triumph was short-lived. The Yorkists rallied around Edward, who was crowned at Westminster on March 4, 1461. Nine days later, as Edward IV, he moved north to confront Henry and the Lancastrian army, routing their forces at Towton with great slaughter on Palm Sunday.

by MARK ROSE

the West Yorkshire Archaeology Service and University of Bradford obtained permission from the landowners to excavate the remaining portion of the gravesite. *Blood Red Roses* is a record of that excavation and its findings. As such, it is a site report, but its authors have taken considerable care to lay out the evidence in a clear, step-by-step fashion that allows readers to easily understand how the data are interpreted and why certain conclusions are drawn from them. For example, there are explanations of how the sex and age of an individual is determined from skeletal remains.

Separate chapters deal with topics such as the context of the discovery, in terms of both history and the battlefield landscape; weapons, armor, and late medieval combat; and the excavation and recording methods used. It should be noted that body recovery was the primary goal, an approach used in the study of mass burials related to war crimes, rather than removal of deposits stratum by stratum. The heart of the book, however, is the series of chapters dealing with the human bones of at least 39 individuals that the excavation produced. Who were these people, and what can we reconstruct about their lives and deaths?

The remains, all of men, fall equally into three age groups: 16–25, 26–36, and 36–50. In height, they stood from five feet, three inches to six feet, averaging about five feet, nine inches. Some showed bone alterations characteristic of dietary deficiencies, and most had back problems resulting from physical stress. There is evidence of gum disease—the men could

have flossed more regularly—but few cavities. In all, not a remarkable population. It is with the battle trauma, to which a chapter is devoted, that the evidence becomes horrifying. While there are wounds to the postcranial skeleton, mainly the right arm, which would have been exposed while a soldier attacked or parried a blow, most of the injuries were found on the skulls. Each skull (only one did not have some sort of trauma) had from one to 13 wounds, with an average of four wounds per skull. The distribution of the wounds was telling. Whether caused by a bladed weapon (sword, ax, poleaxe), blunt force (mace or war hammer), or puncture (arrow or tip of poleaxe or war hammer), most wounds were either on the left side of the skull or on the back of it. Those on the side of the head would likely have happened while the person was facing a right-handed opponent. Those on the back, would have occurred if they were fleeing or had fallen down.

The author of this chapter on battle trauma, Shannon Novak of Bradford University, sums it up:

Detailed study of the Towton mass grave skeletons has helped illuminate the reality of medieval warfare. The romanticism of pageantry and knightly honour has often overshadowed the fact that very efficient weapons of war were developed to kill unthinkable numbers of young men. If the figures from Towton are to be believed, 28,000 men were killed on this single day. If the skeletons from this mass grave attest at least a facet of the battle, these men died in a frenzied killing that involved numerous blows to the head, often after they were incapacitated and unable to defend themselves.

Blood Red Roses is notable on several points. The excavation and study were run on a volunteer basis, so this book represents the personal dedication of its authors and all those who participated in the project. It also shows how a site report can be made accessible to a wide audience, not just to a handful of fellow scholars. At the same time, it documents an approach to ancient remains that draws from the forensic study of mass graves, a real contribution given increasing interest in battlefields and prisoner-of-war camps as archaeological sites. Finally, *Blood Red Roses* carries us beyond the written record of either this particular battle or of the period in general, and beyond our fascination with a romanticized version of the past.

The Ship that Terrorized Europe

VIKING RAIDS WERE MADE POSSIBLE BY THE ELEGANT, EFFICIENT LONGSHIP.

by ALEXANDER BENENSON

Between the eight and eleventh centuries A.D., north-ern Europe was at the mercy of the Norse Vikings and their longships. An elegant marriage of crafts-manship and utility, the longship far surpassed other vessels of the day. Its design, having evolved from prehistoric canoes, was simple and devastatingly effective.

The longships and their Viking crews were a menace throughout Europe and even harassed parts of the Mediter-ranean. Each spring, the sleek hulls and curled prows would appear along the coasts in the North Sea and English Chan-nel. A monk from a monastery on the British island of Lindisfarne, describes a Viking raid in 793 A.D. :

They were like stinging wasps, and they spread in all directions like horrible wolves, wrecking, robbing, shatter-ing and killing not only animals but also priests, monks and nuns. They came to the church of Lindisfarne, slayed everything alive, dug up the altars and took all the treasures of the holy church.

A fleet of several hundred longships pushed down the Seine and reached Paris in 845 A.D., extorting 7,000 pounds of silver from Charles the Bald, king of the Franks. Several years later, nearly 40,000 Norse warriors swamped the French city on a fleet of longships so dense that onlookers thought the river had been swallowed up entirely. A prayer echoed through the churches of France, "*A furore normannorum libera nos domine, Skona oss herre från nordmännens raseri.*" (*Oh Lord, save us from the Nordic people.*)

Though Christians believed the raids were the product of bloodthirsty paganism, the Viking forays were probably the result of recent internal political consolidation and population growth. Raids were a quick and efficient means of acquiring precious goods, and most importantly they did not obligate the Vikings to set up any new long-term settlements. And the longships were key to the Viking's ability to conduct such long-distance raids.

The ships were up to 115 feet in length and narrow. The oak planks, which slightly overlapped each other, were bound together by iron nails and caulked with moss or animal fur covered in tar. The longship tapered at both ends, a simple feature which allowed the Vikings to row the ship in either direction, facilitating maneuverability. The shallow draft of the longship made it easy to navigate in as little as three feet of water. Constructed

Built around 890 A.D., the Gokstad ship and the chieftain's burial in it were excavated in Norway in 1880.

© Museum of Cultural History – University of Oslo, Norway, Eirik Irgens Johnsen

out of a single oak timber, the keel ran from the back of the ship to the front, ending in a tightly wound curled tip or ornate carving, often of a snake or dragon. The headpiece was removed during travel lest it fall off, a bad omen according to the Vikings. The one-piece keel stabilized the hull and helped guide the ship along a straight path in the water. The crew, which could be as large as 300, acted as moveable ballast. The number of oars on a longship varied with its length from only several pairs on smaller ships to nearly 30 on the largest. Oars were usually made out of spruce and were cut to different lengths according to their position fore or aft, so that all the oars entered the water at the same time. As early as the seventh century, Vikings began attaching sails to their longships. The large square sails, made of leather-reinforced wool cloth set upon a single mast in the middle of the ship, increased the ships' range and stability. With favorable wind a longship could attain speeds of up to 14 knots.

The best surviving example of a Viking longship is the "Gokstad Ship," found near Oslo in 1880. It was almost entirely preserved inside a burial mound dating back to A.D. 900. Scraps of the wool sail were found along with portions of the mast, confirming the sail-design suggested by drawings on Nordic ruins. Thirty-two shields were also found buried with the ship, painted alternately black and yellow. The shields probably latched onto the ship's gunwales, or railing, and were meant to both protect the rowers as they docked and to intimidate the enemy. Along with another well-preserved ship, the "Oseberg Ship," the Gokstad Ship has provided the template for a number of re-creations. Working from the with Viking-age materials and basing their plans off the excavated ships, archaeologists over the past century have built several longships that have successfully completed transatlantic journeys, including a replica of the Gokstad Ship which sailed from Bergen, Norway, to New York and was then sent to Chicago for the 1893 World's Fair.

Suppression of the Cathars

A FAIRY-TALE LANDSCAPE IN SOUTHERN FRANCE BELIES A BRUTAL CRUSADE.

by JAMES WISEMAN

In late June 1209, responding to Pope Innocent III's call for a new crusade, an army larger than any seen before in Christian lands assembled on the banks of the Rhône River at Lyon. According to the poet and eyewitness, William of Tudela, it comprised 20,000 knights and 200,000 common soldiers (although scholars view his figures as poetic exaggeration). The soldiers were promised remission of their sins—the same indulgence earlier crusaders had received as they set out to fight Islam in the Holy Land—in return for serving a minimum of 40 days. This crusade, however, was aimed not at a distant land or foreign enemies, but rather at home-nurtured heretics known as Cathars in the Languedoc region of France, stretching north from the Spanish border to the Rhône Delta. Suppression of the heresy, called Albigensian after the town of Albi, where Cathars were thought to be particularly numerous, was marked by more than a century of violence, infamous atrocities, and the birth of the Inquisition.

When we visited last June, the Cathar country of the Languedoc seemed like a fairy-tale landscape dotted with castles, cathedrals, vineyards, and vestiges of ancient towns. At its heart lies Carcassonne, whose well-preserved "old city" has become a major tourist attraction, and near which we made a base for our exploration of the region. The city began as a hillfort, and recent archaeological finds south of the Basilica of St. Nazaire show that imports from both the western and eastern Mediterranean found their way there as early as the sixth century B.C. In Roman times it was known as Carcaso, and lay on the road from Tolosa (modern Toulouse) to the provincial capital of Narbo (now Narbonne) and the Via Domitia, the principal road across southern France to Italy. In the late third or early fourth century it received new, strong fortification walls, which underlie most of the inner fortifications and towers of the late thirteenth century, seen today as they were restored (rather too imaginatively) in the nineteenth and early twentieth centuries. Archaeologists and preservationists are now replacing with red tiles on a gentler pitch the slate shingles and pepper-pot roofs of the towers, mistakenly "restored" by the architect Eugène Emmanuel Viollet-le-duc in the 1840s. The adventurer, soldier, and scholar T.E. Lawrence (1888–1935), also known as Lawrence of Arabia, included illustrations of the restored fortifications of Carcassonne as part of his senior thesis on crusader military architecture at Jesus Col-

lege, Oxford. The thesis formed part of his book, *Crusader Castles,* published posthumously in 1936 (London: Golden Cockerel Press).

A troubadour song in Oc, the French dialect of the region, explains the city's name with a tale of how "la Dame de Carcass" brought an end to a long siege by Charlemagne by having a sow force-fed with the last remaining grain in the city, then hurled from the ramparts. The unfortunate pig burst open at the feet of the attackers, who were astonished that the city had so much food it could squander it in such a way. Discouraged, Charlemagne lifted the siege, and as the army marched away, the lady had the bells of the church rung in triumph, prompting one of the soldiers to say, *"La Dame de Carcass sonne!"* (The lady of Carcass rings!).

The Roman walls, best seen on the northeast, were strengthened over the years and still served the city in 1209, when Viscount Raymond Roger Trencavel VI refused to submit to the crusaders, who wanted Carcassonne as a base of operations, as well as for plunder. The viscount was captured, or betrayed into his enemies' hands, and the city capitulated. The crusaders were so intent on plunder that they seized the homes and all the possessions of the inhabitants, expelling the Catholic population wearing only their underwear. Simon de Montfort, a military leader of the crusade, was awarded the lands of the captured viscount (who soon died) and zealously continued the crusade for nearly a decade until, in 1218, he was struck on the head by a stone hurled from the walls of Toulouse, which he was then besieging. He died on the spot and was buried in Carcassonne.

The people of Béziers, one of Viscount Raymond's principal cities and the first in the Languedoc besieged by the crusaders, had also refused to surrender or to hand over the heretics among them. When the crusaders began to break into the town, one of the attackers asked Arnaud Amaury, the papal legate in command of the army, how they should distinguish between Catholics and heretics. He is reported to have replied, "Massacre them all, for the Lord knows his own!" The town was plundered and burned, and nearly 20,000 people were said to have perished: clergy, women, and children being killed in churches. "So terrible a slaughter has not been known or consented to, I think, since the time of the Saracens!" was the judgment of William of Tudela in his "Song of the Cathar Wars." The massacre so terrified the people of the Languedoc that more than 100 fortified villages submitted to Amaury as he led his army west to Carcassonne.

The following spring, writes Michael Costen of Bristol University in his study, *The Cathars and the Albigensian Crusade* (Manchester University Press, 1997), when new crusaders arrived to replace those who had fulfilled their pledge and returned home with their plunder, the first place besieged was Minèrve, a fortified village northeast of Carcassonne in a dramatic setting between two deep river gorges. Minèrve was the home of a Cathar bishop and known to be providing refuge for a large number of *perfecti* (perfect ones), the most devoted of the Cathar heretics. When the town surrendered following bombardment and the destruction of its water supply, Amaury and Montfort spared the Catholics, but not the perfecti, who refused to recant their beliefs. A great bonfire was built at the edge of town and 140 Cathars, both men and women, were burned to death.

Minèrve gives its name to the region north of the Aude River, the Minervois, extending from near Carcassonne to the sea, and the home of some of the finest wines in the Languedoc. As our little group made its way from Carcassonne to Minèrve, a pleasant drive among the vineyards that line the roads and spread across the rolling hills, we paused in La Livinière, a wine-producing center, to sample the reputedly excellent wine of the Domaine Maris (our tasting confirmed the reputation!), where we discovered that the principal *négociant* (wine company) there commemorates the medieval persecutions with its name, Le Comte Cathare (The Cathar Count). From there we crossed the same winding mountain pass that Simon de Montfort and his army must have taken to Minèrve.

The archaeological museum there was one of the saddest we encountered in France: it was badly maintained, and the displays, ranging from prehistoric stone tools to medieval artifacts, were poorly presented, with little or no signage. A stroll through Minèrve itself, however, was a walk into the past; set against a backdrop of hollowed cliffs, its medieval walls and streets were strongly evocative of the time of the crusade.

The capture of other castles and towns in the Languedoc was followed by executions as horrific as the ones at Minèrve, although many places simply surrendered out of terror. At Lavaur, a town near

Toulouse taken by storm in 1211, Geralda, lady of Lavaur, was thrown into a well and stoned to death; her brother, the lord of Montréal, who had already been dispossessed by Montfort, was hanged with 80 of his knights; and more than 400 Cathars were burned to death. Considerations of politics and profit were a part of the pattern then set, whereby lords of the Languedoc were killed or dispossessed, ostensibly for not rooting out all the heretics, their places and lands then taken by northerners, and heretics identified and burned.

Who were these Cathars, who called themselves Christians and "Good Men" and inspired such affection that some towns risked annihilation by harboring them? They must have been long established in the Languedoc by 1165, when a number of Cathars were invited to a public debate at Lombers, near Albi, with several prominent Catholic churchmen, attended by both aristocrats and commoners. The heresy seems to have spread into the region from the north, where it was known earlier in the century. Ekbert of Schönau, a monk whom Cathar missionaries had tried (and failed) to convert during the 1150s, explained the meaning of Cathar as pure, deriving the word from the Greek *katharós*. They were, indeed, often seen as pure, and so presented themselves to the public, in contrast to the Catholic clergy, many of whom in the Languedoc were considered even by the pope to be corrupt and uncaring. The Cathars believed there were two gods, an evil God of Darkness who created the world and all that is visible, and a good God of Light, who created the spiritual, unseen things, including souls and good

angels. It followed for Cathars that the God of the Old Testament, who created the world, was Satan, and that the human body, a creation of Satan, was therefore evil and should receive as little as possible to sustain it; only the soul within was from the God of Light, and its release from the body was a prospect of joy.

The leaders of the Cathars, the *perfecti*, abstained from sexual intercourse, did not marry, took no oaths, did not eat meat, and even avoided foods related to animal reproduction such as eggs and milk; long fasts were standard. They believed that Christ would never have cooperated with Satan by assuming an evil human body, so that the body and blood of Christ never existed, and the Catholic mass was fakery; they pronounced the Catholic Church an instrument of Satan. The strictures of Cathar doctrine were so severe that only the perfecti were expected to abide by them, while other Cathars, the *credentes* (believers) lived more customary lives, and often became perfecti only near the point of death. At the dawn of the thirteenth century, perfecti in the Languedoc may have numbered some 1,500 and the credentes may have been as many as 15,000.

The perfecti, preaching and teaching, often in poverty, began to be met on their own terms by the Castilian monk Dominic de Guzman, the future St. Dominic, who came to the Languedoc in 1206 on a mission of preaching and living in poverty. When his small band of followers was formally recognized as an order by the Lateran Council of 1215, founded at first as a specific counter to the heretics of Languedoc, he moved his base to Toulouse and began to recruit new canons from the universities of the north before his death in 1221. As the Dominicans became recognized for their skill in teaching and theological debate, especially in disputing heretics, they were given bases in cities across the Languedoc, including Béziers, Narbonne, and Carcassonne.

Despite the Dominicans, despite the crusaders, and despite the deaths of many Cathars, the heresy continued to exist and, at times, even flourish. Finally, in 1233, the church established a new apparatus for the systematic discovery and punishment of heretics, the Inquisition, which was directed by the Dominican brothers. Inquisitors, with the aid of secular authorities, could arrest anyone on suspicion of heresy; prisoners were denied legal assistance, were not confronted by their accuser, and evidence needed not be revealed. They were interrogated in private; only the sentence was public, and there was no appeal. The horrors of the new approach carried with it new fervor: in celebration of the first saint's day of St. Dominic (August 4, 1234), the bishop of Toulouse had a sick woman, who had confessed heresy to him in a fever, carried on her bed to a meadow and burned to death. Even the corpses of dead Cathars were exhumed and burned.

Some Cathars took up arms, some converted to Catholicism, others fled the country or sought refuge wherever it might be found. But any such refuge was only temporary. The castle of Montségur, on a remote and precipitous hilltop at the edge of the Pyrénées, had been refurbished by its owner in 1204 to serve as a gathering place for Cathars; this became a favored refuge for Cathars during the crusade and Inquisition. It withstood a siege in 1241, but when it was finally taken in 1244, after a long siege and perilous assault, some 200 Cathars were immolated below the castle, where a monument now stands. An archaeological museum at Montségur houses artifacts found in excavations at the site since 1958, including everyday objects used by those in the castle and the village below it, as well as remains of two people who are believed to have perished in the siege.

There were other remote castles further east in the Fenouillèdes region, on steep and rocky cliffs that hem in long, verdant valleys. Peyrepertuse, one of the largest of them, surrendered in 1240. From the ramparts of Peyrepertuse visitors may look across a valley to Quéribus; perched on a pinnacle of rock reachable only by a single steep ascent, it seems impregnable. It was the last stronghold of the Cathars to surrender, in 1255.

The Inquisition continued, with intermittent periods of mild activity, until the end of the century, and the end of the Cathars. The castles remain to mark their passing.

Reconstructing Medieval Artillery

ARCHAEOLOGIST PETER VEMMING TAKES A HANDS-ON, EXPERIMENTAL APPROACH TO HIS STUDIES OF CENTURIES-OLD ARMS.

*W*ork has begun on a 22-ton fourteenth-century trebuchet at Warwick castle in southern England. (See page 5 of the photo insert.) The largest reconstructed trebuchet ever attempted, it is the work of medieval-weapons expert Peter Vemming of the Danish Medieval Centre (www.middelaldercentret.dk). Once it is completed in late June, the siege weapon will launch projectiles—sending them up to 300 meters—daily throughout the summer. Vemming recently spoke to ARCHAEOLOGY'S *Alexander Benenson about the new trebuchet and other projects he and his colleagues have worked on, including the re-creation of an early fourteenth-century Scandinavian cannon.*

How did you first get interested in medieval weaponry and, especially, in reconstructing trebuchets?
Very early in my life even before going to the university—probably from reading Prince Valiant. As an archaeologist at a local museum, I suggested we reconstruct a medieval trebuchet for the 700th anniversary of the city Nykøbing Falster.

At that time, in 1989, I think that only Napoleon III had tried something like that in 1851. His machine broke down after a few shots and the first trial shot was minus 70 meters because there was not enough curvature on the iron hook holding the ammunition sling! This was a bad result for Napoleon, but good information for us and we succeeded in building a reconstruction of a medieval siege engine, which still shoots nearly every day for the visitors at the Medieval Centre in Denmark.

How did your early reconstructions lead to the creation of the Medieval Centre in Denmark?

The reconstruction drew so much public attention that the idea of starting a center was born. During the next few years we made several reconstructions of medieval artillery. A few years later the center had been so successful that either we had to close the center, because there were not enough facilities for staff members and the visitors, or invest a lot of money. So the Medieval Centre in Denmark was created!

What is the origin of the trebuchet? When did they first make their appearance on the Western Europe battlefield?

Mechanical devices for warfare are known way back in history, but it is commonly agreed that this type of artillery originated in Asia, and that the idea for trebuchets was born in China. From here the knowledge spread westward in the sixth century and reached the Arabs via Persia and Byzantium. From them it spread to Sicily, and the Europeans then started to experiment with this new technology, which resulted in the creation of the very heavy counterweight trebuchet. This happened in the ninth century, and this new kind of heavy and reliable artillery dominated warfare into the first half of the sixteenth century, together with new and very potent gunpowder artillery.

How effective was the trebuchet?

A counterweight trebuchet is a very simple, very powerful, and very reliable technology. Once you have set it up it can work continuously with high precision for months without much maintenance.

It was used throughout the medieval age to besiege castles and cities. Even though we don't have much information on the construction details of the weapon we have a lot of sources that tell us about its effectiveness in warfare. The counterweight trebuchet was the ultimate heavy artillery of the medieval age and though they surely used a lot of mechanical devices in warfare, many maybe very specialized ones, none had the same effects as the big trebuchets!

We have several accounts of the use of a trebuchet as the decisive factor in the siege of a castle from Edward I in the Welsh wars in the late thirteenth century. We know how many stone bullets were used, how much they cost, how many horses and wagons were used to bring the trebuchet to the castle, the wages of the blacksmith, and even the cost of pigs' fat for greasing the axles. It took 480 great stones to make the castle surrender and not a single attacker was killed. At the rate of a stone every 15 minutes this siege would have taken 80 hours!

In your 1992 article about trebuchet reproduction, published in **Acta Archaeologica,** *you mention a number of earlier attempts to re-create this weapon, including the attempt by Napoleon III. Today, there are hundreds of groups around the world devoted to trebuchets, what makes these siege weapons in particular so popular?*

Again, it is simple and reliable technology that everybody can build. It is fun to play with, but also a bit dangerous. But that is not the whole truth, once you start working with the technology you become fascinated with all the variables that have to be in harmony for the perfect shot—the length of the sling, the curvature of the release pin on the throwing arm, the length of the throwing arm, the weight in the ballast box, the weight of the bullet, etcetera. It sort of grabs you. It is probably the best hobby a "big boy" can get!

From what sources did you draw your plans for the trebuchet? Were you able to consult any archaeological evidence?

Unfortunately, we don't have any archaeological evidence. The only fully preserved machine was excavated under a church in 1890s at Liebemuehl in East Prussia, but shortly after excavation it was cut up for firewood. So the sources we used for the reconstruction are written sources and illustrations, combined with an overall knowledge of medieval craftsmanship—the metalwork and different types of joints in the timberwork. The quality of these sources differs, and a reconstruction cannot be based on a single source alone, but has to be put together from many different places. What

we build could be described as the sum of knowledge at this moment of time—something that might change if we learn more, for example by the excavation of a fully preserved trebuchet—though that is probably very unlikely!

In terms authenticity in construction, do you have a strict set of rules for materials and tools?

The authenticity of a reconstruction always goes hand in hand with the amount of money you have. We distinguish between replicas and copies. A replica is built with the old tools and materials reconstructing the old working processes, while the copy looks like the finished replica, but it is done with modern tools and devices, lifting gear, etc.

Before each reconstruction we agree on a set of rules on which we build the machine and often we choose the replica way, not that it will have any effect on your test results, but because it is very interesting for the visitors to the center to see the old crafts being used. The big machines, though, are built as copies.

Were there any surprises or new problems you encountered in building such a large trebuchet this time?

Not really. We work a lot with models before doing the big machine and we have so much experience from all the years, that we didn't meet any surprising problems.

What can a full-scale reproduction like this teach us about medieval warfare?

What would we know if we didn't build one? Experimental archaeology is a fantastic tool for understanding all the missing links in the working processes. We learn about the effectiveness of the machine itself, but also about the logistics, craft specialization, and handling of heavy machinery, you name it! But it all rests on the quality of the reconstruction; if you don't do your best there—if you use modern solutions or cut corners—the value of your results drops drastically!

What have your reconstructions taught you about the quality and precision of medieval engineering and workmanship?

At the Medieval Centre we have a windmill standing close by the trebuchets. This windmill needs repairs very often, but the trebuchet just keeps shooting and it only needs a little pigs' grease once in a while. The windmill is very recent technology (late eighteenth century), while the trebuchet represents thousand of years of know-how and craftsmanship—knowledge we have lost today.

What plans do you have for the future in terms of medieval weaponry reconstruction?

For the last four years the Medieval Centre has hosted an international seminar on early guns and gunpowder. Scandinavia probably has the oldest medieval gun—the so-called Loshult gun. We have reconstructed this gun and together with the Danish military have tested it with gunpowder made from original recipes and with original materials. This research has shown that even though many scholars think of these guns as being very ineffective, it is quite opposite—these guns and powders are very efficient and the gunpowder is of nearly modern quality. The

interesting question is now, if you had such effective guns in the 1350s then why does it take more than 200 years for these new weapons to conquer the old mechanical artillery on the battlefields around Europe?

The answer, we believe, lies in the raw materials for powder making. The sulfur could only come from Iceland or Sardinia and the saltpeter had to come from Bengali in India, or you had to make it yourself, which wasn't very effective. The saltpeter came with the old trade routes from India, but in 1453 the Turks took Constantinople and this trade stops. It now became vital to find a seaway to India to get the saltpeter. The problem was not using this technology, but securing the stable delivery of raw materials. It took 200 years for the Europeans to solve this logistic problem and from then on they started to conquer the world with these new gunpowder weapons.

How did construction of the trebuchet at Warwick castle go?

The machine itself was built by English carpenters from my drawings, while we made the iron fittings here in Denmark. There are more than two tons of iron on it. All the parts were then sent to Warwick Castle in England, where the two work crews met and put the thing together. The machine sits on a little island by the river Avon and it was not possible to get heavy lifting gear on the island, so the timbers had to be raised by hand using blocks and tackles and a simple A-frame as a crane, exactly as they would have done it in medieval times. It took a lot of manpower, but everything went very smoothly.

Were the test firings a success?

When the machine's frame was up we started rigging it—putting on the ropes for pulling down the arm and then attaching the sling bag. Then, when it was time for the first trials, we pulled down the arm to see if everything worked well, ran in the treadmills (the large wooden wheels that serve as a winch), and checked all details before putting in the counter-weight in the ballast box. The Warwick people wanted the projectile to land 250 meters down the island, so, judging from our experience with our Danish trebuchets, we put two-thirds of the weight of the projectile in the ballast box. The first shot was 280 meters, so we just stopped there and didn't put in more ballast. Subsequent test shootings showed the normal pattern: The bullets landed very close together in a series of shots. But then it started to rain and we had some very strange results. We know that the ropes pull together when they get wet, and that the range of shot changes a bit, but were surprised to see some very long shots when the ropes got wet. It was only days after that we got the explanation from a bright guy, who remembered that the ballast stones we put in for counter-weight were made of soft sandstone, which absorbs water very easily. By accident, we had added a lot of weight suddenly and, therefore, the longer shots.

The throwing arm of the machine is very light—suitable for museum purposes, so to speak—and it will only shoot with a 15-kilo stone. Had this been a real medieval machine the arm would have been made more solid and the ropes, etc., would have been heavier and stronger.

What's your next project?

Our next project will be to reconstruct a very big medieval gun of the so-called "Anholt" type or *Mary Rose* type (as on Henry VIII's warship of that name) and test it with gunpowder made from the original recipes. We have just finished collecting the necessary sulfur from the big deposits in Mamfjall in northern Iceland. Working together with the local Akureyri Museum, employees from the Medieval Center in Denmark reenacted the medieval process of extracting sulfur. This sulfur will be used for making gunpowder using early recipes and then tested in replicas of medieval guns together with the Danish army.

The Danish Medieval Centre's trebuchet is now on display at Warwick Castle in England. For more information visit Warwick Castle's siege weapon site: www.warwicksiege.com

◉EYEWITNESS: The Crusades and the Fall of Constantinople

compiled by MARK ROSE

Literary works, especially nineteenth-century novels like Sir Walter Scott's *The Talisman* and *Ivanhoe,* may focus on the deeds of knights in open battle or courtly competition, but medieval warfare often came down to a brutal trial of endurance between those defending walls and those attacking them. A besieging force might attempt to carry a castle or city by storm, going over its walls or battering through them. Mining beneath walls to collapse them was one ancient strategy, encouraging a betrayal was another. If time and resources permitted, a less costly approach would be to starve the defenders. All these techniques were employed during the crusades. At the end of the era, however, gunpowder and the development of the massive siege cannon altered the paradigm of warfare.

After the capture of Jerusalem by Caliph Omar in 638 A.D., Christians continued to enjoy freedom of religion

Jerusalem's Tower of David, depicted in this woodcut, incorporates ancient, Crusader, and later stonework.

Courtesy Mark Rose

there. But in 1076, Jerusalem came under the control of the Seljuk Turks, who persecuted the city's Christian inhabitants and pilgrims. In 1095, Pope Urban II appealed for a crusade, and the following year two expeditions set out. The first, led by Peter the Hermit, was a disorganized mass march of men, women, and children armed largely with faith. They were killed or captured by Turkish forces before ever reaching the Holy Land. The second was a large-scale military operation by knights and soldiery from France, Flanders, Provence, and southern Italy. With Byzantine aid, the crusaders captured Nicaea, Antioch, and, in July 1099,

Jerusalem. But the kingdoms they established were not long-lived. In less than a century, Saladin recaptured Jerusalem.

This account, by Baha' al-Din Ibn Shaddad, Saladin's biographer, is one of classic siege warfare. Saladin identifies the weakest point in the defenses and moves in his artillery, consisting of trebuchets, to batter down the walls. The siege continues until the fall of the city becomes inevitable and the defenders negotiate terms:

He descended on the city on Sunday 15 Rajab 583 [20 September 1187]. He took up position on the western side. It was crammed with fighting men, both mounted and foot soldiers. Experienced sources estimated the number of soldiers who were there at more than 60,000, apart from women and children. Then, because of an advantage he saw, he transferred to the north side, which move took place on Friday 20 Rajab [25 September]. He set up trebuchets and pressed hard on the city with assaults and a hail of missiles. Eventually, he undermined the city wall on the side next to the Valley of Gehenna in the northern angle. The enemy saw the indefensible position they had fallen into and the signs were clear to them that our true religion would overcome the false. Their hearts were downcast on account of the killing and imprisonment that had befallen their knights and men-at-arms and the fall and conquest of their fortresses. They realized that their lot was ineluctable and that they would be killed by the sword that had killed their brethren. Humbled, they inclined toward seeking terms. An agreement was reached through an exchange of messages between the two sides. The sultan received the surrender on Friday 27 Rajab [2 October].

Two years later, in 1189, the third crusade arrived, led by kings Richard of England and John of France. Though they successfully besieged Acre in 1191, the crusaders ultimately settled for a truce that left Saladin in possession of Jerusalem. Scarcely a decade later, a fourth crusade, of French and Venetians, was on the move. At Constantinople, however, the crusaders became entangled in dynastic struggles and disputes about aid promised by the Byzantines. Instead of proceeding to the Holy Land, the crusaders besieged Constantinople in July 1203 and again in February–April 1204.

Among the Franks was Geoffroy Villehardouin, whose *Conquest of Constantinople* provides a firsthand account of these events. As with Saladin at Jerusalem, here the Franks were confronted with massive

The Venetian leader of the fourth crusade, Enrico Dandolo, was entombed in the Byzantine church Hagia Sophia.

Courtesy Mark Rose

ancient walls, built in the fifth century A.D. by the emperor Theodosius. He details a failed attempt to go over the top, in which the Franks were met by professional soldiers in the pay of the Byzantines. The emperors had long hired Vikings for their elite guard, which in later years included English, armed with traditional battleaxes, from families dispossessed after the Norman conquest.

The French planted two scaling ladders against a barbican close to the sea. The wall here was strongly manned by Englishmen and Danes, and the struggle that ensued was stiff and hard and fierce. By dint of strenuous efforts, two knights and two sergeants managed to scale the ladders and make themselves masters of the walls. A good 15 of our men got up on top, and were quickly engaged in a hand-to-hand combat of axes against swords. The Greeks inside the barbican plucked up courage and fought back so savagely that they drove our men out. …Such was the outcome of the assault as far as the French were concerned. Many were wounded and many were left with broken limbs.

Like the crusader kingdoms, the Latin Empire established by the fourth crusade did not last, and the Byzantines recovered Constantinople in 1261. Two centuries later, Constantinople fell a final time when the Ottoman sultan Mehmet attacked in 1453. Throughout the account of the siege by the Venetian Nicolò Barbaro there are references to the punishing effect of Mehmet's artillery, not the catapults and trebuchets of earlier generations but massive cannon that the city's thousand-year-old walls could not withstand.

> On the eleventh of April, the Sultan had his cannon placed near the walls, by the weakest part of the city, the sooner to gain his objective. ...One of these four cannon which were placed at the gate of San Romano threw a ball weighing about 1,200 pounds...which will show the terrible damage it inflicted where it landed.

San Romano was the weakest point in the walls, and it was there that the Byzantine emperor, Constantine Palaiologos, led the defense. But the cannon demoralized the defenders and wore them down through the effort required to repair the walls.

> On the twentieth of May, there were hardly any attacks or skirmishings by sea or on land, except for the usual cannon fire, which continually brought stretches of the walls down to the ground, while we Christians quickly repaired the damage with barrels and withes and earth to make them as strong as they had been before. Men and women, the old and the young and the priests, all worked together at these repairs.

The final assault was on May 29, with the Turks "firing their cannon again and again," so that "the very air seemed to be split apart." Three waves of troops came at the walls, and the third, the elite janissaries, broke through and carried the city. The use of cannon to break down the walls at Constantinople marked a turning point in warfare. At about the same time, Henry V of England was employing large siege cannon against the French with equal success. "Modern" weaponry had surpassed the old defenses.

THE *MARY ROSE*

RESURRECTING THE PRIDE
OF HENRY VIII'S FLEET

by ALEXANDER BENENSON

Since being raised in 1982, *Mary Rose,* a British warship from the fleet of Henry VIII, has undergone a continuous process of conservation and restoration. (See page 5 of the photo insert.) The ship, built between 1509 and 1511, was part of the newly crowned king's aggressive campaign to create a world-class navy. Threatened by the superior fleet of King James of Scotland and the hostile French, Henry built *Mary Rose,* one of the first warships capable of firing broadside, as part of a fleet that would grow to 58 ships. *Mary Rose* was shuffled between Scotland and the English Channel over the next 35 years during Henry's campaigns against the Scots and the French. Just the presence of the massive 207-gun man-of-war was often enough to decide a battle, as happened in 1514 when the appearance of *Mary Rose* scattered a fleet of French galleys. Later that year the ship would help to burn Cherbourg on

Quality Cargo

Off the rugged coast of northwest Scotland, new finds are shedding light on the Spanish Armada's failed effort to conquer Britain. Near the town of Kinlochbervie, archaeologists from St. Andrews University's Archaeological Diving Unit have found artifacts from a sixteenth-century ship scattered on rock outcrops up to 100 feet below the surface. Though no timbers of the ship remain, project head Martin Dean feels it was probably a galleon from the fleet that Spain's Philip II dispatched to conquer England in 1588. So far his team has found anchors, wine jars, a cooking pot, four cannon, and a depth-sounding lead, all most likely from the ship's bow quarter.

Most intriguingly, the archaeologists have recovered pieces of 26 rare, high-quality Italian majolica jugs and plates. Considered Europe's finest ceramics at the time, some of the majolica is painted with mythological creatures found in frescoes that decorate Nero's Golden Palace in Rome. Clearly the high-end goods are not the kind of tableware normally found in a ship going to war. "This pottery is not meant to be used at sea," says John Wood, a local archaeologist. "They may have been carrying it for the victory celebration they were anticipating." The presence of so much valuable tableware also suggests the Spaniards might have intended the pieces as gifts, or bribes, to win over English officials after the conquest.

by Eric A. Powell

the northern coast of France. In 1545, when the French launched and assaulted the channel and the Isle of Wight, *Mary Rose* was front and center. But early on in the engagement on July 19, 1545, *Mary Rose* heeled over and sank. The French immediately proclaimed they had sunk the pride of the English fleet, while the British accounts maintained variously that the ship had sunk accidentally after strong seas forced water into the unusually low gun ports or that the vessel's notoriously quarrelsome crew was to blame. After a failed attempt to raise her in the following months, *Mary Rose* was all but forgotten for nearly 300 years. In 1836, John Deane, one of the men responsible for developing the first diving helmet, rediscovered the wreck after getting a tip from a local fisherman. He commenced a series of dives in which a number of artifacts, including iron cannons, were retrieved from the wreck. Despite his efforts, no attempts to raise *Mary Rose* were made until its rediscovery in 1966 by military historian Alexander McKee.

After being raised in 1982, conservation efforts focused on stabilizing the fragile timbers of the ship that had been submerged in murky water for nearly 450 years. Titanium beams were installed to replace missing or heavily damaged wooden ones and conservators built an elaborate spray system that doused the hull with cold water continuously for nearly ten years to prevent the wood from drying out and to discourage fungal growth. In 1993, the last timber was replaced and *Mary Rose* entered a new phase of active conservation. The Mary Rose Trust, which oversees the wreck in

Portsmouth, England, began spraying the ship with a solution of polyethylene glycol (PEG 200) in September 1994. This wax-like substance slowly replaced the water molecules inside the wood of *Mary Rose.* Over a period of 15 years, the solution essentially froze the wreck, like petrified wood, preserving it for posterity.

In 2005, the final five-year-long phase of spraying began. For this phase, the solution was made more concentrated. The new solution will act as a sealant on the hull of *Mary Rose.* Once applied, it will take four years to dry completely and to adjust to the controlled conditions of the museum environment. Archaeologists hope that then, after 30 years of tireless effort, the wreck, the only surviving sixteenth-century warship, will finally be open to the public for viewing with no physical barriers between the ancient hull and the visitor.

The Mary Rose Trust in Portsmouth has dedicated a museum to Mary Rose *and her history. More information can be found at www.maryrose.org.*

Death March of Hernando de Soto

ARCHAEOLOGISTS CHART THE CONQUISTADOR'S TRAIL OF HUMAN DESTRUCTION FROM FLORIDA'S GULF COAST TO THE MOUTH OF THE MISSISSIPPI.

by David H. Dye

Four hundred and fifty years ago, on May 25, 1539, the Spanish conquistador Hernando de Soto landed in Florida, probably at Tampa Bay. His fleet of nine ships carried supplies, pigs, horses, war dogs, and 600 conquistadors, accompanied by tailors, shoemakers, stocking makers, notaries, farriers, trumpeters, friars, servants, slaves, and at least two women. De Soto's royal charter from King Charles V of Spain explicitly forbade him from engaging in atrocities in La Florida—the southeastern United States—and ordered him to pacify the land without "death and robbery of the Indians." De Soto and his followers had a different agenda. Their consuming aim was to comb the Southeast for the kind of treasure Spanish conquerors had found in Central and South America. If Indians obstructed their quest, the Spaniards were prepared to pacify them by any means necessary.

Four years later, in the summer of 1543, the 311 surviving members of De Soto's expedition straggled to safety in Mexico. Their looting excursions had taken them thousands of miles through portions of at least ten southern states, as far west as Texas. Their numbers had been cut in half by starvation, desertion, disease, drowning, snakebite, and Indian arrows and clubs. De Soto himself had died in 1542, presumably of fever, as his army camped on the banks of the Mississippi River.

The calamity that befell the Spaniards, however, was nothing compared with the tragedy visited upon the Indians. By the end of the sixteenth century, native cultures in the Southeast were in a state of collapse. While no one can be sure what caused that collapse, many scholars believe that De Soto's expedition, or *entrada,* played a major role. Many Indians met their deaths directly at the hands of the conquistadors. Many more are believed to have perished in the epidemics of new diseases—influenza, whooping cough, and smallpox—that the Spaniards introduced into North America.

Archaeological evidence of De Soto's trek has been elusive. Recent discoveries, however, have begun to shed light on the world through which he passed. At the South Florida Museum in Bradenton, I have had the pleasure of photographing numerous artifacts from all over the Southeast, many of which give direct evidence of the De Soto expedition: iron chain used to bind the Indians; gift kits containing long, blue Nueva Cadiz and faceted chevron beads and mirrors; iron chisels and wedges; sheet brass bells; tubular and sheet brass beads; and fragments of military hardware such as chain mail, swords, lances, and armor.

Recent excavations of an Indian burial mound in Citrus County, Florida, have yielded large numbers of artifacts that may be associated with De Soto. In addition, a mass burial of more than 70 Indians was found in the mound, some of them possible victims of a Spanish-introduced epidemic. Others probably died more suddenly—their bones exhibit sword cuts. Similarly slashed Indian bones found at the King site in northwestern Georgia testify to the "pacification" methods of the Spanish conquerors.

Two years ago a site believed to be De Soto's 1539–40 winter encampment was discovered at a construction site in downtown Tallahassee, Florida. Exploration of the site, under the direction of Calvin Jones and Charles Ewen, is widely regarded as one of the most important Spanish contact period projects under way in North America today. Jones, Ewen, and teams of archaeologists now working together throughout the Southeast hope that the data gathered at the Tallahassee site, and from other possible De Soto sites along the conquistador's route, will enable them to salvage a long-lost social history of the southeastern Indians. For the moment, our most informative sources about De Soto's odyssey remain the records and diaries kept by members of his expeditionary force.

The Indian societies De Soto encountered were impressive. At the time of his expedition the densely populated river valleys of southeastern North America were home to dozens of political groups of varying degrees of complexity. Many scholars believe that chiefdoms, composed of ranked elites and commoners, were the dominant form of political organization. Native elites sought to control sacred and secular power to enhance their status, reduce internal competition, and maintain political order. The search for power and authority was often conducted through warfare, contacts with the supernatural, and economic control. Chronic warfare existed between chiefdoms, and elites led warriors against their neighbors.

De Soto and his men were not always treated as invaders; they were in fact often accepted into a chief's domain as guests. Nor was De Soto above presenting himself as a god to the Indians; he learned quickly enough that many native rulers claimed to have come from the "upper world"—to have a divine nature—and he made that claim for himself.

Because the Spaniards appeared to be from a supernaturally distant realm, many Indian rulers sought their help in fighting their enemies. The chief of Casqui, for example, whose chiefdom may have centered on the St. Francis and Tyronza Rivers in eastern Arkansas, requested aid in fighting his traditional enemy, the chief of Pacaha, whose chiefdom was located near the Mississippi River. The Chicaça Indians, living south of present-day Tupelo, Mississippi, first sought Spanish help in subduing the rebellious Chakchiumas and in conquering the Caluça. (The Chicaça would later turn on De Soto for consuming their winter stores of corn and for demanding 200 burden bearers. The

attack was one of the worst De Soto ever sustained.) In several instances Indian elites tried to secure alliances and kinship with De Soto through marriage. Thus, the chief of Casqui gave his daughter to De Soto, and the chief of Pacaha gave him one of his wives, a sister, and a woman of rank.

When diplomacy failed (as it usually did), De Soto turned to military tactics that were often callous and brutal. One of his most important strategies was to take chiefs captive. Such measures had been successfully used in Spain a century earlier to drive out the Moors, and it had become standard procedure throughout the Indies. Hernán Cortés had conquered the Aztecs at Tenochtitlan in 1521 by capturing Cuauhtemoc; and in 1532 Pizarro had conquered the Inca Empire at Cajamarca by seizing Atauhualpa.

De Soto succeeded in capturing southeastern Indian rulers with relative ease. When he could not, he turned to force. The impact on the Indians of guns, war dogs, horses, and men with crossbows, halberds, lances, swords, and knives was devastating. The Spaniards' technology, however medieval, usually overpowered the masses of warriors posed against them in combat. The Indians were especially vulnerable on open terrain; mounted lancers in combination with halberdiers, arquebusiers, and war dogs routed even the best squadrons the southeastern chiefdoms could field.

The *perro de guerra,* or war dog, was psychologically effective as well as genuinely deadly: the dogs were trained to disembowel their victims and then tear them to bits. Mastiffs, greyhounds, and wolfhounds had been bred and used for centuries in Europe and the Middle East as adjuncts for halberdiers and sword-wielding cavalry. De Soto and his captains used their enormous mastiffs and greyhounds to "dog" uncooperative Indians. Guides who misled the expedition were routinely thrown to the dogs to be devoured as an example to other guides.

Enslavement was also central to De Soto's tactics. The conquistadors carried iron collars and chains for shackling Indians who were used as burden bearers. De Soto may have been interested in the prospect of capturing Indians for the lucrative Caribbean slave market. During his southeastern expedition he enslaved a force of up to 500 men and women. Some of the women were taken for sexual purposes, although others may well have been taken to serve as cooks and domestic workers.

The Indians' ignorance of Spanish ways was one of De Soto's greatest assets. Indian chiefs understood one another, and their conflicts were characterized by centuries-old rituals and customs. Hostilities, for example, normally took place during the warm season, from late spring to early fall, when the rattlesnakes were out. The rattlesnakes had important associations with the Indian concept of the underworld, and hence with death. Since the mobile Spaniards lived off the land by looting, they were unconcerned about the Indians' traditions, and often encountered chiefdoms when the proper season for warfare was past. In many such instances the Indians seem to have assumed that the Spaniards' intentions were peaceful.

Although the conquistadors maintained military superiority on land, they were no match for the southeastern Indian on the Mississippi River. The expedition first saw the Mississippi in early May of 1541, and shortly afterward De Soto ordered his men to begin sawing timbers for four barges. Each afternoon during the construction of the barges an armada of 200 large dugouts filled with men from the chiefdom of Pacaha and its vassal chiefdom of Aquixo crossed the river and showered the Spaniards with arrows. The war canoes were about 60 feet long and carried a crew of some 25 paddlers and 25 warriors. The warriors, painted red and wearing multicolored feathers, held bows and arrows and woven cane shields decorated with feathers with which they protected the paddlers. The chief, as fleet commander, sat under a canopy on a raised platform over the stern.

The greatest naval battle on the Mississippi—and the last of scores of brutal encounters between De Soto's army and the Indians—began on July 2, 1543, when the Spaniards, now under the leadership of De Soto's lieutenant, Luis de Moscoso, headed downriver in their barges and attached canoes toward the Gulf of Mexico. Two days later, a fleet of 100 war canoes of the chiefdom of Quigualtam engaged the Spanish flotilla. The battle continued unabated until noon the next day, when the warriors halted at the southern boundary of their territory. Fifty canoes from the adjoining chiefdom picked up the engagement and pursued the Spaniards until midmorning the next day.

This 48-hour battle took place along 200 miles of the Mississippi ending near Natchez. The conquistadors were without guns or crossbows by this time; they had only their shields and swords with which to defend themselves. The Indians wounded a number of men with their bows and arrows, but the worst Spanish casualties occurred during a small counterattack: a number of Spaniards set out in five small canoes to drive the Indians away. The Indians quickly surrounded and upset the canoes, drowning some 12 men.

The Spanish *entrada* resulted in devastating changes for the Indians. Massive epidemics raced through villages. In some chiefdoms the mortality rate may have been as high as 85 to 100 percent. With rapid depopulation the southeastern towns and villages became smaller; fewer settlements were occupied as outlying towns were abandoned; villagers moved into new territories, seeking new political alliances; and the members of the elite began to lose their power and ability to manipulate their followers. The decline in chiefly organization is witnessed by the demise of mound construction, mound centers, palisade construction, site hierarchy, status markers, and craft specialization.

The psychological shock of defeat in warfare, the subsequent looting, especially of the sacred temples, by the victors, the enslavement of both men and women, but particularly women—these factors had a ruinous effect on the Indian elite. The once vibrant southeastern chiefdoms either disappeared or gave way to new, attenuated political relationships. By the time the English established Charleston in 1670 and the French began their exploration of the Lower Mississippi Valley in 1673, the world of chiefdoms that De Soto had fought and attempted to conquer had vanished.

Until about 15 years ago, it seemed as though that world would remain permanently obscure. A colleague once told me, "We don't even know what to look for. We don't even know what the sixteenth-century artifacts should look like." Since then, things have changed dramatically for the better. Anthropologists, archaeologists, and ethnohistorians have joined their energies and efforts, adopting a three-pronged approach based on artifactual recovery, historical documentation, and anthropological theory. This endeavor has galvanized southern archaeology, as various disciplines have been applied toward a common goal, leading to discoveries that my colleague once despaired of. It would be fitting if the archaeological ferment created by such recent discoveries as the ones in Citrus County, the King site, and the site of De Soto's first winter encampment in Tallahassee were to make the long vanished chiefdoms of the Apalachee, Ichisi, Ocute, Coosa, Pacaha, and many other native groups "come alive" once again.

Pizarro's Family and His Head

A CONQUISTADOR'S FAMILY, FROM CRADLE TO GRAVE

by MARK ROSE

Extremadura, an isolated, poverty-stricken, unfertile region in west-central Spain, was a harsh nursery, and it was there that Francisco Pizarro was born, along with his fellow explorers and conquistadors Cortés, Balboa, and Orellana. Guidebooks will tell you that the pig-raising people of Extremadura eat lizards even today. Pizarro, himself a swineherd in his youth (we don't know whether he ate lizards or not), was one of four illegitimate half-brothers. All four were involved in the conquest of the Inca. Juan was killed in an assault on Sacsayhuaman during Manco's rebellion in 1536. Hernando spent 20 years in prison, where he lived well on his share of the loot, having been accused by rivals of provoking the rebellion. Gonzalo was executed for high treason in 1548. Francisco, governor of Peru, was assassinated in Lima three years later. Of the family, only Pedro, a younger cousin, died in his bed after writing his account of

This woodcut shows Diego Almagro avenging his father's death by assassinating Francisco Pizarro in 1541.

the conquest. Francisco did not record his experiences first-hand; he was illiterate.

In 1541 the Wheel of Fortune turned against Francisco Pizarro, and the conquistador reaped a bit of what he had sown. After the fall of Cuzco in 1533, the Pizarro brothers had cut their rival, Diego de Almagro, out of much of the booty. By way of compensation, Francisco offered him Chile, and the Spaniard marched off in hopes of conquest and gold. He returned two years later, having found no fortune, and helped suppress Manco. His quarrel with the Pizarros led to a battle between their factions at Las

Salinas on April 26, 1538. Captured, the defeated Almagro was garroted on Hernando's order. Francisco, now governor, later stripped Almagro's son, also named Diego, of lands leaving him bankrupt.

The embittered young Almagro and his associates plotted to assassinate Francisco after mass on June 16, 1541, but Pizarro got wind of their plan and stayed in the governor's palace. While Pizarro, his half-brother Francisco Martín de Alcántara, and about 20 others were having dinner, the conspirators invaded the palace. Most of Pizarro's guests fled, but a few fought the intruders, numbered variously between seven and 25. While Pizarro struggled to buckle on his breastplate, his defenders, including Alcántara, were killed. For his part Pizarro killed two attackers and ran through a third. While trying to pull out his sword, he was stabbed in the throat, then fell to the floor where he was stabbed many times.

Alcántara's wife buried Pizarro and Alcántara behind the cathedral. He was reburied under the main altar in 1545, and then moved into a special chapel in the cathedral on July 4, 1606. Church documents, from the verification process for remains of St. Toribio in 1661, however, note a wooden box inside of which was a lead box inscribed in Spanish:

> *Here is the skull of the Marquis Don Francisco Pizarro who discovered and won Peru and placed it under the crown of Castile.*

In 1891, on the 350th anniversary of Pizarro's death, a scientific committee examined the desiccated remains that church officials had identified as Pizarro. In their account in *American Anthropologist* (7:1, January 1894), they concluded that the skull conformed to cranial morphology then thought to be typical of criminals, a result seen as confirming identification. A glass, marble, and bronze sarcophagus was built to hold the mummy, which was venerated by history buffs and churchgoers.

But in 1977, workers cleaning a crypt beneath the altar found two wooden boxes with human bones. One box held the remains of two children; an elderly female; an elderly male, complete; and an elderly male, headless; and some fragments of a sword. The other contained the lead box—inscribed as had been recorded in 1661—in which was a skull that matched postcranial bones of the headless man in the first box. A Peruvian historian, anthropologist, two radiologists, and two American anthropologists studied the remains. The man was a white male at least 60 years old (Pizarro's exact age was unknown; he was said to be 63 or 65 by contemporary historians) and 5'5" to 5'9" in height. He had lost most of his upper molars and many lower incisors and molars, developed arthritic lipping on his vertebrae, fractured his right ulna while a child, and suffered a broken nose.

Examination of the remains indicated that the assassins did a thorough job. There were four sword thrusts to neck, the sixth and twelfth thoracic vertebrae were nicked by sword thrusts, the arms and hands were wounded from warding off sword cuts (a cut on the right humerus and two on the left first metacarpal; the right fifth metacarpal

was missing altogether), a sword blade had cut through the right zygomatic arch, a thrust penetrated the left eye socket, a rapier or dagger went through the neck into the base of skull, and a pair of thrusts had damaged the left sphenoid. The savage overkill suggests revenge as a motive rather than simple murder or death in battle.

The scholars concluded that these were indeed the remains of Francisco Pizarro. The two children might be Pizarro's sons who died young, the elderly female is possibly the wife of Alcántara, and the other elderly male Alcántara. The dried out body long thought to be Pizarro exhibited no sign of trauma as would be expected if it was indeed the corpse of the conquistador. They decided that the interloper was possibly a church official, and replaced the body with the conquistador's bones in the glass sarcophagus.

◉ EYEWITNESS: Cortés and the Night of Sorrows

compiled by ALEXANDER BENENSON

The Aztec king Moctezuma welcomed Hernán Cortés when he arrived at the capital city, Tenotchtitlán, in November 1519. But relations quickly deteriorated. First, Moctezuma was forced to submit publicly to the Spanish. Then, Cortés left Pedro de Alvarado in charge when he had to return to the coast. The latter's brutal treatment of the Aztecs brought matters to a head by the time Cortés came back to Tenotchtitlán. The storm broke on the night of June 30, 1520. Cortés and his men, along with their Tlaxcalan Indian allies, had to fight their way out of the city. Pursued by Aztec warriors in the narrow streets and canals of Tenotchtitlán, the Spanish suffered many casualties. Bernal Diaz, a soldier in Cortés' army, immortalized the bloody encounter as "The Night of Sorrows" in his history, *On the Conquest of New Spain*.

Many squadrons attacked us both by day and night, and the powder was giving out, and the same was happening with food and water, and the great Moctezuma being dead, they were unwilling to grant the peace and truce, which we had demanded of them.

In fact we were staring death in the face, and the bridges had been raised. Thus Cortés decided with all of us captains and soldiers that we should set out during the night, when we could see that the squadrons of warriors were most off their guard. In order to put them still more off their guard, that very afternoon we told them through one of their priests whom we held prisoner and who was a man of great importance among them and through some other prisoners that they should let us go in peace within eight days and we would give them all the gold.

Four hundred Tlaxcalan Indians and 150 soldiers were told to carry this bridge and place it in position and guard the passage until the army and all the baggage had crossed. 200 Tlaxcalan Indians and 50 soldiers were told to carry the cannon, and Gonzalo de Sandoval, Diego de Ordas, Francisco de Sauzedo, Francisco de Lugo, and a company of 100 young and active soldiers were selected to go in the vanguard to do the fighting. It was agreed that Cortés himself, Alonzo de Avila, Cristóbal de Olid, and other captains should go in the middle and support the party that most needed help in fighting. Pedro de Alvarado and Juan Velásquez de Leon were with the rearguard, and placed in the middle between them were two captains, the soldiers of Narváez, and 300 Tlaxcalans; and 30 soldiers were told to take charge of the prisoners and of Doña Marina and Doña Luisa.

After we had learned the plans that Cortés had made about the way in which we were to escape that night and get to the bridges, as it was somewhat dark and cloudy and rainy, we began before midnight to bring the baggage along the bridge, and the horses and mare began their march with the Tlaxcalans, who were laden with gold. Then the bridge was quickly put in place, and Cortés and the others whom he took with him in the vanguard, and many of the horsemen, crossed over it. While this was happening, the voices, trumpets, cries, and whistles of the Mexicas began to sound and they called out in their language to the people of Tlaltelolco [another island in Lake Texcocco, famous for its rowers], "Come out at once with your canoes, for the Teules are leaving! Cut them off so that not one of them will be left alive!"

When I least expected it, we saw so many squadrons of warriors bearing down on us, and the lake so crowded with canoes that we could not defend ourselves. Many of our soldiers had already crossed and, while we were in this position, a great multitude of Mexicas charged at us, removing the bridge and wounding and killing our men who were unable to assist each other; and as misfortune is perverse at such times, one accident followed another, and as it was raining, two of the horses slipped and fell into the lake. When I and others of Cortés' company saw that, we got safely to the other side of the bridge, and so many warriors charged on us, that despite all our good fighting, no further use could be made of the bridge, so that the passage or water opening was soon filled up with dead horses, Indian men and women, servants, baggage, and boxes.

Fearing that they would not fail to kill us, we advanced along the causeway, and we met many squadrons armed with long lances waiting for us. They cried, "Oh villains, are you still alive?" and with the cuts and thrusts we gave them, we got through, although they then wounded six of those who were going along.

Then if there was some sort of plan such as we had agreed upon it was an accursed one; for Cortés and the captains and soldiers who passed first on horseback, so as to save themselves and reach dry land and make sure of their lives, spurred on along the causeway, and they did not fail to attain their object; and the horses with the gold and the Tlaxcalans also got out in safety. I assert that if we had waited at the bridges, we should all have been killed, and not one of us would have been left alive; the reason was this, that as we went along the causeway, charging the Mexica squadrons, on one side of us was water and on the other rooftops [which made it easy for the Mexicas to hurl stones and darts] and the lake was full of canoes so that we could do nothing beyond what we accomplished, which was to charge with sword thrusts against those who tried to lay hands on us, and to march and advance to get off the causeway.

Had it been in the daytime, it would have been worse, and we who escaped did so only by the grace of God. To one who saw the numbers of warriors who fell on us that night and the canoes of them coming along to carry off our soldiers, it was terrifying. So we went ahead along the causeway in order to get to the town of Tacuba, where Cortés was already stationed with all of the captains.

Gonzalo de Sandoval, Cristóbal de Olid, and others of those horsemen who had gone on ahead were crying out: "Señor Capitan, let us halt, for they say that we are fleeing and leaving them to die at the bridges; let us go back and help them, if any of them survive"; but not one of them came out or escaped.

Cortés' reply was that it was a miracle that any of us escaped. However, I promptly went back with the horsemen and the soldiers who were unwounded, but we did not march far, for Pedro de Alvarado soon met us, badly wounded, holding a spear in his hand and on foot, for they had already killed his sorrel mare, and he brought with him four soldiers as badly wounded as he was himself, and eight Tlaxcalans, all of them with blood flowing from many wounds.

Relics of the Kamikaze

EXCAVATIONS OFF JAPAN'S COAST ARE UNCOVERING
KUBLAI KHAN'S ILL-FATED INVASION FLEET.

by JAMES P. DELGADO

Stepping off the dock into the warm, murky waters of Imari Bay, I swam to the bottom, then followed a line staked out down a steep slope. The visibility was poor, particularly as excavations had stirred up soft mud, but suddenly I saw the wreck. Unlike other sites I've dived on, the seabed here was not dominated by a large hull. Instead, clusters of timbers and artifacts suggested that a ship, or ships, had crashed into the shore and been ripped apart.

There were bright-red leather armor fragments, a pottery bowl decorated with calligraphy, and wood with what seemed like fresh burn marks. My heart started to pound when I swam up to one object and realized it was an intact Mongol helmet. Nearby was a cluster of iron arrow tips and a round ceramic object, a *tetsuhau,* or bomb. Scholars had doubted whether such bombs, filled with black powder, existed this early, yet here it was. I just floated there, lost in thought that the detritus of this ancient battle lay here as fresh as if the ship had sunk yesterday, not seven centuries ago. The experience brought the story of Kublai Khan's invasions of Japan and the kamikaze—the legendary "divine wind" said to have destroyed his fleets in 1274 and 1281—into the realm of the tangible, touchable past.

Working in this small cove on the shore of Takashima, an island off Japan's Kyushu coast, underwater archaeologists led by Kenzo Hayashida of the Kyushu Okinawa Society for Underwater Archaeology (KOSUWA) have excavated the broken remains of a massive Chinese warship, lost during the khan's invasion of 1281. This past August, I was privileged to join the KOSUWA team as the first Western archaeologist to dive on the site. The fragments of the ship and the artifacts being recovered here—from weapons, provisions, and personal effects to the remains of the crew—are giving the world its first detailed view of a ship from a famous battle that ended when a storm smashed the khan's fleet.

Broken into fragments and scattered by the storm that wrecked it, the ship has already yielded thousands of artifacts, many remarkably well preserved by centuries of burial in silt. As amazing as the artifacts is the ship itself. The hull, made of iron-fastened planks with a large keel that has just started to emerge from the sea floor, had watertight compartments. Although the Japanese archaeologists caution that they have not yet completed excavation of the site, the warship appears to have been about 230 feet in length, twice as big as contemporary Euro-

pean ones. The huge anchor, indicative of the vessel's size, is a massive wood-and-stone assembly weighing more than a ton. Its red oak stock, now broken, was 23 feet long. Analysis of the wood and the granite used in the anchor shows that they originated in China's Fujian Province, site of a major trading port and a marshaling point for the fleet that attacked Japan in 1281. As subjects of the Mongols, China's Sung Dynasty provided most of the fleet—4,400 ships according to Chinese records—and many of the troops for the invasion.

In the 1920s, Japanese archaeologists began excavating remains of a 12.4-mile-long defensive wall built in and around the ancient port of Hakata (modern Fukuoka) in anticipation of the 1281 invasion. These investigations were part of a nationalistic drive to find and restore portions of the wall in order to reinforce the story of Japan's miraculous rescue, thanks to the emperor and his divine ancestors who sent the kamikaze. The story of the invasion and the kamikaze grew in importance to the Japanese government's reinterpretation of its past as the nation prepared for war.

After the end of World War II, archaeological work around Fukuoka occasionally yielded stone anchor stocks thought to be from the Mongol fleets, although Hakata's long history as a port might have accounted for such finds. The possibility of discovering more concrete evidence of the invasions led Torao Mozai, a Tokyo University engineering professor, to Takashima in 1980 to see what might lie on the seabed there. On Mozai's first trip, local fishermen who had trawled the bottom of Imari Bay for generations showed him ceramic pots and other finds brought up in their nets that hinted at a number of shipwrecks. One find piqued Mozai's interest. Discarded in a fisherman's toolbox was a square bronze artifact. Engraved in Chinese and in Phagspa, a written form of Mongolian, it was the personal seal of a Mongol commander. The seal was clear evidence that the fishermen were pulling up relics from Kublai Khan's lost fleets.

Mozai, known as the "father of underwater archaeology" in Japan, used sonar to survey the sea floor. Divers checking promising sonar contacts in 1981 recovered iron swords, stone catapult balls, spearheads, stone hand mills for grinding rice (although some may have been used to prepare gunpowder), and stone anchor stocks. Mozai's finds paved the way for a new generation of Japanese archaeologists to work in the waters off Takashima, among them Kenzo Hayashida.

Since 1991, Hayashida and KOSUWA, which he founded, have conducted annual field seasons at Takashima, surveying the bottom of Imari Bay and performing limited excavations to gauge the number of potential wreck sites and the range of material culture remaining on the seabed after centuries of typhoons and generations of fishermen using dragnets and trawls. In 1994, KOSUWA discovered three wood-and-stone anchors at Kozaki Harbor, a small cove on Takashima's southern coast. The largest anchor was still set, its rope cable stretched toward shore. Buried in mud about 500 feet from the shore and in 70 feet of water, the anchor was a tantalizing clue that a wreck lay nearby. But no

massive target appeared in the probes of the surrounding area, just a number of smaller anomalies. Suspecting that this might be a wreck that had broken up, either in 1281 or through the action of typhoons, Hayashida began excavation. In the 1994–1995 season, KOSUWA recovered 135 artifacts near the shoreline, then slowly traced the finds back into deeper water through the 2001 season.

That October, the years of fieldwork paid off with the discovery of the ship's remains. After 20 years of investigation, the waters of Imari Bay finally yielded, albeit in more than one piece, one of the khan's ships. But government-financed construction of a new fish-farming installation directly atop the wreck site was slated to begin shortly. While that project provided funds to KOSUWA's investigations, the 2,600-square-foot site had to be completely excavated by the end of 2002. Work proceeded rapidly, aided by a large team of divers, underwater communication systems, and an intensive program of excavation in cooperation with the Takashima Museum of Folk History and Culture and the Fukuoka City Museum.

In a series of dives, I was able to watch as the site yielded an incredible array of well-preserved features and artifacts. The main portion of the wreck site lies in 45 feet of water and is buried beneath four feet of thick, viscous mud. Working with a documentation crew, I watched as they mapped each artifact, photographing and then recovering ceramics, tortoiseshell combs, scraps of red leather armor, hull planks, and part of a watertight bulkhead.

Facing the Khan's Wrath

Kublai Khan's ascendancy to leadership of the Mongols, fraught with internal dissension and civil war, coincided with his long and difficult conquest of China. Needing to obtain additional resources and to demonstrate his power and legitimacy as the Mongol ruler, Kublai, grandson of Genghis Khan, opened a second front in Japan even as he fought the last remnants of China's Sung Dynasty for control of the mainland.

The khan sent envoys, demanding the Japanese submit, but the bakufu, Japan's military rulers, rebuffed them. In 1274, with the assistance of his Korean vassal state of Koryo, the khan assembled a fleet that historical accounts suggest was as large as 900 ships to ferry 23,000 troops across the narrow, 110-mile straits of Tsushima, which separate the Korean peninsula from Kyushu. Sailing from Koryo in early October, the fleet overwhelmed Japanese defenders on the islands of Tsushima and Iki before landing at the ancient trading port of Hakata (modern Fukuoka).

The Japanese were waiting for them with a force of about 6,000 samurai and gokenin, or armed retainers. Japanese sources suggest that the battle, while hard fought, was going badly for them. The samurai, who fought as individuals, were no match for the Mongols with their tactics of fighting en masse, and their use of poison-dipped arrows and catapult-launched exploding shells. After a week of battle, the Japanese had retreated ten miles inland to Daizafu, the fortified capital of Kyushu. The invaders looted and burned Hakata but, wary of Japanese reinforcements and perhaps the weather on a coast notorious for typhoons, the fleet commanders prepared to withdraw. On October 20, the wind shifted and blew hard. The fleet, with some ships dragging anchor and drifting to shore, departed. Most historical accounts claim as many as 300 ships and 13,500 men were lost in the "storm" that ended the first invasion, but others suggest that the majority of ships simply escaped with the changing wind, with only a handful wrecking on the beach.

Kublai Khan sent more envoys to demand subservience from the Japanese, but the bakufu, emboldened by the retreat from Hakata, continued their defiance, executing the khan's ambassadors. The bakufu also strengthened their defenses, relocating loyal samurai to estates near Hakata and, in 1276, ordering them to build a 12.4-mile-long stone wall along the coast; it was completed in six months' time. The samurai at

The artifacts range from personal effects, such as a small bowl on which was painted the name of its owner, a commander Weng, to provisions and the implements of war. The provisions include a large number of storage jars in various sizes, all of them hastily and crudely made. They hint at the rapid, if not rushed, pace of the khan's mobi-

Hakata organized local fishermen and traders into a coastal naval force of small craft and trained the local inhabitants as a defense force.

The khan and his vassals had not been idle. Chinese histories report that Kublai ordered Koryo to build 900 ships and assemble 10,000 troops for a new invasion. In China, drawing from the newly defeated Sung navy and new ships built expressly for the invasion, Kublai reportedly gathered a force of 3,500 ships and 100,000 troops. Sailing separately in May 1281, the two fleets were supposed to rendezvous at Iki Island in the straits of Tsushima.

But the Korean force, after recapturing Iki from the Japanese, sailed on for Hakata without waiting for the larger Chinese force. The Japanese, alerted by spies, were waiting for them. Thwarted by the stone wall fortifying the beach, the invaders fell back to Shikanoshima Island in the middle of Hakata Bay. Japanese defense craft raided the fleet as it lay at anchor, samurai warriors springing onto the decks of the enemy ships to fight it out with their crews. Other craft were set on fire and sent drifting into the mass of enemy warships. Finally, the Koryo fleet retreated to Iki Island, its role in the invasion over.

The Chinese contingent, after a delay, finally sailed in June and arrived at the small island of Takashima in Imari Bay, 31 miles south of Hakata. Weeks of battle on the small island's shores and hilly countryside were at best a stalemate for the defenders when a sudden storm mauled the fleet on the evening of July 30. According to Japanese records, most of the invading ships were driven ashore and sank, killing nearly all of the 100,000 invaders. At the entrance to Imari Bay, says one Japanese account, "a person could walk across from one point of land to another on a mass of wreckage."

Kublai Khan never again sent a force against Japan. He abruptly canceled plans for a third invasion in 1286. The Japanese embarked on a series of punitive raids against Korea and China, many of them more piratical than naval. If there was a policy, it was found in Japan's ultimate retreat into the solitude and security of their home islands, which they now believed were protected by the gods, who twice had sent winds and storms to thwart an enemy's ambitions. The myth of that protecting force, the kamikaze, would not die until seven centuries later, in the last desperate months of World War II.

by JAMES P. DELGADO

lization for the invasion. So, too, do the anchor stones. Chinese anchor stones of the period are usually large, well-carved, single stones that were set into the body of the stock to weight the anchor. Those found at Takashima are only roughly finished and made of two stones. More easily and quickly completed than their longer, more finished counterparts, they are not as strong as the single stone anchors. It may be that these hastily fabricated anchors contributed to the fleet's demise in the storm that dashed Kublai's hopes for the conquest of Japan.

The weapons recovered from the site include bundles of iron arrow tips or crossbow bolts, spearheads, and more than 80 swords and sabers. During one dive, I saw a Mongol helmet upright on the bottom, fish swimming in and out of its projecting brow. Close to the helmet was perhaps the most amazing discovery yet made—*tetsuhau,* or a ceramic projectile bomb. KOSUWA has recovered six of these from the wreck. They are the world's earliest known exploding projectiles and the earliest direct archaeological evidence of seagoing ordnance.

Chinese alchemists invented gunpowder around A.D. 300, and by 1100 huge paper bombs much like giant firecrackers were being used in battle. Chinese sources refer to catapult-launched exploding projectiles in 1221, but some historians have argued that the references date to later rewritings of the sources. In his recent book *In Little Need of Divine Intervention,* which analyzes two Japanese scrolls that depict the Mongol invasion, Bowdoin College historian Thomas Conlan suggests that a scene showing a samurai falling from his horse as a bomb explodes over him was a later addition. Conlan's research masterfully refutes many of the traditional myths and commonly held perceptions of the invasion, downplaying the number of ships and troops involved and arguing that it was not the storms but the Japanese defenders ashore, as well as confusion and a lack of coordination, that

thwarted the khan's two invasions. But his suggestion that the exploding bomb is an anachronism has now been demolished by solid archaeological evidence. Moreover, when the Japanese X-rayed two intact bombs, they found that one was filled just with gunpowder while the other was packed with gunpowder and more than a dozen square pieces of iron shrapnel intended to cut down the enemy.

The site has yielded fragmentary human remains. A cranium, resting where a body had perhaps been pushed face down into the seabed, and a pelvis, possibly from the same individual, now rest in the conservation lab awaiting analysis. This state-of-the-art lab, at the Takashima Museum of Folk History and Culture, is filled with containers of freshwater in which artifacts rest. Initial study of the artifacts has revealed new information about the khan's forces. Only one percent of the finds can be attributed to a Mongolian origin; the rest are Chinese. The Mongol invasion was Mongol only in name and in the allegiance of the invading sailors and troops.

The future of the finds is uncertain. While the excavation has been fully funded by the Japanese government, it has only committed funding for conservation of ten percent of the collection. For now, the rest will remain in freshwater tanks. The existing museum is too small to house all of the artifacts, and Japan remains firmly gripped by economic recession. Given widespread interest, and the significance of the discovery, perhaps the time has come for an international funding effort to assist the expensive but archaeologically and culturally rewarding work being accomplished there.

Takashima Island's local government is interested in further exploration of the lost fleet of Kublai Khan, and Kenzo Hayashida and his colleagues continue to work off the island's shores. Hayashida believes, like Thomas Conlan and other historians, that the khan's fleet size was exaggerated, and that hundreds, not thousands, of wrecks lie buried here. Even so, the remains now emerging from the mud and water are one of the greatest underwater archaeological discoveries of our time, providing critical new information about Asian seafaring and military technology, as well as an invasion crushed by a legendary storm.

Digging Napoleon's Dead

A MASS GRAVE IN LITHUANIA IS GRUESOME EVIDENCE OF THE CATASTROPHIC FRENCH RETREAT FROM MOSCOW.

by JARRETT A. LOBELL

Now a prosperous, post-Soviet city, the Lithuanian capital of Vilnius has had a turbulent and often violent history. Since its founding in the mid-thirteenth century, Lithuania, and especially its capital, was often at the center of conflicts between Russia and Poland, and more recently, the Soviet Union and Germany. When a mass grave was discovered by construction workers in the Siaures Miestelis ("Northern Town") section of Vilnius last fall, archaeologists called to the site suspected the bones belonged to Lithuanian victims of the Soviet KGB, or its predecessor, the NKVD. The intelligence agency's brutality over the 47 years of the Red Army's occupation of Lithuania is well known—more than 250,000 Lithuanians were sent to Siberian work camps. The location of the gravesite next to the former barracks of a Soviet tank division fueled this theory.

Between 1941 and 1944, when Nazi Germany occupied Lithuania, the Gestapo and the SS annihilated the Jewish community, murdering some 200,000 people, the circumstances of whose disappearance have never been fully documented. In a country that is 96 percent Catholic and which seeks to distance itself from its difficult past, the Jews of Lithuania are seldom discussed, even though the city was once known as the "Jerusalem of the West" because of its large and influential Jewish population. Excavators feared that the mass grave might contain victims of Nazi oppression. In all, it is estimated that more than 30 percent of Lithuania's population perished between 1940 and 1953, the year of Stalin's death.

Archaeologist Justina Poskiene and physical anthropologist Rimantas Jankauskas of the University of Vilnius eventually solved the mystery. In addition to 1,000 to 2,000 human skeletons, they recovered buttons, medals, coins, and scraps of fabric, all pointing to the Napoleonic era. What they had found was the first mass grave of soldiers from Napoleon's Grande Armée.

Experts in the study of mass graves from France's Centre National de la Recherche Scientifique and University of Marseille were called in to assist in the excavation and lab analysis. Michel Signoli and Olivier Dutour joined the Lithuanian team bringing with them not only expertise gained at other mass graves sites, but also sophisticated digital cameras, computers, and software not generally available in Lithuania. This allowed the scientists to search for the DNA of microorganisms that may help to determine causes of death.

Courtesy Mark Rose

Forced to retreat from Russia during the winter of 1812, Napoleon abandoned his army to its fate.

A historian and the chair of archaeology at the University of Vilnius, Poskiene had an extraordinarily difficult job. Working under a tight deadline, she completed the excavation of the 98-foot-long, 20-foot-deep grave in April 2002, when real-estate developers who own the site resumed construction. She thinks there are other mass graves in the area, which once lay on the outskirts of the city. Negotiations are underway between city officials, archaeologists, and several television companies such as the BBC to fund work at these sites, even as rapid development threatens them.

The grim story of Napoleon's retreat from Russia in the winter of 1812 is well known. As many as 450,000 soldiers died during the Russian campaign from France, Italy, Spain, Croatia, Germany, and at least 15 other countries. The retreat from Moscow to Vilnius lasted from October 19 to early December, and it is thought that only 50,000 reached Lithuania and that as many as 20,000 may have died there. One of Napoleon's sergeants wrote in his diary:

On December 9th we started out for Wilna [Vilnius], with the temperature at -28 degrees Celsius [-18 Fahrenheit]. Out of two divisions totalling over 10,000 men...only 2,000 actually made it to Wilna. The hope of making it to the city where we were to find food in abundant supply had restored strength in me, or rather, like my fellow men, I produced supernatural efforts to make it there.

The city that had welcomed Napoleon on June 28, only six months before Sergeant Bourgogne's diary entry, now saw his decimated army return from its disastrous campaign in Russia. What is less well known is what happened to those who perished. This excavation may provide some of the best clues.

Jankauskas, dean of the University of Vilnius Medical School, came to the site daily, bagged the hundreds of excavated bones, and drove them to a university lab where he could try to put the skeletons together. When he first saw the site, he said, "I thought this could be a unique chance for independent and objective testing of often biased or incomplete historical sources." Jankauskas also noted, "From a human point of view, I felt sorry for those young men. From a professional point of view, I was excited. I never thought I would have so many skeletons in my closet." Surprisingly, the soldiers were buried along with women. "Although war is generally considered a man's job, there are a certain number of females in the grave," he declared. "What was the role of women in a military campaign and do historical sources neglect or underestimate their role?" In addition to the human skeletons, there are also hundreds of horse bones, which are now being studied—more evidence of the fate of one of the world's greatest armies.

One of the best descriptions of the desperate conditions in Vilnius during the winter of 1812 is a journal entry by General Robert Wilson, a British military observer in Lithuania, upon his visit to a Vilnius monastery that the French had turned into a makeshift hospital:

The hospital at St. Bazile presented the most awful and hideous sight: seven thousand five hundred bodies were piled like pigs of lead over one another in the corridors...and all the broken windows and walls were stuffed with feet, legs, arms, hands, trunks, and heads to fit the apertures, and keep out the air from the yet living.

At first, the people of Vilnius cremated the thousands of bodies piling up all over the city, but eventually the smoke and smell of burning flesh became overwhelming, and they began burying them in mass graves dug by Napoleon's surviving soldiers. Most of those in the first grave excavated by Poskiene were between 15 and 20 years old, and forensic analysis shows few were veterans of previous campaigns, as some of the historical records indicate. Jankauskas says that soldiers with long experience often suffer foot fractures, and their bones show signs of healing, but none of these skeletons had evidence of this kind of trauma.

It is clear that many soldiers died from the cold, as some of the skeletons were found in the fetal position usually taken when freezing to death. Some scholars believe Napoleon exaggerated the harshness of the winter to make his defeat and the staggering loss of life appear beyond his control, but Dutour says the skeletons corroborate historical accounts that the winter was extremely cold.

Many soldiers also died of starvation—the army had taken little food with it during the retreat and traveled across a countryside devastated by the Russians' scorched-earth campaign. According to some accounts, soldiers went to the very medical school of which Jankauskas is now dean and ate the alcohol-preserved organs kept there for anatomy students. It is almost certain that many of the soldiers died of typhus, a disease often called "war fever," because of its close association with filthy wartime conditions. The presence or absence of typhus may be determined by the DNA study to be conducted by the French scholars.

The scientific value of the Siaures Miestelis excavation is enormous, but per-haps just as important, the team successfully dealt with the delicate task of removing over 1,000 skeletons under extreme time pressure. "I am impressed with how the excavation of the remains was undertaken," says Clark Spencer Larsen, a physical anthropologist at Ohio State University. "The work was sensitive and carried out in an appropriate manner." Nothing illustrates this more than plans developed for the final disposition of the remains. Almost 200 years after their unceremonious burial in an anonymous mass grave, Napoleon's soldiers will be reburied in Vilnius' main cemetery, next to many of Lithuania's heroes.

Napoleon's Lost Fleet

DIVERS DISCOVER WHAT REALLY HAPPENED AT THE BATTLE OF THE NILE.

by ANGELA M.H. SCHUSTER

ABOUKIR, EGYPT

Six-foot waves propelled by a small weather system over the Mediterranean rock the research vessel *Princess Duda,* anchored at the entrance to Aboukir Bay, as divers prepare for another foray into the deep. Falling overboard one by one, they submerge, meeting at the anchor line for a group descent. Near the seabed some 40 feet below, the waters are quiet. Waterlogged timbers—the center section of Napoleon's 120-gun warship *L'Orient*—lie among a scatter of bronze cannon, twisted and torn; gold, silver, and copper coins minted in Malta, Venice, Spain, France, Portugal, and the Ottoman Empire; cooking pots and silverware; bits of clothing; human bones; and a heap of lead type from a shipboard printing press. The strong scent of gunpowder permeates the site; you can smell the battle. The ship's 35-

foot-long rudder, emblazoned with the words Dauphin Royal, *L'Orient's* original name, lies on its side 200 feet from the wreckage. Anchors of Napoleon's ships *Guerrier, Conquérant, Spartiate, Aquillon, Peuple Souverain,* and *Franklin* are scattered about the site.

Here, 15 miles east of Alexandria, an international team under the direction of French marine archaeologist Franck Goddio is exploring ships sunk at one of the most decisive battles in maritime history, the Battle of the Nile, or more accurately, the Battle of Aboukir. Waged on the night of August 1–2, 1798, the engagement pitted Britain's finest, under the command of Rear Admiral Sir Horatio Nelson, against a French fleet led by Admiral François Paul Brueys d'Aigailliers; its outcome ended forever Napoleon's dream of conquering Egypt and the east.

Having pursued the French fleet for nearly four months, Nelson happened upon it late in the afternoon of August 1 during a sweep of Egypt's north coast. As he rounded what is now known as Nelson Island and entered Aboukir Bay, he saw 13 French battleships moored in a north-south line near its western shore. Four frigates were anchored still closer to the shoals.

Against Napoleon's wishes, Brueys had selected the bay over the harbors at Alexandria, believing it afforded his cumbersome, deep-draft vessels a better anchorage and, with its wide-open mouth, would be hard for the British to blockade.

Nelson noticed that the French ships were anchored at the stern only and that enough room had been left between them so they could swing on their anchors with the tide. More importantly, he surmised, enough room had been left between the ships and the shoals so that his vessels, far more agile and of shallower draft, could sail inside the French line.

Nelson and his "band of brothers," as he would later call his men, seized the opportunity to attack. In a bold move, the first in line of the British ships, *Goliath,* under the command of Captain Thomas Foley, sailed between *Guerrier,* the leading French ship, and the shore. *Zealous, Orion, Theseus,* and *Audacious* followed. As each ship passed *Guerrier,* then *Conquérant* and *Spartiate,* it delivered a thunderous broadside. Anticipating attack from the seaward side, the French were caught off guard. Within 20 minutes these three French ships were silenced. The remaining British ships stormed down the seaward side, bombarding the French fleet and breaking through the line.

In the hours that followed, the battle escalated as the British ships picked off the French vessels one after another. A fire broke out aboard *L'Orient* during the melee. At about 10:30 p.m. it ignited *L'Orient's* aft powder magazine and the ship exploded. The blast was so great that it was heard in Rosetta, ten miles to the east. Stunned by the explosion, both sides ceased fire for a quarter of an hour.

"Victory is not a name strong enough for such a scene," Nelson would later write as he recalled the smoldering, sinking hulks of his enemy's fleet. By daybreak all but two French battleships, *Guillaume Tell* and *Généreux,* had been sunk or captured. Some 1,700 Frenchmen had lost their lives; 800 were killed instantly in the explosion aboard *L'Orient.* The British had lost only two ships and 218 men. Some 3,000 French were taken prisoner, only to be released a short time later when Nelson could no longer feed them.

Discovered in 1983 by the late underwater explorer Jacques Dumas, the wreck of *L'Orient* is spread over a quarter mile square. "The scatter of debris, along with the remains we have found of the frigates *Sérieuse* and *Artemise* and anchors left behind by French ships attempting to flee," says Goddio, "are providing a wealth of new information on the battle. We know, for instance, that there were two nearly simultaneous explosions aboard *L'Orient* rather than one as previously thought. It is quite clear from the wreckage that when the aft powder magazine blew, flaming debris ignited auxiliary powder stores in the front of the ship. From the burning and scarring of the forwardmost timbers of the center section, we know that the bow as well as the stern was blown off and probably burned up, leaving only the ship's center section to founder. All that remains of the stern is its bronze and wood rudder. Its distance from the rest of the wreckage suggests that the explosion of the stern propelled the ship forward several hundred feet.

"We also know just how poorly positioned the French fleet was. According to historical sources, the French ships were both closer to shore and to each other. The anchors, which are separated by more than 400 feet, tell a different story. We have a snapshot of the position of the French forward guard at the moment the battle began and it is clear that they were in no position to close up gaps in the flotilla."

"The conventional story of how Nelson's fleet sailed behind the French line is a bit simplistic," says Royal Naval Museum deputy director and Nelson biographer Colin White, who, along with French naval historian Michèle Battesti, was in Alexandria this past June to inspect the wrecksite firsthand. "Nelson did catch the French fleet by surprise, and their landward guns were not prepared for battle," says White. "But the problems the French faced were far greater. Brueys simply did not understand Nelson's strategy. The French were prepared for a traditional one-on-one naval engagement, a battle for which the fleets were well matched in both size and number." The British fleet comprised 13 warships carrying 74 guns each and one with 50 guns which delivered 18- to 32-pound shot; the French fleet, 13 warships, carrying between 74 and 120 guns each delivering 24- to 36-pound shot, and four frigates.

Ships delivered what are called broadsides; teams of gunners responsible for manning pairs of guns, one on each side of the ship, would all fire from one side of the vessel. Knowing that there were not enough crew to fire all port and starboard guns simultaneously, Nelson split his fleet, sending vessels down both sides of the French line.

In addition to details of the battle, Goddio notes other inconsistencies in the historical record, particularly with regard to the ship's manifest. "We were surprised at the number of coins we found minted at so many different locations. According to historical sources Napoleon looted the Maltese treasury before sailing to Alexandria, unloading the booty on his arrival. That he looted the treasury is not a question, why so much of it remained aboard *L'Orient* is."

"Perhaps the most important aspect of this excavation," adds White, "is that it has given a life to the story of the battle that simply cannot be conveyed in history books. To read a description of the battle and the explosion aboard *L'Orient* and then actually to see the damage makes for a far more compelling narrative."

The gathering between site excavators and naval historians ended with a handshake between Anna Tribe and Louis Napoleon Bonaparte-Wyse, descendants, respectively, of Nelson and Napoleon. Artifacts raised from *L'Orient* are being conserved by the Supreme Council for Egyptian Antiquities. Human remains are to be reburied on Nelson Island where the British admiral interred the dead from both sides more than two centuries ago.

⊚ EYEWITNESS: The Battle of the Nile

compiled by MARK ROSE

D ominique Vivant Denon, one of the civilian scholars or savants accompanying Napoleon's expedition to Egypt, described the Battle of the Nile between the French and British fleets on August 1, 1798. The fight, despite its name, took place at Aboukir Bay on the Mediterranean coast east of Alexandria. Denon recorded his observations of the battle, which he viewed at a distance, and its aftermath in his book *Travels in Upper and Lower Egypt* (1803). At first Denon and his colleagues believed their fleet was victorious, only later did they realize the magnitude of the disaster:

The first shot was fired at five o'clock; and shortly after, our view of the movements of the two fleets was intercepted by the smoke. When night came on we could distinguish somewhat better, without, however, being able to give an account of what passed. ...Rolls of fire incessantly gushing from the mouths of the cannon evinced clearly that the combat was dreadful, and supported with an equal obstinacy on both sides. ...At ten o'clock, we perceived a strong light, which indicated a fire. A few minutes after we heard a terrible explosion, which was followed by a profound silence. ...At eleven o'clock a slow fire was kept up; and at midnight the action again became general: It continued until two in the morning. At daybreak I was at the advanced posts; and ten minutes after, the fleets were once more engaged. At nine o'clock another ship blew up. At ten, four ships, the only ones which were not disabled, and which I could distinguish to be French, crowded their sails, and quitted the field of battle, in possession of which they appeared to be, as they were neither attacked nor followed. Such was the phantom produced by the enthusiasm of hope.

In this way we cherished illusion, and spurned at all evidence, until, at length...we found that our situation was altered, and that, separated from the mother-country, we were become the inhabitants of a distant colony, where we should be obliged to depend on our own resources for subsistence until the peace... We learned that it was the L'Orient *which blew up at ten o'clock at night, and the* Hercule *the following morning; and that the captains of the ships of the line, the* Guillaume Tell *and* Généreux, *and of the frigates,* Diane *and* Justice, *perceiving that the rest of the fleet had fallen into the enemy's hands, had taken advantage of a moment*

of lassitude and inaction on the part of the English to effect their escape.

We reached the seaside at midnight, when the rising moon lighted up a new scene. The shore, to the extent of four leagues, was covered by wrecks, which enabled us to form an estimate of the loss we had sustained at the battle of Aboukir. To procure a few nails, or a few iron hoops, the wandering Arabs were employed in burning on the beach the masts, gun-carriages, boats, &c. which had been constructed at so vast an expense in our ports, and even the wrecks of which were a treasure in a country where so few of these objects were to be found. The robbers fled at our approach; and nothing was left but the bodies of the wretched victims, drifted on the loose sand, by which they were half covered.

In April 2005, the remains of 30 British sailors and soldiers and their families were interred with a solemn ceremony at the British Military and War Cemetery at Al-Shatby. An Italian archaeologist, Paollo Gallo, discovered the remains, including those of two women and three children, while searching for classical sites on Nelson Island in Aboukir Bay. They date to the 1798 battle and to the landing of a British expeditionary force there three years later. One of the individuals, Master and Commander James Russell, could be identified from his uniform.

The Great Wall's Patchwork History

SATELLITE IMAGES SHOW CENTURIES OF CONSTRUCTION PRECEEDED THE MING DYNASTY'S FORTIFICATIONS.

by ALEXANDER BENENSON

The Great Wall of China is one of mankind's most ambitious and enduring military building projects. Throughout the dynastic period of China, emperors increased the size and length of the wall not only to bolster security but also to stand as a symbol of strength and unification. The earliest evidence of a wall dates back to B.C. 695 when the Chu state built a U-shaped fortification around their northern border to keep out other rival states. Similar walls were built by kingdoms in the following centuries. In third century B.C. the short-lived Qin Dynasty sought to connect the disparate sections and create one single wall as well as build a new section in Inner Mongolia. When China was unified in B.C. 221, the wall turned into a defense against Mongolian raiders. Only small sections of these ancient walls remain, many of which, like those from the sixth and seventh-century A.D. Sui Dynasty are almost entirely obscured by sand and sediment. Most of what stands today was built during the Ming Dynasty, which lasted from A.D. 1368 to A.D. 1644. The Ming wall took nearly 200 years to complete and required the labor of over a million workers. The wall is peppered with thousands of watchtowers, gates, and storehouses, which stood as the first line of defense against invaders.

The images of the wall seen on page 4 of the photo insert were acquired on April 10, 1994 by the SIR-C/X-SAR radar onboard the space shuttle *Endeavor* and show a segment of the Great Wall in a desert region of north-central China, about 700 kilometers (435 miles) west of Beijing. The image at left shows an area 25 kilometers by 75 kilometers and the right images show an area 3.1 kilometers by 2.2 kilometers. The wall appears as a thin orange band, running from the top to the bottom of the color image on the left. The black and white images on the right correspond to the area outlined by the box and represent the four radar channels of the SIR-C radar. Each channel is sensitive to different aspects of the terrain, including two generations of the Great Wall. The bright continuous line running from top to bottom in this image is the younger wall, built during the Ming Dynasty about 600 years ago. Immediately to the right of this wall is a bright discontinuous line that is the remnant of the Sui Dynasty wall, built about 1,500 years ago.

PART IV:

The Wars of North America

The Forgotten Fight for America

THE CENTURIES-LONG STRUGGLE FOR CONTROL OF THE CONTINENT BEFORE 1776

by MARK ROSE

The enemy advanced with shouts & dismal Indian yells to our intrenchments. ...[the French] from every little rising–tree –stump–stone–and bush kept up a constant galding fire upon us.

On July 4, 1754, a young British officer led his exhausted and demoralized soldiers in retreat from western Pennsylvania. The night before, in a driving rainstorm, he had surrendered to the implacable adversaries who had surrounded his "fort of necessity" and decimated his troops in a grueling nine-hour battle. The defeat was a low point in George Washington's military career, but it was only one battle in the French and Indian War, and just one more battle in the largely forgotten, centuries-long struggle for possession of North America.

Excavations in the 1950s unearthed remains at a scatter of places, such as the palisade of Washington's Fort Necessity and skeletons of the garrison of Fort William Henry in New York, site of the French and Indian War massacre immortalized in James Fenimore Cooper's *The Last of the Mohicans.* But today, archaeologists are at work throughout the Atlantic seaboard, investigating early French settlements in the Southeast, homes of rebels and rulers in Maryland, shipwrecks in the frigid waters of Québec's Gulf of St. Lawrence, and the camp of merchants who supplied forts in the Lake Champlain corridor of New York and Vermont. At these sites, they are rediscovering the settings of the fight for America, telling of individuals who were swept up in sectarian strife and international wars, and discovering new evidence and asking new questions that will take us beyond history based on documentary sources alone.

CONFLICT MARKED THE initial occupation of America by Europeans, as countries staked out rival claims. Nowhere was this played out as brutally as in South Carolina and northern Florida, where archaeologists are tracking down the sixteenth-century French sites Charlesfort and Fort Caroline, vestiges of a colonization attempt that ended catastrophically.

The Spanish had explored the Southeast for decades by the time French Protestants seeking religious freedom—and perhaps a base from which they could intercept Spanish treasure fleets—arrived in 1562. An expedition led by Jean Ribault reached what is now South Carolina and built Charlesfort

on Parris Island. Ribault returned to France, leaving 27 men behind and promising to return with supplies. Religious civil war in France forced Ribault to England, where he was imprisoned as a spy. Growing desperate, the men at Charlesfort built a ship and sailed for France. Running out of food, they ate their leather shoes and jackets; eventually they drew lots and ate the loser before being rescued by an English ship.

Undeterred, the French launched another expedition, this one under René de Laudonnière, who sailed for America in 1564 with three ships. The expedition reached the St. Johns River, where its 300 soldiers, settlers, and craftsmen built Fort Caroline, somewhere near modern Jacksonville, Florida. Lack of food and other hardships led to desertions, and the colony was failing, like its predecessor, but in August 1565 Ribault arrived with five ships and reinforcements. Meanwhile, Phillip II had sent Pedro Menéndez de Avilés from Spain with orders to oust the French. Menéndez's fleet of 10 ships made landfall on September 4, only a week after Ribault's.

Deciding on a preemptive attack, Ribault sailed for the Spanish base at St. Augustine. But a storm scattered the French fleet, blowing four vessels ashore. Menéndez took advantage of the situation, surprising Fort Caroline in a dawn attack. Some 132 French male colonists were killed and 50 or so women and children captured. Menéndez then tracked down the survivors from Laudonnière's ships, telling one group that offered to surrender that he was "bound to pursue them with a fire and blood war to extermination." For Menéndez, the Protestant French were not only trespassers but also heretics. Except for the few Catholics among them, he slaughtered all of the men.

Where did these disastrous attempts at colonization take place? Four years after Charlesfort was abandoned, the Spanish founded the town of Santa Elena in the area, yet their documents do not identify where the French post was. And visitors to the reconstructed Fort Caroline, built in 1964 by the National Park Service, likely aren't aware that the accuracy of the early engravings, on which it is based in part, has been questioned. Nor are they likely to know that excavations there in 1952 and nearby in 1973 turned up no French artifacts. But now archaeologists have found Charlesfort and are hot on the trail of Fort Caroline.

In 1982, archaeologist Stanley South found several possible French pottery sherds among Spanish majolica and redware at the site of Fort San Felipe in Santa Elena. But he attributed them to the presence of French privateers in the area. Seven years later, Chester DePratter excavated at possible locations of Charlesfort and found nothing. He concluded that the fort's remains had eroded into Port Royal Sound. Then, in the mid-1990s, they reexamined pottery from Santa Elena, and confirmed the French stoneware identified from Fort San Felipe. Moreover, they found that French sherds came only from the fort and nowhere else at the site. Rather than razing the French fort, as they were ordered to do, the Spanish, South and DePratter believe, simply reoccupied it.

This offers clues also to the location of Fort Caroline, says archaeologist Jerald Milanich. Earlier researchers had been looking for French faience pottery, not the wares found at Charlesfort/Fort San Felipe. With that in mind, Rebecca Gorman, a graduate student working with Milanich, has gone back and checked pottery collections made in the region. She has turned up French and Spanish ceramics of the right period in dredge in the St. Johns River. The task now facing Gorman is to pinpoint where the spoil came from, if such records exist, and then determine if anything remains of the site that might identify it as Fort Caroline.

RELIGIOUS PREJUDICE ALSO played a role in the struggle for dominance. In seventeenth-century Maryland, faith and social divisions, exacerbated by civil war in England, led to rebellions that tore the colony apart. In recent excavations, archaeologists have uncovered the homes of Nathaniel Pope, a leader of the revolt in the mid-1640s, and of Charles Calvert, third Lord Baltimore, who ruled the colony until an uprising in the 1680s. Finds from the sites provide insights on the course of the first rebellion and how Calvert used his residence to symbolically reinforce his right to rule.

The Calverts, who were granted the colony by Charles I, envisioned Maryland as a manorial society of large landholders and tenant farmers living in a spirit of religious toleration. But seeds of division were embedded in the colony from the start. Many of the elite were Catholic, like the Calverts, while most of the lower class were Protestant.

The first crisis took place when the war that erupted between Charles I and Parliament in 1642 crossed the Atlantic. The Calverts, with their ties to the royal court, were targeted by a group aiming to install a pro-Parliament, Protestant government. Among those involved were Richard Ingle, captain of the tobacco ship Reformation, and Protestant freemen such as Nathaniel Pope.

Ingle received a commission from Parliament authorizing the capture of vessels from royalist ports. On February 14, 1645, he sailed to St. Mary's and seized a Dutch trading ship. It was the beginning of what became known as "The Plundering Time." After a brief resistance, the governor, Leonard Calvert, retreated to Virginia. Houses of those loyal to the Calverts were ransacked and their property stolen (the loot being taken to Pope's home in St. Mary's). Many fled; others were killed in fighting.

The rebels fortified Pope's home, and its excavation has revealed a sophisticated pentagonal ditch and palisade with three bastions enclosing the house. But although the north and east sides were carefully laid out, the south and west were not. Similarly, the ditch was very shallow on the west side, barely two feet deep. Archaeologist Timothy Riordan believes that the plan and initial work may have been directed by Ingle, while later, less competent work was done after he returned to England in the spring of 1645. The ditch also appears to have been quickly filled in with domestic debris, animal bones, and oyster shells. All this suggests that any threat to the rebels from Calvert faded quickly.

Indeed, it was nearly a year before Leonard Calvert was able to assemble a large enough force to return and reestablish control. By then the colony was shattered. St. Mary's population was reduced from 500 to fewer than 100—less than when it was first settled.

Although the colony recovered, by the mid-1680s the tobacco economy was in a severe depression; discontent and old antagonisms resurfaced. Many Protestant colonists strongly supported Charles Calvert, Leonard's uncle and the third Lord Baltimore, but others felt that they would never benefit from his political patronage. These men, known as the Protestant Associators, spread rumors of combined Catholic and Indian plots to wipe out Protestant settlers. In July 1689, when Baltimore was in England, the Associators marched on St. Mary's City and seized the State House, then went on to take over Calvert's plantation at Mattapany.

Beginning in 1666, Calvert had set about building a major plantation and port at Mattapany. Conventional wisdom among scholars was that nearly all planters in the Chesapeake region, even the wealthiest, lived in impermanent houses with timber frames set directly into the ground. But excavations at Mattapany during the 1990s by archaeologists Ed Chaney and Julia King revealed massive brick foundations of a house at least two stories tall that measured 25 by 50 feet and had a tile roof, glass windows secured by lead frames, plaster walls, and fancy fireplace tiles. Calvert also shifted the colony's weapons magazine to Mattapany (excavations there yielded hundreds of pieces of shot and a gun barrel). Though St. Mary's City continued to function as the legislative capital, he governed from Mattapany. "A colonist approaching Mattapany—and most with any business on the Patuxent River had to stop there—would see, perched atop a 20-foot bluff overlooking the water, the colony's principal magazine and, rising behind it, Calvert's impressive brick dwelling. This was an extremely symbolic landscape, and there is no doubt that he intended it to be," says King.

Excavation also revealed traces of a log palisade around the house. "The logs were set only about two feet in the ground," says King, "suggesting it had been built hastily. It may have been erected either by Calvert loyalists when they learned the Associators were marching on Mattapany or by the Associators after they seized it." In England, Lord Baltimore tried to take his colony back, but King William refused, preferring to take control himself, and sent a royal governor to Maryland in 1691.

ON CHRISTMAS EVE 1994, diver Marc Tremblay spotted muskets, glass wine bottles, and timbers on the floor of the Gulf of St. Lawrence at Baie-Trinité. For archaeologists, his discovery opened a window on the lives of those swept up in an ill-fated invasion of Québec after war broke out between England and France in 1689. Both sides used their Native American allies as fast, quickly mobilized proxies at the start of this war. In August, the settlement of Lachine, near Montréal, was attacked, and 24 French were killed and 72 taken captive. Retaliation was swift: Schenectady, Salmon Falls, and Casco were all attacked by French and allied Native Americans in the first half of 1690. These raids would soon be followed by major, European-style military operations.

Louis XIV had already approved a plan to seize the city of New York, but the British colonists struck first with a large-scale expedition. After taking Port Royal, Nova Scotia, in the spring of 1690 with a fleet of seven ships, Sir William Phips of Boston led a fleet of 32 ships against Québec. Phips' plan was to preoccupy the French with a feint against Montréal by a land force, but the diversionary troops never made it past Lake Champlain. When Phips arrived at Québec with his 2,300 militiamen and some Native American allies, he was outnumbered by forces under Count Frontenac, governor general of New France. The assault failed, and while the expedition was returning to Boston, disaster struck as stormy weather sank four of the ships, including the one found in 1994.

An archaeological team from Parks Canada and the Québec Ministry of Culture and Communications excavated the wreck site in the summers of 1996 and 1997. It was clear from the artifacts that the wreck was British and from the late seventeenth or early eighteenth century. Clues to the ship's identification were found in the form of a musket with the initials ct and a shallow metal bowl with mis engraved on the handle. These could be compared to names on lists of Massachusetts militia companies. Cornelius Tileston of Dorchester appeared on one list. For the other, Increase Mosely, also of Dorchester, is likely. His wife's name, Sarah, completes the initials. Both Tileston and Mosley sailed on the *Elizabeth and Mary*.

Considering that the wreck was in less than 15 feet of water at high tide, the integrity of the remains and preservation of the artifacts are astonishing. At the wreck's bow, bricks and cast-iron kettles defined the galley area, where meals were prepared while at sea. The central part of the vessel, the location of the human cargo of militiamen, contained the bulk of the individual belongings, including muskets and pistols, swords and belt axes, cartridge pouches, leather shoes, buttons and buckles, tobacco pipes, and spoons. In the stern area of the wreck, navigation instruments, numerous tools, and various types of containers reflected the small ship's operation and maintenance, as well as the equipment and provisions brought along for the expedition against Québec.

The wreck and material culture of the *Elizabeth and Mary* brought the archaeologists an unexpectedly personal look at those who sailed in it. "The image of military invaders sailing to Québec on a large fleet of 30-some vessels, as evoked in the historical documents, gave way to a more moving story," recalls Parks Canada's Marc-André Bernier. Oil lamps made from lead and brass scraps probably reflect attempts by the men to generate heat to fend off the November damp and cold of the St. Lawrence. Another man, trying to keep his belongings together in the cramped hold of the vessel, wedged his shoes and his belt ax between frame timbers, where they were found four centuries later. A silver-crowned, heart-shaped brooch, a love token of the period, bespeaks a soldier's desire to carry with him a reminder of a loved one left waiting at home.

"None of these soldiers knew what to expect when they boarded the ships en route to New France to retaliate for the French raids on their own villages in a global war for which they probably could barely understand the European origins," says Bernier. "They certainly did not think that they would bring back smallpox, an affliction that would do as much harm to them as any French incursion in their territory. As ships trickled back to Boston, some of them returning only the following spring, the disease that had decimated the troops spread through the colony."

THE LAKE CHAMPLAIN CORRIDOR from New York to Montréal and Québec was a vital route for trade and for armies during the French and Indian War 250 years ago and, later, from the Revolutionary War. Many of its sites have been picked over by souvenir hunters and by early archaeologists. These include Fort William Henry, Ticonderoga, Crown Point, and the Saratoga battlefield. Here, archaeologist David Starbuck is confronted with two questions: Is there anything left to dig? And is there anything left to learn?

For the past 14 years, Starbuck has been excavating at Fort Edward on the Hudson River at the southern end of the Champlain corridor. At the time of the French and Indian War, Fort Edward was the largest British post in North America. Today, work is focused not on the fort but on the camp of the sutlers, the merchants who supplied the army in the 1750s. "For the past three summers we have been excavating the richest site ever found at Fort Edward. We've found a complete, burned sutler's warehouse absolutely packed with artifacts. I've never seen anything like it before," says Starbuck.

Finds from this past summer include wine bottles, a bayonet, hundreds of tobacco pipes, pottery, and dozens of British and Spanish coins. The excavation of a sutler's warehouse is a first, and is leading to new research questions. "We're finding so many pieces of wineglasses," says Starbuck. "In the military camps, there aren't many wineglasses. Does that mean these are things being sold only to officers? Or does it mean that the sutlers were making so much money off the army that they personally were living high on the hog?"

Ironically, excavation at the sutlers' camp was prompted in part because of looting there. Military artifacts have a high dollar value, according to Starbuck. "If you dig up a regimental button, or a gunflint, or a musket ball even, these things are all over eBay right now. A lot of military stuff gets sold there, and somehow that market has to be closed off." He fears that privately owned sites will be gone in 50 years if treasure hunters aren't reined in.

That danger is particularly disturbing because archaeology is critical to understanding not just the French and Indian War but all of the early conflicts in the struggle for North America. "The number of historians who are willing to use material culture to understand the past is still very low. A few younger historians are willing to use archaeological evidence, but most of the older ones are still into the big names and big events of history," says Starbuck. "I think they are leaving out a huge part of the story. They aren't finding new documents. You can rehash the same old documents only so

many times. As we go out and dig military camps, as we go out and collect material culture, as we go out and study housing types, I think archaeologists are the only people right now who really are adding to the historical record."

Anatomy of a Massacre

AN UNPUBLISHED 1950s EXCAVATION AND MORE RECENT SKELETAL ANALYSIS YIELD GRAPHIC NEW DETAILS ABOUT THE SLAUGHTER OF A BRITISH GARRISON DURING THE FRENCH AND INDIAN WAR.

by DAVID R. STARBUCK

The siege of a frontier fort in upstate New York and the massacre of its British garrison during the French and Indian War were immortalized in James Fenimore Cooper's *The Last of the Mohicans.* Published in 1826, Cooper's book graphically describes the assault on Fort William Henry at the southern tip of Lake George and the subsequent slaughter of British captives by Indians loyal to the French. The story of the siege and massacre has also inspired several films, the most recent of which was released in 1992. Both Cooper and the filmmakers embellished history to suit their purposes, and no doubt the truth concerning the Fort William Henry garrison has suffered from these dramatizations. Nonetheless, historical archaeologists excavating the fort some 40 years ago found concrete and often chilling evidence of life and death at the garrison. Now an osteological study of remains found there may provide further insight into what transpired during those fateful days in the summer of 1757.

This much we know for certain. In the early morning of August 9, 1757, Lt. Colonel George Monro and his 2,300 British regulars and provincials surrendered Fort William Henry to 10,000 French, Canadians, and Native Americans, led by the Marquis de Montcalm. Named after two grandsons of King George II, the fort was built to block the advance of French forces from Canada. Its 30-foot-thick walls of pine logs and earth formed the front line of British defenses in the north. Montcalm's superior forces had surrounded the fort and bombarded it for six days before Monro surrendered. The terms were generous. The British were not asked to surrender their possessions as booty. And after pledging not to fight against the French army for the following 18 months, Monro's troops were to be escorted to Fort Edward, a British base of operations on the Hudson River, 16 miles to the south. The sick and wounded would remain at Fort William Henry under Montcalm's protection.

Later that day, British and provincial troops marched out of the fort to stay overnight in Montcalm's camp, and the French took possession of the fort. Trouble, however, was brewing. The French paid their Indian allies for military service by allowing them to loot the possessions of the defeated British and provincial armies. Native American warriors considered it shameful to return to their villages without scalps or booty. After the military ceremony accompanying the transfer of power, some of the 1,600 Indians attached to the French army searched Fort Henry William for loot. When they found little and realized they might not be compensated for their service, the Indians killed, scalped, and in a few cases beheaded the 17 sick and wounded British soldiers who remained inside the fort. They also dug up some of the bodies in the British military cemetery and scalped the corpses. Some of those buried there had died of smallpox. The Indians were soon infected and carried the disease back to their villages in Canada.

The following morning, August 10, war whoops signaled an Indian attack on the captives who were being led to Fort Edward. The French escort could do little to protect the men, women and children. Probably no more than 200 soldiers and civilians were actually killed in the massacre, but the terrified survivors clearly believed that the number had been far greater. Many were taken to Canada, where some were adopted into Indian tribes, some sold into slavery, and others eventually ransomed and returned home.

Montcalm was victorious, but the slaughter of prisoners under his protection became a blot on his otherwise spotless reputation. Seeking to clear the area of enemy buildings and reclaim the land for France, Montcalm burned Fort William Henry to the ground after removing its cannon and stores.

Nearly two centuries later, in 1952, Harold Veeder, an Albany, New York, real estate broker, formed a stock company and purchased the Lake George site, intending to

Five victims of the massacre found in a casemate room underneath the brick floor of the East Barracks in 1957.

Courtesy the Fort William Henry Museum and David Starbuck

build a replica of the fort as a tourist attraction. They hired contract archaeologist Stanley Gifford to direct excavation of the vague outlines of a dry moat and diamond-shaped bastions visible on the surface. Accurate rebuilding would be possible because detailed written descriptions and measurements of the original fort were available, along with copies of the 1755 construction plans, housed in the British Archives in London, the Canadian Archives in Ottawa, the Library of Congress in Washington, and the New York State Department of Education in Albany. The original plans, however, would have little value without an archaeological determination of the location of each structure.

The drawings revealed that the fort consisted of four bastians, four curtain walls, and four wooden barracks. The north and south barracks were two stories high, the east and west barracks consisted of one story underground and two stories above ground. One entered the fort by crossing a bridge over a deep dry moat, which surrounded the structure on three sides. The fourth side faced Lake George.

Intensive trenching began in the spring of 1953 and lasted through 1954. Gifford found the stone- and brick-lined rooms that had been built underneath the east and west barracks, where women, children, and the sick were sheltered during battle. Underneath the the brick floor of the east barracks, Gifford found six human skeletons, some missing their skulls and one intermingled with eight musket balls. These skeletons may well have been the remains of those killed on August 9; a Jesuit priest had described an Indian leaving the fort carrying a human head.

Gifford also discovered a layer of black sand. Fastidious about sanitation, British Lord Jeffrey Amherst, in preparing to camp there during a summer campaign in 1759, sterilized the site by burning the ground and covering it with beach sand. In the northeast corner of the parade ground, Gifford's crew also excavated the original 60-foot well from which the soldiers drew their water. The tens of thousands of artifacts recovered from the fort's ashes included cannon balls, mortar shells, axes, bayonets, parts of muskets, projectile points, coins, animal bones, and wine bottles. The number of bottles prompted Gifford to conclude, tongue in cheek, that "the war was fought by each side throwing rum bottles rather than firing their muskets."

Perhaps most unusual was the discovery of a live eight-inch mortar shell still loaded with black powder. A bomb squad from Fort Jay on Governor's Island in New York Harbor found traces of a human scalp with black hair embedded on the surface of the shell. The mortar shell was presumably lobbed into the fort, where it had glanced off the head of a soldier, tearing off part of his scalp. It may have landed upside down in the fort's sandy soil, extinguishing its fuse.

It has been estimated that as many as a thousand soldiers died at Fort William Henry between 1755 and 1757. Gifford located a corner of a cemetery outside the southern wall and excavated ten graves. The soldiers seem to have been buried hastily, without coffins, although one was found lying on what appeared to be a slab of pine bark. Most of the bodies had probably been wrapped in blankets.

A promotional view of one of the skulls discovered at the fort in the 1950s.

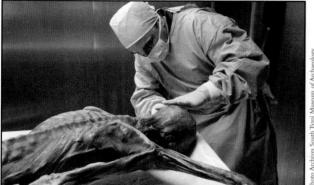

A decade after he was first discovered, an x-ray in 2001 revealed that the 5,000-year-old "Iceman" known as Ötzi had been shot with an arrow. Other tests showed he was attacked by several assailants.

The Crow Creek mass burial, uncovered in 1978, held remains of nearly 500 men, women, and children, apparently killed when their village on the Missouri River was overrun around 1325 A.D.

The mid-third millennium B.C. "Standard of Ur" depicts a king and his army, both foot soldiers and heavy four-wheeled chariots, with captured and killed enemies.

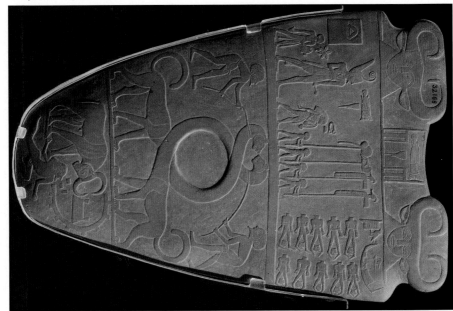

Narmer, an early Egyptian king of about 3100 B.C., appears on this ceremonial stone palette walking in a procession to inspect dead and mutilated enemies and smiting a captured rival with a mace.

Known today as Egypt's last great pharaoh, Ramesses III (1185–1153 B.C.) led his forces against the Sea Peoples, an invading coalition of tribes from the central Mediterranean and Aegean.

The menorah from the temple in Jerusalem is paraded in a relief on the Arch of Titus commemorating the Roman victory of A.D. 70.

A panorama of the east fortification wall of Troy VI in 1932. Blegen identified stratum VIIa as 'Homer's Troy', but the fortification wall built in stratum VI remained the defense of the citadel, with a few patches.

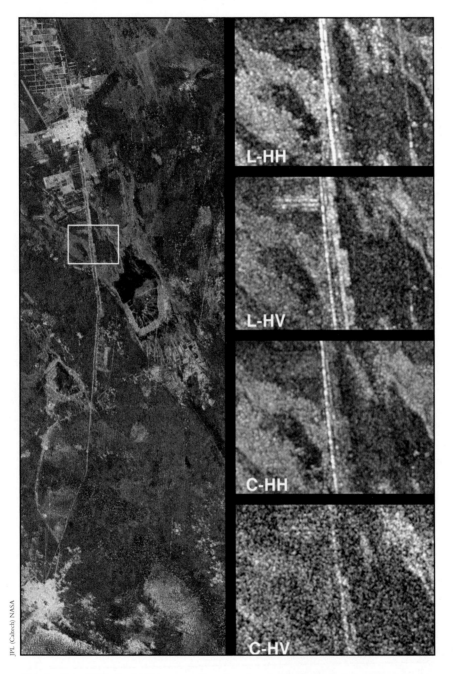

L-HH

L-HV

C-HH

C-HV

China's Great Wall is familiar to tourists through restored sections of its Ming Dynasty (1368–1644 A.D.) version, but radar imaging from the space shuttle has revealed much older fortifications from the Sui Dynasty of the sixth and seventh centuries A.D.

Even with a lightweight throwing arm intended for demonstration purposes only, this replica trebuchet built at Warwick Castle in England can throw a 33-pound stone more than 900 feet.

The pride of Henry VIII's fleet, Mary Rose *sank in 1545. Since it was raised in 1982, the ship has undergone nonstop conservation efforts. A wax-like substance is being sprayed on the timbers to replace the water that saturated them and to seal the wood.*

This cameo with a solid gold band was excavated at the Johnson's Island Civil War POW camp in Ohio. It may have been worn or used by one of the Confederate prisoners there.

Archival records suggest that this sub, once thought to be Pioneer, *is an unknown Confederate vessel.*

In 2000, the Confederate submarine Hunley *was recovered intact from the bottom of Charleston's harbor where it went down with all hands after sinking the Union warship* Housatonic *in 1864.*

Excavated in 1964, the Union ironclad Cairo *has been rebuilt in skeletal fashion. An electronically detonated mine sank the ship in the Yazoo River in December 1862.*

This lantern is one of the many artifacts that have been brought up from Monitor.

The revolving turret, one of several innovations on the Union warship Monitor, *was recovered in 2002.*

An American ICBM flies through a Soviet flag in this example of Cold War art now preserved in the Minuteman Missile National Historic Site.

A diver swims near the propeller of the battleship Nagato, *which was sunk in an atomic test at Bikini Atoll in 1946.*

The replica of Fort William Henry was completed in 1956; limited archaeological work continued until 1960. The exposed skeletons became a major tourist attraction for the resort community near Lake George. In 1993, the Fort William Henry Corporation, a group of businessmen who won the replica fort, decided it was no longer appropriate to display the skeletal remains and arranged for their reburial.

Before reinterring the bones, however, the group asked Maria Liston, a physical anthropologist at Adirondack Community College, to reanalyze the skeletons. Advances in osteology in the 40 years since the Gifford excavation suggested that more could be learned from the bones. Liston's first task was to remove the plastic coating applied to the bones to preserve them. She X-rayed the bones and examined them for signs of chronic stress (from carrying heavy loads), diseases, amputations, and wounds. Most of the skeletons were identified as Caucasian males between the ages of 15 and 25, although some of the bones were from two women and a small child. The skeletons reflect injuries such as herniated discs in the backbone, and scars on the bones of the shoulders, arms, and legs as muscles were overused and town away from the bone. "This is not surprising," says Liston, "since the men were portaging heavy material back and forth between Fort William Henry and Fort Edward like two-legged pack mules." Liston's initial survey also revealed a catalog of traumatic injury; a soldier who may have been scalped, another who may have died during the amputation of a leg, a third who suffered broken ribs from a fall after being hit by canister shot that shattered his ribs and the lower part of his left arm. Liston and associate Brenda Baker of Moorhead State University also found evidence of long-term chronic diseases such as tuberculosis.

"I'm used to working with [dead bodies, with] skeletons," Liston says. "And yet sometimes it is very moving to realize that these men were in bad health, often were [hurting] a great deal, and then either died of disease or died very violently. . . . At times it really comes home to you just how rough life was at that time."

The skeletons from the exhibit areas were reburied during a memorial service at Fort William Henry's cemetery in May 1993. Chief Paul Waterman, of the Onondaga Nation, joined representatives of New York State's government, the British Consulate, and the British military in eulogizing the dead and in placing a wreath over their remains. Many had died at Fort William Henry struggling for control of the continent—English, provincial, French Canadian, and Native American. Unfortunately, archaeology has not been able to give names or ranks to any of the dead who lie within Fort William Henry's cemetery, nor can we say for sure which skeletons were British and which were American provincials. Still, by studying their remains, we are learning more about how these soldiers lived and how they died.

Turtle
Dives Again

RE-CREATING GEORGE WASHINGTON'S
REVOLUTIONARY SUBMARINE

by TOM GIDWITZ

A t midnight, September 7, 1776, a strange craft on a deadly mission made its way down the Hudson River. Shaped like an egg, with a windowed copper conning tower, two spindly propellers, and a 100-pound time bomb on its back, the seven-foot-tall wooden submarine *Turtle* was the most daring invention of the Revolutionary War.

The brainchild of David Bushnell, a frail Connecticut ex-farmer and mechanical genius, *Turtle*'s task was to affix the bomb to *Eagle,* the 64-gun flagship of the British fleet anchored in New York Harbor. Hundreds of men-of-war, transport ships, and gunboats also crowded the waters, and 30,000 British troops were bivouacked on Staten Island and Long Island. The force threatened to cut the colonies in half and crush the Continental army. If *Turtle* could destroy *Eagle,* it might alter the course of the war.

As the sub approached its target, its only occupant, Sergeant Ezra Lee, feverishly cranked two propellers and let

enough water into the ballast tanks to submerge the craft and slip beneath the ship. But
the auger mounted atop the sub, meant to
penetrate *Eagle's* hull and attach the bomb,
bounced off. When Lee tried again, the sub
skidded out from beneath the British ship and
shot to the surface.

Dawn was breaking, and Lee turned the
ungainly *Turtle* back to Manhattan. As he
powered past Governor's Island, British sen-
tries spotted him and gave chase in a barge.
The *Turtle* couldn't even make one mile an
hour and as the barge caught up, Lee
released the time bomb. It drifted on the
surface, and the Red Coats, sensing danger,
hurried back to shore. An hour later, not
long after *Turtle* was back in Manhattan, the
bomb exploded, rocking the harbor and
blowing a column of water high in the air.

A month later Bushnell was transporting
Turtle up the Hudson aboard a sailboat when
the British attacked, sinking the ship and
destroying the innovative vessel in the
process. The sub was the first ever used in
warfare, but Bushnell never built another.
The only surviving evidence of its design to
survive are eyewitness accounts and letters
Bushnell wrote at the request of a fellow
inventor, Thomas Jefferson, 15 years later.

But now *Turtle* sails again, thanks to
Rick and Laura Brown, two Massachusetts
artists who resurrect lost technologies to
help them better understand human ingenuity over time. With the help of historians,
archaeologists, timber framers, blacksmiths,
glassblowers, museum curators, U.S. Navy
cadets, and the Browns' students at Boston's
Massachusetts College of Art (MassArt), they
built a new *Turtle* faithful to the design,

materials, and techniques that Bushnell used
himself. The result is an ungainly, oddly
beautiful vessel reminiscent of a mad wiz-
ard's flying machine, with a nut-brown hull
of carved wood and hammered metals bearing the marks of many hands.

The Browns are experts at revealing the
past, but not with archaeological excavations.
In their MassArt classes, they re-create
ancient objects with rigorous exactitude,
using the same materials and tools used for
the originals. By tracking down "very specific skills to a very specific location to a very
specific material and a very specific time
frame," Laura says emphatically, they can
access the past through "the world of objects
that reflect the humans that made them."

The Browns began their careers thinking
more about contemporary sculpture than the
past. But they were always fascinated by the
history of the tools and materials they used.
Soon they began to incorporate time itself as
an integral part of their art, creating environmental installations from sculpted earth or
concrete that eroded in the weather or that
they altered themselves in response to events
in the world. When they were asked to lend
their skills to the re-creation of a pair of
medieval trebuchets, or catapults, in England,
they realized that experimental archaeology—
replicating history's forgotten or misunder-
stood objects—would allow them, Laura says,
"to better understand these innovations and
the complexity of the people and places that
surrounded them." They would test the
boundaries of art and archaeology both.

They have gone on to re-create a sixteenth-century, five-story, human-powered
crane and are currently reconstructing the

wooden cupola of an eighteenth-century Polish synagogue destroyed by the Nazis. In 1999, in a Chelmsford, Massachusetts, stone yard, they settled the mystery of how the ancient Egyptians raised their obelisks by using a ramp, a pile of sand, and a 112-person crew tugging hemp ropes to gently set a 36-foot-tall granite obelisk upright. Their most ambitious projects are assembled in near round-the-clock marathons that can stretch for more than a week, with scores of helpers, ringing axes, flying wood chips, and long tables of artisans and students sitting down to share stories and soup.

In their pursuit of accuracy, the Browns and their students study the history, science, literature, technology, and art that shaped the original object. They strive to put themselves into the minds of the original makers, and, in essence, experience the past from the inside out. The Browns then bring the experience to the larger public through museum exhibitions and documentary films.

Rick, 56, is a round-faced, white-haired man with a gentle voice and a relaxed manner. Laura, 53, is energetic and spirited, with narrow eyes and a Southern twang. Natives of Georgia, the Browns are sculptors. Rick is also a trained architect, and Laura is skilled at welding, timber framing, concrete construction, and can operate backhoes and bulldozers. They have built houses in Boston; immersed themselves in the folkways of Africa, Central America, and Asia; and have embraced the idea that the hand-fashioned object, well wrought and communally made, can reveal a truth as deep as that of any artist's masterpiece. Although they exhibit their own art in museums, their true love is teaching. "One of

our objectives is to give education kind of a shot in the arm," says Rick.

Their headquarters is the Handshouse Studio, a tall, graceful post-and-beam workshop in the pinewoods of Norwell, Massachusetts, half an hour south of Boston. The building is a testament to their eclecticism and sense of community. Laura and Rick spent a year cutting its timber frame, using Roman, medieval European, and nineteenth-century American wood construction techniques. They then staged an old-time barn raising, welcoming dozens of colleagues and friends who helped them erect the structure in two days.

In April 2002, the producers of *Ancient Arsenal,* a series on pioneering war machines, proposed that they rebuild *Turtle* for an episode of the show. Unlike the Browns' previous re-creations, the sub was a one-time product of a single individual, not a device refined over years of use. But David Bushnell intrigued them. His *Turtle* boasted the world's first sealed submersible chamber with an exhaust system for carbon dioxide, the first two-bladed propeller, the first depth gauge, a modern snorkel, and a time bomb with a flintlock detonator. "Bushnell's submarine was the greatest technological advancement of the American Revolutionary War," says Rick. "With it, Yankee ingenuity was born."

Other people had built or drawn versions of *Turtle,* but they included modern parts or components that never could have worked. To re-create *Turtle* accurately, the Browns had to explore the era's European, Native American, and Yankee raw materials and crafts.

They also studied Bushnell's original letters to Thomas Jefferson until they knew much of them by heart. In 1785, Jefferson was ambassador to France. An inventor himself, he was eager to foster innovation and technological self-sufficiency in the fledgling United States. He asked for details from Bushnell's original supporters, including George Washington, who called the sub "an effort of genius." Bushnell sent Jefferson a thorough description of *Turtle,* which Jefferson later published in the *Transactions of the American Philosophical Society.*

Bushnell was a farmer, not a shipwright, and he described the sub with a landsman's terms. "The external shape of the submarine vessel bore some resemblance to two upper tortoise shells of equal sizes, joined together," Bushnell wrote. It was egg-shaped with "the place of entrance into the vessel being represented by the opening made by the swell of the shell at the head of the animal." Pilot Ezra Lee described the hull as "composed of solid pieces of oak scooped out and fitted together," and "bound thoroughly with an iron band." After poring over these accounts, the Browns realized the hull had been cut from a single log, with the same techniques local Native American Pequots used to carve out their canoes.

The pilot sat on a bench inside a chamber that held enough air for a 30-minute dive. To submerge he tapped a foot-operated valve that let water into ballast tanks; to surface he worked two hand pumps to force the water out. He cranked two foot-long, windmill-shaped propellers to move forward, backward, up, and down. A compass provided direction, and a cork afloat in a glass tube connected to the water outside indicated depth; both were coated with

foxfire—a glow-in-the-dark fungus—for visibility in the underwater gloom. On top, said Bushnell, "was a brass crown or cover, resembling a hat with its crown and brim" and the hull-piercing auger. Aft was a rudder and the mounted bomb. Secured to its bottom with iron straps were hundreds of pounds of lead ballast.

The Browns conferred with Joe Woods, head of MassArt's Small Metals Department, to come up with the appropriate eighteenth-century materials and tools for the scores of metal pieces. They studied leather and brass water pumps from the period at the American Museum of Firefighting in Hudson, New York, and spent an entire weekend with timber framers and engineers discussing how to carve and assemble the shell. They consulted specialists at the Smithsonian Institution, Boston Museum of Science, Winterthur Museum, Mystic Seaport, and Connecticut College Arboretum about the metals, marine technologies, and wood that Bushnell might have found available at the time. Archaeologist Kevin McBride of the Mashantucket Pequot Museum in Connecticut told them how the era's Native Americans burned out the centers of large logs and shaped them to make canoes, a process that Bushnell himself might have used. The project's educational reach extended to the U. S. Naval Academy in Annapolis, where Lew Nuckols, then a professor of ocean engineering, incorporated *Turtle* into his courses. "It was really a very good educational tool for the Naval Academy," Nuckols says. History students searched archives for information and midshipmen helped design the hull and analyze the ballast and propulsion requirements.

In late December 2002, MassArt students and faculty, naval cadets, and artisans gathered in the cold at Handshouse to re-create *Turtle*. On one side of the studio, the Browns and MassArt colleague Matt Hinc-man set up a blacksmith shop to forge and hammer out the sub's iron parts, and a machine shop to fashion dozens of rivets, pins, brackets, bands, and other pieces.

A 12-foot-long Sitka spruce log, seven feet in diameter, arrived from British Columbia. (A huge piece of East Coast oak, although historically more accurate, would be nearly impossible to obtain legally today.) Ten professional woodwrights and engineers from the Timber Framers Guild split the giant log with wedges, then used traditional hand tools to round and hollow out the hull's two halves. Back at MassArt, faculty members, alumni, and students cast the bronze window frames, hatches, and hinges. They attached them to the conning tower, which Joe Wood had hammered from a single piece of copper. The assembly was taken to Handshouse, where the hull and conning tower were cinched together with iron straps and sealed with felt gaskets slathered in a goo of beeswax, turpentine, boiled linseed oil, and lard.

Despite his long letters, Bushnell never recorded how he joined the various sections of *Turtle* together. "It was always a temptation to use silicone to seal the thing," says Rob Duarte, a MassArt student. "Then you realized that someone else had to figure this out with the same limited resources that we were using. That's just an interesting way to learn. You can't do it any other way than by actually doing it."

After 12 days of labor, the Browns immersed the completed Turtle in the chilly harbor of Duxbury, Massachusetts. Inside was Matt Hincman, who reported that the seals were watertight and the parts worked properly. Then, in March 2003, they launched the sub in an indoor test tank at the U.S. Naval Academy, where Nuckols made 10 dives. Inside, he says, "you feel very isolated from the outside world," for the six-inch-thick hull is virtually soundproof, and the three view ports let in little light. "If you had any sense of claustrophobia it would not be a very good experience." The sub moved slowly no matter how hard he cranked, and to steer he had to yank the tiller and use the rudder like an oar. Yet, after 227 years, *Turtle* finally completed its mission, albeit with the assistance of some modern technology. With directions relayed by radio from the surface, after three attempts he successfully planted a replica of the bomb on a mockup of *Eagle's* hull.

On April 6, 2003, at the North River in Massachusetts, the Browns launched the sub from a horse-drawn cart. Rick Brown took the vessel for a one-hour surface cruise. It was hot, exhausting, and edifying. "You have to experience firsthand the kind of things this guy had to confront, and I can understand how difficult it was," he says. Back in 1776, Ezra Lee in the primitive sub attacked "the most powerful navy in the world single-handedly, one man against the Royal Navy. That was a pretty courageous moment."

Benedict Arnold Gunboat

Re-enactors man a replica of the 1776 gunboat Philadelphia II, originally used by Benedict Arnold against the British. Constructed by staff and volunteers at Lake Champlain Maritime Museum (www.lcmm.org), it now serves as a centerpiece for interpretation of the Revolutionary War era.

Courtesy Lake Champlain Maritime Museum

A vessel that was part of a 15-ship squadron led by Benedict Arnold in a Lake Champlain engagement with a superior British fleet on October 11, 1776, has been found in the lake, its 50 feet of mast still standing and its large bow gun, a 12-pound cannon, still in place. Two ships were lost and ten percent of Arnold's men were killed in the first five hours of fighting. The remaining 13 ships attempted to slip past a British blockade during the night, their oars wrapped in greased rags. One ship was captured and another sank. The following day, the British engaged the remaining rebel ships,

in a second battle, which ended when Arnold intentionally destroyed five vessels to keep them from falling into British hands. Arnold and his men escaped overland to Fort Ticonderoga, to which only four of the original 15 ships safely returned.

Art Cohn, director of the Lake Champlain Maritime Museum, believes that the newly discovered gunboat is the one lost during the blockade run. It is similar to the Philadelphia, a gunboat sunk in the first engagement, which was discovered in 1935 and is now in the Smithsonian Institution. Cohn dove to the well-preserved wreck, and a remote-operated vehicle took photographs and videotaped the ship. The gunboat was found during a survey of the lake bottom begun in 1996 in reponse to an invasion of non-native zebra mussels that threaten the lake's archaeological resources. The Lake Champlain Maritime Museum will be working with the appropriate federal agencies and the states of New York and Vermont to develop a management plan for the gunboat, and to decide whether to leave the ship in place or raise, conserve, and exhibit it.

by JESSICA E. SARACENI

Remains of a Sumptuous Feast

EXCAVATIONS AT VALLEY FORGE REVEAL HOW SOLDIERS COPED WITH INSUFFICIENT SUPPLIES AND FOOD.

by Nathaniel Ralston

The Valley Forge encampment of the Continental Army during the winter of 1777–1778 is one of America's most famous Revolutionary War sites. In September 1777, General George Washington's men had suffered a major defeat at the hands of British forces at Brandywine Creek, and shortly thereafter were repulsed at Germantown. In late November, the loss of American forts on the Delaware left General Howe and his British forces in full control of Philadelphia and the surrounding area. As Howe settled his men in the city for the winter, Washington led his 11,000 to Valley Forge.

George Washington's choice of Valley Forge offered him an ideal defense position. There, on the level summit of a hill, the encampment was protected by a river that flowed at the base of the hill on one side, and two creeks provided natural barriers that would slow any attack. The army's safe arrival at Valley Forge on December 19, gave the Continental Congress enough optimism to call for a "sumptuous Thanksgiving to close the year of high living," according to the account of Joseph Plumb Martin, a Connecticut soldier there. Martin details the feast as having been composed of "half a gill (cup) of rice and a tablespoon of vinegar." Unfortunately for the brave souls at Valley Forge, this "sumptuous" meal only foreshadowed the hardships to come. Daily life involved hunger, disease, freezing cold, and death for thousands of the Continentals.

Excavations at Valley Forge in 2000, led by National Parks Service archaeologist David Orr, have provided archaeologists with a clearer picture of exactly how the camp looked and have added to our knowledge of what daily life was like for the soldiers who struggled to survive. In planning the dig, Orr and others drew on the archival records, including, for example, Washington's explicitly detailed orders on the construction of housing: "The Soldier's huts are to be... fourteen by sixteen each, sides, ends and roofs made with logs...fireplace made of wood and secured with clay on the inside eighteen inches thick."

Following the arrival of the Prussian officer Friedrich von Steuben at Valley Forge in February 1778, Washington's men received extensive training from the best in the world. Archaeologists got some help of their own from Von Steuben, in the form of a map he drew of the encampment. By matching the surface topography—for example, depressions in the soil—with features shown on Von Steuben's map, identified three areas for investigation. Occupied by

two Pennsylvania brigades, the areas were representative of the whole encampment: the officer's huts, the enlisted men's huts, and the camp support area. Three officer's huts were explored. Two well-constructed stone hearths were unearthed, work that could have only been accomplished by skilled men. Other finds included personal effects that were probably brought from home by the officers. These included high-quality dinnerware, a cufflink, and civilian buttons. Several bits of weaponry—including musket and pistol balls, gunflints, and a musket lock—were found scattered in this area. Meanwhile, the enlisted men's quarters provided much evidence, left behind in the contents of a stone-rimmed fire pit, including fish remains and bones from cows and pigs. A preliminary study shows that they were from low-quality cuts of meat and old animals. To make up for lack of quality, the soldiers most likely boiled the meat for a long time in order to tenderize it. Archival evidence indicates that the men needed a lucky day to get even the poorest cuts of meat; diaries speak of the men surviving off of "fire cakes," which were a mixture of flour and water fried on a griddle. The final area examined was the camp support area, where food was officially stored and cooked; here bread was baked and livestock kept. Two large, circular depressions in the ground, which appear to mark the locations of large earthen mounds in which bread was baked and around which food was cooked, were discovered. Unfortunately, excavations at this site revealed no significant finds.

Some of the most intriguing finds were the numerous military buttons found dispersed

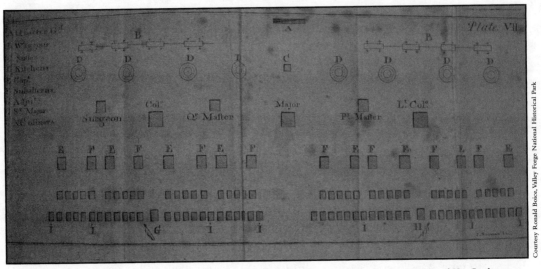

In planning their excavations, archaeologists used this map of the Valley Forge encampment by the Prussian general Von Steuben.

around the enlisted men's site. The buttons would be significant finds alone, but the fact that they were from the uniforms of British troops added to the intrigue. This can be readily explained by the fact that the Continental Army had so few supplies that they used whatever they could get a hold of. Apparently, supplies including uniforms were meant to reach the British King's Eighth Regiment—evidenced by the "K8" inscribed on the button—but were intercepted by continental soldiers. This circumstance can be explained by, and gives physical evidence to support, a letter from the Quartermaster General of the Continental Army that instructed troops to boil British coats with chestnuts, in order to change the color from red to brownish. So the continentals would discard the British buttons along with whatever else had been cooked but had no use.

Excavations at Valley Forge have added to our perceptions of how the Continental Army set up camp and how difficult the struggle to survive each day there really was. As Bruce Stocking, branch chief of Interpretive and Visitor Service at Valley Forge National Park put it, "The individual artifacts uncovered offer insight into the personal lives of the soldiers who battled for America's freedom."

The Guns of Palo Alto

BATTLEFIELD SURVEYS INDICATE THAT MEXICAN MAPS
DISTORTED THE OPENING ENGAGEMENT OF THE
MEXICAN-AMERICAN WAR. WHY?

by CHARLES M. HAECKER

When he wrote his memoirs, an aged and terminally ill Ulysses S. Grant could still vividly recall his introduction to battle almost 35 years earlier. A baby-faced second lieutenant, he, along with some 2,200 other American soldiers, had marched in column formation through shoulder-high grass "almost as sharp as darning needles" in the opening battle of the Mexican-American War. The future general of the army and president remembered cannonballs "whizzing thick and fast." This was the battle of Palo Alto, fought on a warm south Texas afternoon, May 8, 1846.

Young Grant and many of his comrades would experience battles of far greater complexity and bloodshed during the Civil War, which in time would overshadow the Mexican-American War of 1846-1848. Many Americans would quickly forget the far-reaching results of the earlier war, which wrested more than one million square miles of land from Mexico. Palo Alto was a testing ground for a new generation of professional officers, West Pointers like Grant, whose familiarity with tactical advances such as the fast moving, accurate, "flying" artillery—so called because each man in a battery had his own mount—would lead a new and bloodier form of warfare.

Mexico had severed diplomatic relations with the United States following the annexation of Texas in February 1845. Fearful that the U.S. Army intended to claim their entire country, many Mexicans agitated for war to recapture Texas. Meanwhile President James K. Polk was convinced he could force Mexico into recognizing the state, and in May 1845 he ordered General Zachary Taylor to move 1,500 regular troops from Fort Jessup, Louisiana, to Corpus Christi, Texas, 140 miles north of the newly established Rio Grande border. By the end of July, Taylor's troops had been supplemented by 2,800 men, including infantry from the Indian frontier in Kansas and artillerymen from defenses on the Gulf Coast of Florida.

Learning through diplomatic channels of Mexico's eagerness "to settle the present dispute in a peaceful, reasonable, and honorable manner," Polk tried to persuade Mexico to accept the Rio Grande boundary by promising to pay several million dollars worth of property damage and unsatisfied debt claims filed against Mexico by Americans living or doing business there. He also hoped that the nearly bankrupt Mexico would settle for a sliding scale of payments for the additional Mexican lands beyond Texas: $5 million for New Mexico and up to $25 million for California. When Polk was snubbed by Mexico's secretary of foreign relations, he increased the pressure with a show of force, ordering Taylor to move his troops to the Rio Grande.

In March 1846 Taylor took 2,800 troops to the northern bank of the river, where they built a star-shaped earthen garrison, called Fort Texas, opposite the Mexican town of Matamoros. In late April, Mexican forces crossed the Rio Grande, intent upon severing the fort's supply line to Port Isabel 20 miles to the north. General Anastasio Torrejón crossed ten miles west of Matamoros with about 1,600 troops; shortly thereafter his commander, General Mariano Arista, forded the river 13 miles east of the town with some 3,500 troops. Learning of Torrejón's crossing, Taylor sent out patrols to determine his position. One was attacked, and 11 men were killed, six wounded, and 46 captured. The engagement led to an official declaration of war by the House of Representatives, which Polk signed on May 13. But by then the first major battle of the war had already been fought.

Taylor was convinced that the Mexican army, which now numbered more than 5,000 troops, would march toward Port Isabel, cutting off his supply route. To block such a move, he left 500 men in Fort Texas and on May 1 took 2,300 to protect Port Isabel and bring back supplies. The Mexican army followed, confident it could prevent Taylor from returning to relieve Fort Texas, under bombardment from Matamoros since May 3.

Taylor delayed his return to Fort Texas until sufficient reinforcements could be gathered to ensure the safety of Port Isabel, where he left more than 50 men in need of medical attention. Heading back on May 8 with 300 loaded supply wagons, he found the road to Fort Texas blocked by Mexican troops spread out before him on a broad prairie known as Palo Alto, or "Tall Timber," named for the mesquite forest that surrounded it. The field was covered with shoulder-high grass, and recent heavy rains had turned shallow depressions and old riverbeds into stagnant marshes.

Arista had arrayed his men and cannon in a mile-long line on the southern end of the battlefield, east of the Port Isabel-Matamoros road. Mounted troops armed with lances blocked the road and protected the army's flanks. When Taylor's regiments advanced, Mexican artillery opened fire. The Americans formed a battle line, with light artillery in front of the infantry and out of the range of Mexican musket fire.

The American guns rained six-, 12-, and 18-pound exploding shells on the Mexicans, whose antiquated four- and eight-pounders were no match for the American cannon in accuracy or destructive power. It soon became obvious to Taylor that his superior artillery made an infantry charge unnecessary. Mexican cavalry and light infantry tried flanking maneuvers, but were turned back by the devastating artillery fire. The broad marsh between battle lines discouraged a frontal attack. The battle ended at dusk, with Arista's mauled and retreating army now encamped beyond the range of American artillery. Search parties from both sides brought in wounded under a flag of truce. Some 250 to 400 Mexicans had been killed or wounded; only seven Americans had been killed and 43 wounded.

The following morning, Arista's army retreated to a more defensible position at Resaca de la Palma, a marshy area seven miles south of Palo Alto, where he was reinforced with fresh troops. Taylor's army, in hot pursuit, struck again, driving the Mexicans back across the Rio Grande. Taylor's smaller force had won the day.

The Palo Alto prairie was littered with battle refuse: fragments of exploded shells, cannonballs, ox- and horseshoes, and the bodies and belongings of dead soldiers. The victors took lances, swords, and regimental badges as souvenirs. Seven months later a soldier from a volunteer unit stationed near Palo Alto visited the battlefield and identified the Mexican line as a roughly linear scattering of bones in tattered rags, the remains of soldiers lying where they had fallen. The Mexicans had only managed to bury a handful of their dead. Grasses eventually hid the ground laid bare by fighting, and flooding deposited new soil on the battlefield. In time the wagon road from Matamoros to Port Isabel was abandoned, its traces obliterated and forgotten.

In June 1992 Congress passed the Palo Alto Battlefield National Historic Site Act, which recognized the significance of the engagement in American history. In so doing, it authorized the National Park Service to study Palo Alto and provide a plan for managing and interpreting the battlefield park for the public. My investigation began that year with archival research. I was intrigued by two maps of the battle sketched by Captain Jean Louis Berlandier, one of Arista's staff officers. Berlandier's drawings formed the basis of an official government document on the battle published in Mexico in 1846, a few months after the event. During the next 100 years, maps based on these sketches were published in several major American and Mexican histories of the war. Berlandier had labeled the regiments of both armies, showing their movements during the battle. The final phase of the encounter on one sketch showed an aggressive pivoting advance by the entire Mexican line. According to Berlandier, the Fourth Regiment had been stationed on the left flank, or western end, of the line, close to the Matamoros–Port Isabel road, and had acted as the "hinge" for the advancing battle line. It had thus remained largely stationary, while the other three Mexican regiments extending to the east had swung toward the American line.

An official Mexican account of the battle stated that the Fourth Regiment had suffered heavy casualties from the American 18-pounders. As pivot for a final attack, it would have been a nonmoving target. I correlated topographic features found at Palo Alto today with those labeled on Berlandier's sketches, including the broad marsh that had separated the two armies and the hillock that had anchored the Mexican army's right flank, now known as Arista Hill. I then delineated sample survey areas where Fourth Regiment artifact concentrations should exist. A team of local volunteers and I walked through the survey areas with metal detectors, later recording the locations of pieces of weapons, uniform fittings, and fragments of explosive shells and cannonballs. We hoped to find concentrations of Mexican buttons, badges, and personal belongings mixed with American

ordnance where this regiment had supposedly stood. We found none. More than 1,000 feet to the east, we did find a concentration of Mexican-related artifacts, including badges of the Fourth and other regiments. Were Berlandier's sketches inaccurate?

Prior to our 1993 field season, I searched the Library of Congress and found several battle maps produced by American officers who had fought at Palo Alto. The American and Mexican maps are similar, except for the final phase of battle. Lieutenant Jeremiah M. Scarritt, a topographical engineer, had drawn four maps in a letter to his superior, Colonel J.G. Totten, each depicting a particular phase of the engagement. Scarritt's final sketch shows that both armies had moved from their original east–west orientation to a north–west orientation. American units were now aligned along the road, with cannon directed at the Mexican army to the east. Another American officer had produced a map for a pro-war propaganda pamphlet published a few months after the battle. This map also showed the final Mexican line as parallel to that of the Americans along the road. A third American battle map in *Campaign Sketches of the War with Mexico,* a popular book written by Captain W.S. Henry and published in 1847, shows the final phase of battle as a retreat of four Mexican regiments, including the Fourth, toward the southeast and well away from the road that they had guarded. It appeared that the Mexican Fourth had not functioned as a hinge for the other regiments advancing toward the Americans.

It was still possible, however, that traces of the Mexican Fourth lay somewhere between the road and the area 1,000 feet to the east where we had found the concentration of Mexican artifacts. If regimental badges from the Fourth were found in the immediate vicinity of the road, it would lend some support to Berlandier's interpretation. No more artifacts were found, however, until I extended the survey some 2,000 feet east of the road. We focused on this area of the battlefield, hoping that the patterns of artifacts found here might provide a clue to the orientation of the Mexican line. They did. One area contained a 20- to 30-foot-wide band of Mexican-related artifacts extending 500 feet north–south, to the edges of the test area. Here was conclusive evidence that the American maps were truer than the official Mexican one to what had actually happened.

We now know that toward the end of the battle American artillery had forced the Mexican left flank to the east or southeast and away from the road. This retreat would have compressed the Mexican units, offering an even better target for American artillery. A crowded army under constant artillery attack could not have performed the type of aggressive pivoting advance reported by Berlandier. Additional sampling of the Mexican line yielded numbered badges from four Mexican regiments within a three-acre area, testifying to the compression of regiments during the confusion of the final phase of battle.

To the north and east of the concentration of numbered badges, we found widely dispersed Mexican-related artifacts, perhaps reflecting a rapid movement of troops over a broad area and within a short time span. In fact both Mexican and American battle accounts describe such a charge by the Mexican army's right flank. This tactic was a final, desperate attempt to get around the American left flank and destroy the lightly defended wagon train parked in the rear. The charge was a brave but costly failure. Survivors of this attack retreated in disorder onto the already compressed Mexican left flank, causing even greater confusion and leading to a general retreat.

Why should there be discrepancies between Mexican and American battle maps? Granted, the fog of battle will result in some misinterpretations, but there may be an additional explanation. I believe Berlandier's map was an attempt to put the best face on an otherwise ignominious defeat. It was better to explain the heavy casualties as the result of a bold, final attack rather than the result of poorly used troops slaughtered by the superior cannon of an outnumbered enemy. I suspect that Berlandier created these battle sketches for Arista's use in his defense at a board of inquiry, where he was cleared of charges of incompetency. The sketches became part of the Mexican explanation of what had happened at Palo Alto. Mexican and American historians working from them when writing of the battle unknowingly republished the false information.

Battlefield archaeology has only recently gained respectability as a valuable way to analyze combat experience. A decade ago most scholars felt such investigations were pointless, since any recovered artifacts would have been deposited randomly in the confusion of battle and then picked over by generations of relic hunters. But studies beginning in 1984 at the site of the Battle of the Little Bighorn convinced many scholars that battlefield surveys were not only useful but could lead to dramatic reassessments of military engagements. In the Battle of the Little Bighorn study, the findings from archaeological surveys were used to create a unique computer simulation of the final, fatal moments of the battle. Formerly undetected Indian positions indicated a skillful, coordinated encirclement of the cavalry by the Sioux and Cheyenne forces. This archaeologically based reconstruction significantly altered our traditional notions about how this battle was fought. Similarly, in the case of the battle at Palo Alto, fought over 150 years ago, archaeology helped determine the veracity of conflicting accounts of the engagement's final phase found in historical documents. One can only imagine how such investigations might bear on the study of other battles, ancient or modern.

Doing Time

HOW CONFEDERATE POWS
WEATHERED CAPTIVITY

by DAVID R. BUSH

I t is 1863 and your Confederate infantry unit has been captured. Union soldiers take you by train from one holding pen to another until at last you are ferried across Ohio's Sandusky Bay to the Johnson's Island POW camp. Two rows of barracks face each other across a courtyard, latrines behind each row. Guards patrol a raised platform enclosing the compound. As a prisoner, you cannot choose your companions and are never alone. Your family is far away; there are no visitors. You cook your own food—what little you're given. You scavenge for the rest. You have three options: endure it, escape, or collaborate.

By the end of the civil war, more than 400,000 soldiers had become POWs, almost evenly divided between Union and Confederate troops. There were 32 prison camps in the North, 33 in the South. The camp at Johnson's Island in western Lake Erie, built in 1861, was the only Union prison

Confederate officers at Johnson's Island POW camp pass the time playing chess.

designed expressly for enemy officers. Of the 9,000-plus men held there, some 300 never made it out alive, dying of disease or malnutrition. Men were shot at with little provocation. Those caught trying to escape were shackled and fed only bread and water. Packages from home were opened, their most prized contents—cake, catsup, and brandy—confiscated. Rats overran the compound, and the stench from overflowing privies fouled the air.

Johnson's Island prisoners were among the educated Southern elite, and they left hundreds of personal accounts of their expe-

riences. The volume of letters, diaries, maps, and drawings is unrivaled by any other Civil War prison, North or South. These sources and recent archaeological work tell us how prisoners passed long hours, how they attempted escape, and how they were rewarded for cooperating with their captors.

By mid-1863 accusations of the mistreatment of prisoners abounded, and Northern and Southern prisons responded by cutting rations and limiting purchases from the sutler, the prison store. Recalling the months he spent at Johnson's Island, former Captain John H. Grabill of the 35th

Virginia Cavalry reported in a Confederate veterans' journal in 1906:

> *Some of the prisoners ate candles, purchased at the sutler; but this was kept secret, as it was feared that we would not be permitted to buy candles if it were known they were used as food. ...Rats that lived upon the sinks [latrines] were an article of diet among the officers confined at Johnson's Island. Some prisoners were so hungry that when their two days' small rations was delivered to them on Saturday, they would eat it all at once, and would not have a mouthful to eat until Monday morning. ...I know that I suffered the pangs of hunger for months at a time. While I could not now establish the fact, my own opinion is that a number whose bodies lie in the little cemetery on the borders of Sandusky Bay were the victims of starvation.*

In 1990, after years of archival research that brought me in contact with descendants of prisoners, I led a group of Earthwatch volunteers seeking evidence for ways the POWs coped with their surroundings. We wondered if the tactics of endurance, resistance, and collaboration would be visible in the archaeological record.

Today, the shores of Johnson's Island are dotted with beach homes, and amid the brush inland there is little trace of the prison. In 1861, however, the 300-acre island, leased from one Leonard B. Johnson, was ideal for a POW camp. Because it had no permanent residents it was easily guarded, while its proximity to Sandusky allowed access to the railroad transporting Confederate prisoners.

The journey to Johnson's Island was nonetheless rigorous. Capture was often followed by hours or even days of marching with little food or water, under heavy guard, until transport facilities were reached. As soon as was practical, officers were separated from enlisted men to prevent the former from using their authority to organize insurrections. Better living conditions awaited officers, perhaps to diminish the threat of rebellion further, but more likely because officers were considered gentlemen deserving of better facilities than their subordinates. In his diary, Lieutenant W.B. Gowan of the 30th Alabama Infantry described his new home:

> *We were marched through a door and found ourselves inside of the Prison walls. The grounds enclosed by [th]is wall is ten acres square in extent. The wall is about 12 feet in heighth [sic] of plank set up end ways, around the outside of the wall and about three feet from the top is a walk for Sentinels on duty. The U.S. Government has gone to considerable expense here in fixing up for the accommodation of prisoners of war. For this purpose houses have been erected in two rows parallel to each other with 6 houses in each row and a street between of about 50 yards in width, also one house in the middle of this street at one end making 13 in all. The buildings are framed, two stories in height with glass windows of good size and sealed inside. They are about 120 feet in length by 30 feet in width. Each building is denominated a*

block and numbered accordingly from 1 to 13 these are divided into rooms which are also numbered, each room being furnished with a stove and bunks for the accommodation of five & six men on each bunk a straw matrass [sic] and one blanket. To each block there is a cook room furnished with a good cooking stove and utensils to cook in, a table and cupboard & several long shelves, adjoining to this is a dining room furnished with tables and benches. Tin plates tin cups table spoons knives and forks.

Each of the 13 blocks had a sink (latrine) associated with it. We felt the undisturbed latrines held the most archaeological potential and hoped to uncover disposed contraband or personal items that might have fallen from pockets. Such items might indicate prisoners' survival strategies. We began our search for the sinks built in 1864 and associated with blocks 6, 8, and 10. We decided to first identify two large features—the ditch that once traced the perimeter of the compound just within the outer wall, and the deadline, a staked boundary beyond which prisoners were not allowed to pass. Once we had established the location of those features, Union maps would enable us to locate the sinks.

The ditch had been dug by July 12, 1864, when the prison compound was expanded to the northwest, to thwart efforts to tunnel out. Today it would appear as a long, dark stain. We armed ourselves with an 1864 Union map of the camp and aerial photos taken in the early part of this century. Exposing the subsoil, we immediately recognized the six-foot-wide ditch. We used a soil

corer to track it around the entire circumference of the prison. Now we could reconstruct the deadline, established by William S. Pierson, first commandant at Johnson's Island, in March 1862. Pierson had issued ten general orders, the ninth of which read:

No prisoner will be allowed to loiter between the buildings, and the north and west fences [outer walls], and they will be permitted north of the buildings, only when passing to and from the sinks, nor will they approach the fences anywhere else nearer than thirty feet, as the line is marked out by stakes.

We know from this order that the deadline was 30 feet in from the ditch, and that the sinks were located just inside the deadline. Prisoners crossing the deadline were presumed to be contemplating escape, and many of them complained in their journals that turning the wrong way when leaving the latrine put them in jeopardy of being shot. Having located the ditch, we took a week to plant stakes at regular intervals 30 feet in, trampling vines, poison ivy, and secondary growth. We then dug trenches about 150 feet apart just within our reconstructed deadline. From the maps, we speculated that these three trenches would reveal the 1864 sinks. We knew what the latrines had once looked like—10-by-14-foot structures sheltering eight-by-12-foot pits dug two to five feet deep. But we were not sure what the latrines would look like when we came across them now.

As we dug through the plow zone and topsoil, we encountered jagged limestone

Union Soldiers Identified

Four Union soldiers, whose remains were found on a farm bordering the Antietam battlefield, have been identified as members of the Irish Brigade, famous for its fierce fighting during the Civil War. The location of the burials (where the 63rd and 88th New York were positioned during the 1862 battle), and the discovery of cuff buttons bearing the New York state seal, Roman Catholic medals, a fragmented rosary, and samples of the brigade's special issue .69 buckshot (used in combat shotguns) aided in the identifications. Forensic and archival evidence has allowed scientists to narrow the identity of one of the men to three soldiers who fought with the 63rd New York.

After the Civil War, the government paid area farmers to exhume shallow battlefield graves and move the remains to the newly created National Cemetery in Sharpsburg, Maryland. Portions of these four skeletons were left behind. According to Douglas Owsley, an anthropologist at the Smithsonian Institution, one of the partial skeletons was that of a 40–49 year old man, considerably older than the average soldier, with pronounced tooth wear

and evidence of arthritis in the scapula. Stephen Potter, regional archaeologist for the National Park Service, who had excavated the remains of the four men, checked the New York State register for soldiers in their forties who had died at Antietam and found seven likely candidates. He then accessed a new National Park Service computer database of the Union dead buried in the National Cemetery, but none of the seven names turned up, meaning that the remains belonged to an "unknown" soldier buried in the cemetery. A search of Army service, medical, and pension records at the National Archives eliminated four of the seven men, who had died in or on the way to field hospitals, and would not have been buried on the battlefield. The unknown soldier may have been one of the three remaining candidates, identified as private James Gallagher, 41, a stonecutter born in Kilkenny, Ireland; private Martin McMahon, 41–49, a laborer born in County Clare, Ireland; and James McGarigan, or McGaffigan, 44. The occupations listed would be consistent with the presence of arthritis.

by Jessica E. Saraceni

backfill not typical of either the subsoil or the limestone bedrock. We removed another five inches and found mixed clay and wood fragments, further indication of backfilling...of the sinks? Union records tell us that the procedure for closing a sink was to cover the "night soil" (feces) first with a layer of clay, then with a layer of boards. We brought our meter-square units down another foot and a half and hit pay dirt. Beneath a layer of clay

was a deposit of night soil. Here, in vivid corroboration of our sources, were the sinks of blocks 6, 8, and 10. After another week's work we had exposed the entire block 8 sink.

What we found indicated how prisoners choosing to endure their lot managed the monotony of daily life. One pastime unique to Johnson's Island was much in evidence. Prisoners purchased hard rubber or gutta-percha combs, pipes, and buttons from the sutler and carved them into rings and brooches. Our investigation has recovered more than 150 such items.

Surrounding themselves with objects from home also helped prisoners endure. (See page 6 of the photo insert.) In the sink associated with block 8, we found a beautiful gold pocket watch, perhaps a family heirloom, made in Liverpool in 1805. One August day in 1990, a volunteer, Stella Eismann, was digging in this same sink when she uncovered a gold disk about two inches in diameter. Volunteers abandoned their tasks and gathered around the sink. As she removed the object from the earth, we saw that it was a locket, a deteriorated photograph on one side, a lock of hair, braided, coiled, and tied with ribbon on the other. Stella began to cry, thinking of the homesick soldier who had lost the locket.

Other evidence points to efforts by prisoners to resist. Some ten succeeded in escaping; among them was Lieutenant Charles E. Grogan. In 1865 Captain William Peel of the 11th Mississippi Infantry wrote:

> *Lt. Charles Pierce, of New Orleans, who was one of the party that attempted to break out about a month ago, has made several attempts since, to get out by strategy. The Yanks came in the other night and caught him, at the head of a party, in a tunnel. The Federal Officer told him it was useless to attempt to get out by that means as they knew of his designs within half an hour after he began his work. He satisfied Pierce of the truth of his statement, too, by telling the time he had commenced to dig. They*

> *are kept perfectly posted on all these points and it seems impossible for us to catch their spies.*

Almost all the sinks from the earlier period of the prison (April 1862 through July 1864) show evidence of tunneling toward the stockade wall. The remains of these tunnels are collapsed cavities that have filled with topsoil. We have found remains of wooden planks used to barricade the tunnel against the privy's waste. What did prisoners use to excavate so many tunnels? The archaeological evidence has provided us with some answers. Within the tunnels of the block 8 latrines we found a large iron bar and a cow bone worn on one end from digging.

Some prisoners sought to supplement their provisions by collaborating with Union guards, ratting on anyone contemplating escape. Others went so far as to pledge the Oath of Allegiance; those who did so were spoken of as pigs, not people:

> *Several other razorbacks have taken quarters in Block 1, swelling the number to about 55. ...They expected, by taking the Oath of Allegiance to the Federal Government, to get out of prison. The Yanks, however, are building a kitchen for their special benefit, and this does not look as if they are disposed to let them go yet awhile. They draw more commissaries, however, than we do. Their ration being 20oz. bakers bread, 16 oz. meat and small quantities of beans or hominy, salt, vinegar, etc. per day.*
>
> —Captain William Peel,
> February 2, 1865

We found evidence of special treatment in the 1864 sink associated with block 1, where Confederates swearing allegiance to the North were relocated. At a time when most prisoners were coping with cut rations, the bottles in block 1 reveal that collaborators were given a large quantity and variety of wine, whiskey, champagne, and beer. Alcohol seems to have been readily available to other inmates only at the hospital, where it was used medicinally.

Exploration of Johnson's Island continues. This year's field season will focus on block 2, used for general housing. We hope to learn more about the prisoners' daily life by excavating the floors of their quarters. We will continue to make contact with descendants of prisoners and guards, adding more personal stories to the camp's already rich record.

Excavation has demonstrated that the POW experience on Johnson's Island was hardly uniform. Despite their similar backgrounds as Southern gentlemen, prisoners responded differently to their plight, many choosing to suffer on for their cause despite being a signature away from better treatment. The gold locket, escape tunnels, and the array of liquor bottles are poignant reminders of their choices.

Civil War Espionage

A DIG AT A UNION CANNON FOUNDRY UNEARTHS ARTIFACTS AND A TALE OF INTERNATIONAL INTRIGUE.

by ANDREW SLAYMAN

Archaeologists investigating a Civil War cannon foundry near the U.S. Military Academy at West Point have uncovered evidence of a secret weapons program in which Russian spies helped the Union in a critical arms race against the Confederacy. In an article published in *Federal Archeology,* Joel W. Grossman of Grossman and Associates, a New York City contract archaeology firm, reports on his discovery, excavation, and conservation of a 12-foot-square oak and cast-iron platform on which a sophisticated 13-ton rifled cannon was mounted and tested. With a maximum range of five miles, the cannon became one of the deadliest weapons of its time. Firing shells armed with a precursor of napalm, it was partly responsible for the 1863 burning of Charleston. Development of the weapon helped the Union defeat the Confederacy.

According to Grossman, foundry director R.P. Parrott initially took credit for developing the cannon, a claim he later retracted in congressional testimony. Hearings of the Joint Committees on Ordnance and the Conduct of the War between 1864 and 1867 revealed that Russian agents working in England had obtained plans for a secret British cannon and passed them on to Parrott. Czar Alexander II regarded the United States as an ally against Britain and France, recent enemies in the Crimean War, and was willing to support a Union arms buildup.

More than 150,000 artifacts found in association with the testing platform and at a nearby workers' housing complex point to the presence of highly skilled munitions experts. Instead of the artifacts of poor laborers, Grossman's team found imported ceramics, glass, and jewelry as well as a broad range of scientific and foundry equipment used in testing high-caliber weapons. The European origin of many of these artifacts suggests that the technicians may have come from the continent to work on the cannon.

From the 1950s to the 1970s, the site was used by the Marathon Battery Company, which made nickel-cadmium batteries for Nike missiles. When the company left, parts of the old foundry and waterfront along the Hudson River remained contaminated with cadmium. In 1983, the Environmental Protection Agency ordered the site cleaned up, and Grossman and Associates was hired to excavate before work began.

Iron Warships of the Civil War

THE IRONCLADS, MONITORS, AND SUBMARINES OF THE CIVIL WAR LAID THE FOUNDATION FOR ALL MODERN WARSHIPS.

by ALEXANDER BENENSON

The first modern conflict, the American Civil War gave birth to a number of new military technologies. Repeating rifles, electrically controlled mines, and aerial reconnaissance were all invented during the Civil War. But some of the period's most incredible feats of engineering were its new naval vessels: ironclads, monitors, and submarines. Despite their importance, it is only in the past few decades, with the discovery of several intact submarines and the well-preserved *Monitor,* that archaeologists have had a chance to study these Civil War Era innovators first hand.

The term ironclad is often used as a blanket term to describe many of the innovative ships of the Civil War, but it specifically refers to ships that had wooden hulls plated in iron. The Confederacy's most famous ironclad, *Virginia,* is the prototype of such vessels. It rose out of the ashes of the Union steam frigate USS *Merrimack,* which had been

Courtesy Vicksburg National Military Park

Cairo was typical of the shallow-draft ironclads built by the Union for service on rivers.

burned by Union forces as they retreated from Norfolk harbor in Virginia. Working with what was left of *Merrimack*'s wooden hull, Confederate Lieutenant J.M. Brooks built a radically new type of ship in July 1861. He encased the hull in iron sheathing an inch thick, and he added a sloping wooden casemate, to which he fastened four-inch-thick plates. The power to turn the ship's two screw propellers came from the sea-soaked engines that had been salvaged from *Merrimack*. The 275-foot-long vessel, which sat in the water like an inverted washbasin, was virtually impervious to cannon fire. On each side of the ship four guns extended out of small portals in the casemate, with one more cannon each end.

Virginia was armed with one extra weapon—not a new invention, but a relic from the triremes of the ancient world, an iron ram. The ram was both an effort to conserve gunpowder and to provide the ship with a failsafe weapon.

Virginia's sloping iron casemate became the template for a number of other Confederate ironclads such as *North Carolina, Georgia,* and *Louisiana,* a converted paddle wheeler. Like *Virginia,* most were slow and difficult to maneuver. The Union used the same ironclad casemate design for the "city class" boats. So-called because they were named after cities, like USS *St. Louis,* they had a shallow draft, making them ideal for river duty. Built under the direction of James B. Eads, they also featured separated bulkhead compartments to reduce the risk of sinking.

On the whole, however, the Union was reluctant to accept radical new ship designs. They controlled the seas and their blockade had a stranglehold on the Confederacy. Moreover, they already had a superior fleet of "modern" warships. It is no surprise that Swedish engineer John Ericsson never received a response when he first wrote to Abraham Lincoln with his plan to build *Monitor,* an impregnable "floating battery that he had originally designed for Napoleon III's fleet. A few weeks later, upon presenting a scale model of it to a group of naval officers, Ericsson was flatly rejected. Eventually, the plan for *Monitor* was adopted, and construction began in Brooklyn in October 1861. *Monitor* featured a host of new innovations and looked nothing like any other ironclad. The 172-foot-long deck sat only about 18 inches above the water. Because *Monitor* was not based on the traditional hull shape of an oceangoing vessel, much less of its body was submerged. The shallower draft meant the boat had much better mobility along the coasts and in the rivers than large wooden ships. It was also the first ship to have both water pumps and ventilation tubes powered by its coal-fired steam engine, innovations Ericsson hoped would make operation more efficient. But the most striking feature of the ship was its large circular gun turret, which gave the ship its nickname, the "cheesebox on a raft." Covered with eight-inch-thick iron sheets, the turret housed two 11-inch guns and could be swiveled 360 degrees on circular tracks. This was a huge step forward in combat

mobility compared to ships like the Confederacy's *Virginia* whose fixed guns made tracking a moving ship incredibly difficult.

Monitor gave its name to entire new class of ships, these "monitor class" ships having characteristic low-deck profiles and revolving gun turrets. Eads, the master Union naval engineer, built a wide range of single- and double-turreted craft that patrolled both the Eastern seaboard and inland rivers.

Submarines, though far less strategically successful in the Civil War than ironclads and monitors, have garnered an exceptional amount of notoriety for both their bizarre designs and tragic demises. The first Civil War submarine called *Alligator* or *Alligator Junior,* was commissioned by the Union in 1862. The oars that were originally used for powering the submarine were quickly abandoned in favor of a hand crank running down the center of the hull that attached to a propeller. A diminutive 47 feet in length, *Alligator* was capable of traveling at only three to four knots. It had no ballast tanks to regulate its dive, only buoys the crew could deploy once at its desired depth, probably no more than a few feet. *Alligator* had no weapons. Instead, once it had approached a target, a diver carrying explosives would be sent out. It had a simple, but effective air purification system that drew carbon dioxide out of the air by blowing it through a sheet moistened with limewater. The submarine was originally designed as an ironclad-buster to combat warships like CSS *Virginia*. In 1863, while being towed to Port Royal, South Carolina, *Alligator* sank in a storm, having never seen combat. Another Union submarine, *Sub Marine Explorer,* was equally

Georgia On My Mine

A backhoe operator inadvertently dug up a cast-iron Confederate "torpedo" while excavating a trench for a pipeline on Elba Island, near Savannah, Georgia. Two-and-a-half-feet long, weighing 200 pounds, and encrusted with rust, the weapon, which operates something like a modern-day mine, would have been attached to a fixed pole in Savannah harbor sometime in 1863. Jeff Reed, a historian at Fort Stewart, Georgia, says the mine is an excellent example of the improvised munitions of the period. "Confederate weapons weren't always made in foundries. During the war, small laboratories specializing in munitions sprung up in Savannah." Fort Stewart's 38th Explosive Ordinance Disposal Company, an army bomb squad, was called in to recover the artifact. They heard water inside the shell, leading them to believe that its gunpowder was probably soaked. Nonetheless, historians at Fort Stewart aren't taking any chances. "In the worst case scenario, we'd render it inert. We'd blow it up," says Reed, who would prefer that the mine be left intact for further study. "A good portion of it might survive."

How do you curate an artifact that might blow your arm off? While the Fort Stewart Museum negotiates a minefield of red tape in an attempt to answer that question, the torpedo awaits its fate on a bed of sandbags in a concrete bunker.

by Eric A. Powell

---

as unsuccessful. Built in 1865, but never commissioned, it was eventually exported to Panama to assist pearl divers. After a dive in 1867, her entire crew contracted a "fever" and died. The crew probably had gotten the bends from surfacing too quickly. Soon thereafter she was abandoned.

In the summer of 1864, *Harpers Illustrated Weekly* published a drawing of an electrically powered Confederate submarine called *American Ram*. Though this fueled Union fears that the South had won the underwater arms race, in reality *American Ram* was just a fantasy. The Confederacy was actually using a submarine design scheme almost identical to that of the Union—basically a small tube with a hand-crank powered propeller. Of the submarines built by the Confederacy (including *Pioneer, American Diver,* and *Hunley*), the most famous is *Hunley,* named for its creator Horace L. Hunley. (See page 6 of the photo insert.)

Hunley differed from the Union submarines in its ingeniously designed weapon system. Extending out from the bow of *Hunley* was a long wooden spar, at the end of which was a large black-powder charge. A fuse running from the charge back to the submarine allowed remote detonation. In spite of two early mishaps—in which accidents caused *Hunley* to dive unexpectedly, both times killing its entire crew—the submarine eventually managed to sink USS *Housatonic,* which was blockading Charleston. But its crew probably never had time to celebrate. Minutes after securing its place in history as the first successful attack submarine, *Hunley* mysteriously sank as well.

Courtesy Friends of the Hunley

An enigmatic find in Hunley *was a medal once worn by a Union soldier named Ezra Chamberlin.*

Though marred by mechanical difficulties and tragic accidents, the story of the Civil War submarine is ultimately one of perseverance, ingenuity, and bravery.

Most Civil War ironclads and monitors were broken up and sold in the years following the end of the war. Few were capable of traveling in the open sea, and very few were in good working order; there simply was no use for them anymore. Ironically, the ships we know the most about now are the ones which were thought to be lost forever during the Civil War. They are the few vessels that archaeologists have recently been able to locate and study. The most ambitious mission was to find and excavate USS *Monitor*. Shortly after its famous encounter with *Virginia*, *Monitor* went down in bad weather off the coast of North Carolina. It was finally located in 1973, over a century after its disappearance, by marine archaeologist Gordon P. Watts and geologist John Newton. Designated a marine sanctuary by the National Oceanic and Atmospheric Administration (NOAA) in 1975, it became the site of frequent dives, which yielded hundreds of small artifacts. The recovery process was a slow and often frustrating process because of the depth of the wreck (240 feet). Complicating matters further was the fact that the ship had landed upside-down resting awkwardly on its turret and making a full recovery impossible. However, large portions of the ship have since been raised including its anchor and propeller, and in 2002, its 150-ton turret was finally raised with the help of spider-like claw attached to a 500-ton crane. (See page 7 of the photo insert.) It has since been placed in the Mariners Museum in Newport News, Virginia.

Another monitor built by Ericsson, *Tecumseh,* lies mired in mud at the entrance to Mobile Bay, Alabama, where it sank in 1864. A recovery and conservation plan drafted in 1997 estimated the cost of recovering *Tecumseh* at at least $80 million, a bill that no one has been willing to foot so far. For now, a single buoy marks *Tecumseh's* resting place, and despite attempts at conservation by the Smithsonian Institute, most of its contents remain hidden by mud and silt.

Attempts to recover *Monitor's* rival, CSS *Virginia*, have also yielded little. *Virginia* was burned to prevent capture in 1863 and then its remains removed in the following years, leaving little behind. Only scraps of *Virginia* have been located along with a few small artifacts, confirming accounts of its destruction. The wooden husks of a handful of other ironclads from both sides have been recovered and conserved in museums including those of CSS *Neuse,* CSS *Jackson,* and USS *Cairo.* (See page 7 of the photo insert.) Three other ironclad rams (*Manassas,*

Louisiana, and *Arkansas*) were magnetically located in 1981 by the National Underwater and Marine Agency, an organization founded by the novelist Clive Cussler. All three ships were found along the Mississippi, not underwater, but wedged into the earthen banks and levies. Like *Tecumseh,* these wrecks may never be raised because of the prohibitive cost and difficulty of excavation. The CSS *Georgia,* another Confederate ironclad, which was abandoned and set ablaze after Sherman's invasion, now lies in a clay bank on the Savannah harbor where it is protected and monitored by the U.S. Army Corps of Engineers and local Port Authority. Recent dives on *Georgia* have focused on monitoring the rate of corrosion rather than the recovery of artifacts. Researchers, working together with the Army Corps, hope the lack of sedimentary buildup around the wreck will facilitate recovering portions of *Georgia*'s casemate sometime in the future.

Located after four previously unsuccessful attempts, *Hunley* was raised in August of 2000. Conservation of *Hunley* will take years to complete as workers must slowly and carefully remove the mass of sediment that has collected inside the iron hull. The remains of eight men were found inside *Hunley,* along with a number of small personal artifacts. Archaeologists were shocked to find that one of the men was wearing a Union dog tag. Was there a Yankee spy aboard *Hunley* when it sank? Further investigation proved that the age of the man inside the submarine was about 30 years, where as the dog tags belonged to a 24-year-old named Ezra Chamberlin. The man found inside *Hunley*

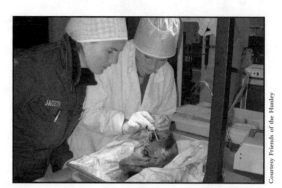

Hunley *excavators examine one of the crewmember's leather shoes.*

had probably kept the dog tag as souvenir.

The wreck of USS *Alligator,* the first Civil War submarine, has yet to be found. A search by NOAA in 2004 was cut short by bad weather. *Sub Marine Exporer,* however, has recently been found off the coast of Panama's San Telmo Island.

Union forces eager to examine the "infernal machine" raised *Pioneer,* the Confederacy's first submarine experiment, shortly after it was scuttled in 1862. For years, researchers thought a small submersible displayed at the Louisiana State Museum since the early 1900s was *Pioneer.* (See page 6 of the photo insert.) But the discovery of a contemporary drawing of the *Pioneer* by historian Mark Ragan in the National Archives proved the museum's submarine could not be *Pioneer.* The final resting place of *Pioneer* remains a mystery along with the true identity of the submarine in Louisiana. But seafloors and riverbeds are not the only places where the remnants of the revolutionary Civil War ironclads, monitors and submarines should be sought; their legacy can still be easily found in all of today's modern warships.

Fire Fight at Hembrillo Basin

BUFFALO SOLDIERS HOLD THEIR GROUND IN A NIGHTTIME SKIRMISH WITH THE APACHE.

by KARL W. LAUMBACH

On April 6, 1880, just four years after Custer's defeat on the Little Big Horn, Captain Henry Carroll of the Ninth Cavalry cautiously led 71 cavalrymen toward an Apache camp in the Hembrillo Basin of south-central New Mexico. Suddenly, volleys of gunfire rang out from the surrounding ridgetops and puffs of smoke marked the discharge of black-powder cartridges. Rushing to the top of a low ridge, the troops dismounted, every fourth man holding horses. Forming skirmish lines, they returned fire until the sun went down. Then they held their ground and waited for reinforcements.

The Ninth was one of six black regiments formed after the Civil War to help keep the peace on the frontier. Its members were called Buffalo Soldiers by the Cheyenne because their curly hair reminded the Native Americans of buffalo hides. At Hembrillo, two companies of the Ninth Cavalry pursuing the Apache war chief Victorio had been surrounded by a superior force of 150 Chiricahua and Mescalero Apache. Unlike the Battle of the Little Big Horn, the Buffalo Soldiers' nightlong battle against two-to-one odds was largely forgotten. Until recently, the record of the fight was based on reports of white Sixth Cavalry officers who credited themselves with saving Carroll's soldiers from "a condition of helplessness." Recent battlefield archaeology and historical research tell a different story, one of bravery in the face of a highly organized Apache force.

In 1987, an archaeological crew from Human Systems Research returned from a field survey in the White Sands Missile Range with stories of amazing panels of Apache rock art. The crew had found the art near a spring in the Hembrillo Canyon, which drains the high-walled Hembrillo Basin of the San Andres Mountains. On a follow-up trip, White Sands Missile Range archaeologist Robert Burton and I visited the painted images of mounted warriors and miniature depictions of cougar, javelina, deer, and dragonflies. The rock art indicated the area had long been a sacred Native American site.

In reviewing the literature on the local Apache, we discovered General Thomas Cruse's Indian War memoir, *Apache Days and After,* which noted that a major battle of the Victorio War had taken place in the canyon. The two-year war began when Victorio's Chiricahua Apache band lost their promised reservation and were forced by the Indian Bureau to share land with several other Apache bands. In his account of the ensuing war, Cruse described a desperate battle around a spring, with troopers surrounded by Apache positioned on a semicircle of higher ridges and rock breastworks where there was no natural cover. Excited by the prospect of finding the battleground, we surveyed around the Hembrillo Canyon spring for evidence, only to come up empty-handed. Oddly enough, it would ultimately take a treasure hunt to find the battlefield.

The best-known feature of Hembrillo Basin is Victorio Peak, a 400-foot-high hill named after the Apache chief and allegedly the site of a fabulous treasure. An itinerant foot doctor named Milton "Doc" Noss is said to have discovered stacks of gold bars in a crevice there in 1937; the gold was subsequently lost in a cave-in. Stories about the treasure's origins attribute the cache to the Aztecs, Spanish bandits, or Victorio's Apache. Descendants of Doc Noss' wife made an attempt to retrieve the treasure. Hoping to find evidence of the battle, Burton accompanied them and found a couple of cartridges ejected from Springfield .45 caliber carbines on a low ridge well within the basin. Then Harold Mounce, a volunteer who had been a 16-year-old participant in a 1949 hunt for Noss' gold, led us to more cartridges and one of the rock breastworks mentioned in military reports.

The interior ridges of the basin are formed by a series of limestone uplifts, each capped with gray outcroppings that provided cover for the combatants. We found our first cartridges in a pack rat nest below an impressive breastwork that looked down on a series of lower uplifts. On one of these we found clusters of cartridges fired from

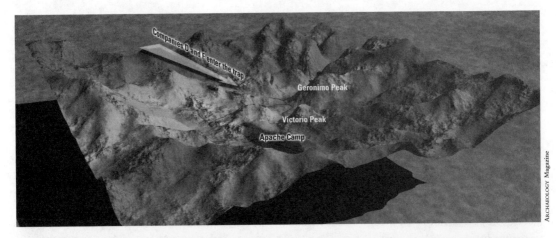

The Ninth Cavalry's D and F companies entered the Hembrillo Basin in the late afternoon of April 6. Surrounded by Apache, the troopers held their ground until the next morning, when they were reinforced by companies A and G, the Sixth cavalry, and 100 White Mountain Apache scouts. The combined force then drove the Apache chief Victorio and his followers out of the basin.

the .45-55 caliber carbines used by the Buffalo Soldiers; those with head stamps (numbers and letters on the head of the cartridges) had been manufactured in 1877 and 1878.

Since we assumed that the clusters of cartridges marked the defensive position of Carroll's besieged soldiers, volunteers with metal detectors swept the area, paying particular attention to positions that could have provided cover for the attacking Apache. As we moved farther up the ridge, we found clusters of .44 caliber Henry cartridges mixed with other non-military ones (Apache used whatever arms they could buy or capture), suggesting that the Apache had fired from this protected position. More Apache breastworks were discovered, some along the edges of arroyos, others on the limestone outcroppings of adjacent ridges.

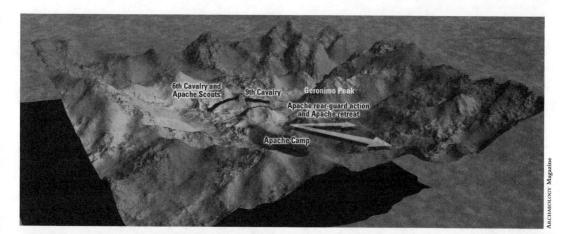

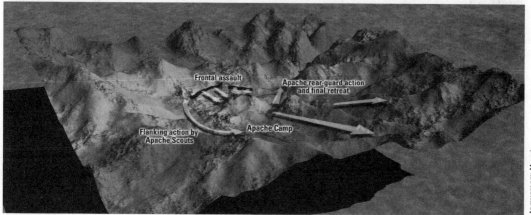

The metal-detector reconnaissance took more than two years, and with the help of 59 volunteers we covered 900 acres of the battlefield. Each artifact, including every cartridge, was carefully mapped and replaced in the ground by a numbered tag. Jim Wakeman, then an associate professor of surveying at New Mexico State University, used a global positioning system (GPS) and sophisticated software to produce a map that faithfully reflected the undulating topography. Wakeman's high-resolution map and the artifact database were then entered into a geographic information systems (GIS) program, that plotted each artifact on the computerized map.

Douglas Scott, an archaeologist for the National Park Service's Midwest Archaeological Center in Lincoln, Nebraska, helped us analyze our finds. In the mid-1980s, Scott pioneered the use of police-style forensic analysis of artifacts recovered from the Custer Battlefield. His analysis resulted in a significant reinterpretation of Custer's tactics during the battle. After comparing firing pin and ejector marks on the cartridges under a microscope, Scott reported that the 800 cartridges collected from Hembrillo were fired from 145 different rifles or carbines and 39 different pistols. Because marks on the cartridges vary with the ejector mechanism of the weapon, he could even identify the make and model of the guns that fired them. When this analysis was added to the GIS program, we could track individual weapons across the landscape and watch the battle unfold on the computer screen. As the archaeological information became more complete, the historical record began to expand as well. The oft-quoted Sixth Cavalry accounts portrayed the Buffalo Soldiers as incompetents who, sick on bad water from nearby Malpais Springs, had wandered helplessly into Hembrillo looking for good water, only to find the springs guarded by Victorio's Apache.

There are no Ninth Cavalry accounts of the battle of Hembrillo in the published literature, and for 115 years history provided the Buffalo Soldiers no defense against the bigoted reports of the Sixth Cavalry. In 1995, Charles Kenner, noted Buffalo Soldier historian, drew attention to an unusual 1903 article on the Victorio War published in an obscure military pamphlet, *The Order of Palestine Bulletin*. The article was written by John Conline, a First Lieutenant who had commanded Company A of Carroll's Ninth Cavalry during the army's pursuit of Victorio.

Conline's report tells of watering with the Ninth's other three companies at Malpais Springs on April 4, 1880. The next morning he led two scouts and 29 troopers south to Hembrillo Canyon, where he found tracks of Apache driving cattle up the canyon. Cautiously following the tracks, Conline soon found himself embroiled in a two-hour skirmish with about 50 Apache. One of Conline's scouts, fluent in Apache, heard Victorio shouting orders. Withdrawing after dark, Conline rejoined Carroll's command, bivouacking on the old Salt Trail, a wagon path used by southern New Mexico communities to access salt beds in the Tularosa Basin.

Now that Victorio was aware of their presence, it was imperative for the Ninth to act quickly lest the Apache melt away in front of them. The next morning, according to Conline, Carroll took Companies D and F into the San Andres by a northern route, sending Companies A and G south to find an alternate route into the mountains. The Ninth was moving aggressively to engage Victorio until help could arrive. But once in the mountain canyons, Carroll had second thoughts about his strategy. A courier was sent to Companies A and G with instructions to follow Carroll's trail into the mountains.

Carroll entered the Hembrillo Basin sometime between 4:30 and 6:00 P.M. on April 6. He did it with the knowledge that Victorio was in front of him and that he had two companies following his trail into Hembrillo. These were hardly soldiers sick on bad water, stumbling blindly into Victorio's camp, as portrayed in Sixth Cavalry accounts. Furthermore, the Ninth had been carrying their own water, according to a previously overlooked letter from one of the Ninth's officers to his mother.

To avoid an ambush, the Ninth approached Victorio's camp across the mountains from the north rather than the more obvious eastern route through Hembrillo Canyon. The distribution of Apache cartridges on the western side of the basin, previously unexplained, suddenly made sense to us. Victorio recognized the tactical advantage of occupying the combined ridgelines on the north side of his camp. When Carroll's Buffalo Soldiers came down the northern rim of the basin, those ridges became Victorio's first line of defense.

The Apache waited as Carroll's command moved deep into a V formed by two ridgelines on the north side of Hembrillo Basin. When they opened fire, the range was still several hundred yards, too far for an effective ambush. Carroll took the prescribed action for dealing with an attack on both flanks and the front. He led his troops forward, driving some Apache from the central uplift of what is now called Carroll's Ridge. Cartridges from those Apache guns were found along the U.S. skirmish lines.

The Apache encircled the Buffalo Soldiers, but nightfall came to the troopers' rescue. Records indicate that the moon did not rise until 4:30 A.M. and was then only a thin sliver. Despite the dark, some Apache managed to creep close. At least three of them, firing either 1866 Winchester or Henry rifles, reached a low uplift just 150 yards from the skirmish line. Their rifles, utilizing a double firing pin, easily jammed. The cartridges often did not fire when first struck and had to be carefully rotated in the chamber and re-struck. Scott's analysis showed some had been struck as many as 23 times. It was obvious that the Apache riflemen had spent some time in one location, patiently forcing each precious cartridge to fire.

The distribution of the cartridges across the battlefield reflects Victorio's superb control over his fighters. Just as the Henry ammunition was found together, cartridges from 15 .44-40 caliber 1873 Winchesters were clustered by a nearby spring. Victorio probably concentrated those short-ranged repeating rifles to keep soldiers from reaching water during the night. Cartridges from certain .45-70 and .50-70 caliber Springfields were also consistently associated, suggesting that the Apache were fighting as highly organized units.

Unaware their comrades were pinned down, Companies A and G camped north of Hembrillo Basin, waiting until morning to join Carroll. From the west came one company of the white Sixth Cavalry, together with 100 White Mountain Apache scouts, the Chiricahuas' bitter enemies. After stumbling toward Hembrillo through the brush and the rocks of the Jornada del Muerto (Dead Man's Journey, a desert basin aptly named for the many travelers who had perished there), they arrived early the next morning. At the same time Companies A and G also descended into the Hembrillo Basin.

Victorio was quickly aware of both groups of reinforcements. His Apache withdrew from their tightening circle around Carroll and took positions on Victorio Ridge, a natural fortress formed by a group of four consecutive limestone uplifts overlooking the troopers from the south. From that vantage, Victorio's rearguard stymied the cavalry for several hours as Apache women and children fled the basin. At this point, the battle involved 300 U.S. troops and 150 Apache, the largest number of combatants of any battle during the Victorio War.

The Apache guns on Victorio Ridge were not the short-ranged Winchesters, but rather long-range .50 or .45 caliber Springfields, Remingtons, and Sharps, all capable of keeping the attackers at bay some 600 yards away. Cartridges indicate that when the frontal assault on Victorio Ridge finally began, the Apache moved to the west to meet the attack on the westernmost uplift. When flanked by the White Mountain Apache scouts, Victorio abandoned the ridge, moving south to confront the scouts.

Victorio's Apache were doing what they did best, fighting a defensive battle with a mountain at their backs. A trail of cartridges marks the Apache route and their successive defensive positions as they fought their way out of the Hembrillo Basin, always keeping the pursuing troops below and in front of them. According to Conline, the Apache front was as much as two miles wide at this point.

Once the Apache disengaged from their final position on Victorio Peak, the Battle of Hembrillo was over. Scouts reported the bodies of three Apache in the vicinity of the Apache camp. Carroll had been hit twice and seven Buffalo Soldiers were wounded. Two would later die at nearby Fort Stanton, an army outpost near the Mescalero Reservation.

That night 400 U.S. troops and more than 300 horses and mules tried to make do with the limited spring water available in the basin. The next morning, a combined force of Buffalo Soldiers and White Mountain Apache scouts reconnoitered the south rim only to find a rear guard of Apache waiting to see what would happen next. A brief skirmish ensued and again the Apache rear guard retreated. Late in the evening of April 8, the troops marched east across the White Sands desert to meet the 10th Cavalry (also Buffalo Soldiers) at the Mescalero Reservation, where Apache sympathetic to Victorio were disarmed and a significant part of Victorio's support base was lost to him.

The battle in Hembrillo was the largest confrontation of the Victorio War. The pressure broke up Victorio's large camp, forcing him west to the Black Range and finally into Mexico. In October 1880, his band was surrounded by Mexican troops at Tres Castillos, an isolated range of low desert mountains in northeastern Chihuahua. In an ensuing massacre (the Apache were out of ammunition), Victorio was killed and his men almost totally wiped out. The few who remained joined the rest of the Chiricahuas in their exile in Oklahoma after the surrender of Geronimo in 1886.

The archaeology of the Hembrillo Battlefield has given us new insight into Victorio's tactical abilities, particularly his control and disposition of available firepower.

Archaeology has also stripped the veil from Carroll's long night, revealing an aggressive strategy and defensive positioning in the face of an attack from established positions. It is now possible to walk the ground the Buffalo Soldiers held, and look out on the basin from the ridges Victorio defended. Standing behind the stacked rock breastworks, visitors can grasp the tactical situation and understand the Apache style of defensive warfare and mobility that became a standard lesson plan for future West Point officers. Today, the U.S. Army uses the battlefield as a "walk around," a place where junior officers can study and analyze the U.S. and Apache battlefield strategies.

PART V:

War in Modern Times

In Flanders Fields

UNCOVERING THE CARNAGE OF WORLD WAR I

by NEIL ASHER SILBERMAN

The Belgian city of Ieper—better known by its French name, Ypres—is really two cities. One is a growing center of high-tech entrepreneurship and commerce with light manufacturing, biotechnology laboratories, and software-development firms clustered around the city in office complexes and industrial parks. The other is a place of cemeteries and war monuments: Flanders fields is where "the poppies blow/between the crosses, row on row," according to the poem by World War I Canadian combat surgeon John McCrae. For four hellish years during World War I, huge armies were bogged down here in a bloody stalemate. By the time of the Armistice in November 1918, this once-proud city, with its massive gothic Cloth Hall, step-gabled shop facades, cathedral, and medieval town square, had been pulverized by incessant bombardment. Its surrounding farmlands were transformed into a cratered, treeless wasteland. It was here that brutal trench warfare claimed the lives of nearly half a million British, Irish, Canadian, Australian, Indian, South African, New Zealand, German, French, and Belgian soldiers. Today, battlefield tours of the "Ypres Salient," as the Allied position deep in German-held territory was known during the war, the 144 official war cemeteries, and memorial ceremonies annually attract hundreds of thousands of visitors to Ieper. A new, state-of-the-art museum, In Flanders Fields, offers a sobering multimedia vision of trench warfare for tourists, descendants of World War I veterans, and a steady stream of school groups.

Now archaeologists have been thrust into a new battle for the soul of Ieper that pits the city's physical expansion against the commemoration of its tragic past. A plan for a new major highway, intended to bring economic development to the region, threatens its vast archaeological remains. Just beneath the surface of the fields, farmyards, and roads all around Ieper for at least three miles in every direction are the remains of trenches, fortifications, ammunition dumps, bunkers, and dugouts; unexploded munitions; discarded equipment; and the unrecovered bodies of at least one hundred thousand soldiers who are listed as missing in action on the various memorials erected throughout the battlefield.

The struggle over Ieper's future has highlighted many of the challenges facing battlefield archaeology the world over: What right does a community have to expand and develop land that is the site of a historic battlefield? What are the obligations of the present generation to preserve the integrity of battlefield landscapes as a memorial to the

fallen and a reminder of the horrors of the past? And what role can archaeology play in examining the nature of modern warfare and preserving its physical remains?

High-tech Ieper and war-memorial Ieper have always lived in polite coexistence, but in 2002, a new regional transportation plan suddenly brought their conflicting interests into sharp relief. The A19, a major eight-lane highway that currently ends at the edge of the battlefield, was slated to continue its northward extension from France, eventually connecting Ieper to the Belgian coast of the English Channel, with its heavily visited tourist spots and ferry ports. Supporters argued that A19 would be a boon to Ieper's economy and draw off summertime traffic congestion from its narrow secondary roads. The plan for an initial four-and-a-half-mile extension was approved by Ieper's city council and sent for final approval and funding to the regional Flemish government.

Naturally, the farmers whose lands would be expropriated for road building immediately objected. But wider and more pervasive protests soon began to be heard: Historians, veterans' groups, preservation activists, and commemorative organizations were outraged that the new highway would rip through a four-and-a-half-mile swath of Flanders fields, almost certainly obliterating all traces of the bodies, trenchworks, and fortifications.

In response to these complaints, the Flemish ministry of culture ordered the Institute for Archaeological Patrimony (IAP), the public research body responsible for excavation and archaeological preservation in Flanders, to undertake a detailed assessment of the proposed route of the A19 extension. The project would provide an opportunity to learn more about Ieper's World War I artifacts. Archaeology in the region has long been focused on the prehistoric, Roman, and medieval periods. Twentieth-century archaeology, and particularly twentieth-century battlefield archaeology, was something new. "At first, I wasn't particularly enthusiastic about this assignment," says Marc Dewilde, head of the IAP West Flanders regional office and a specialist in the area's medieval period. "But we all now recognize how interesting and important this work is."

Over the years, battlefield archaeology at Ieper has been a sporadic, ad hoc affair. Year after year, a grim harvest of bones, twisted metal, and unexploded ordnance has complicated and sometimes endangered the inhabitants' lives. Even today, more than eighty-five years after the end of fighting, a Belgian army bomb-disposal truck makes weekly rounds of the rural roads around the city collecting bombs, artillery shells, and rusted clumps of ammunition and hand grenades that have turned up in the plowing and tending of fields. On rare occasions local farmers have been injured or killed. At building sites and roadworks on the expanding fringes of Ieper, workers regularly uncover trenches, bunkers, military equipment, and human remains. It is impossible to tell how many finds have been dug up and kept or sold as relics by the area's World War I buffs, working with metal detectors and digging in secrecy. Buried artifacts from World War I are protected by the antiquities laws of Flanders, but in practice they are vulnerable: Because the region is so archaeologically rich, it has been impossible for local IAP archaeologists

Trenches, like this one, were on the front lines of the brutal tactics used during World War I.

to effectively patrol the entire area.

In other places along the Western Front, World War I archaeology has been limited to small-scale research projects on select French and Belgian battlefields. But here at Ieper the potential size of the dig was unprecedented. To get a better sense of the nature of the fighting and the places most likely to contain extensive battlefield remains, an enormous cache of contemporaneous documents was studied: military maps, reports, requisition orders, personal snapshots, diaries and letters, and World War I aerial photos.

Assisted by British colleagues from the University of Greenwich, the Imperial War Museum, the National Army Museum, and University College London, Dewilde and his team began work in the spring of 2002. Using the archival maps and documents, first they plotted the recorded locations of trench lines and other fortifications on modern topographical maps of the survey area. They then field walked the entire four-and-a-half-mile strip to spot concentrations of artifacts on the surface and tie them into documented battle sites. This turned up several intense concentrations of material: wire, supplies, tracks, bunkers, dugouts, pipelines, glass bottles with markings, shovels, helmets, concretized sandbags, bullets, cartridges, shells, and indications of trenches. The location of the finds closely matched the documentary record.

Nine areas were selected for excavation on the basis of the surface finds, and digging on two started right away. The IAP archaeologists began with a site identified from the World War I maps and accounts as "The High Command Redoubt," the German front established after the second Battle of Ieper, in April 1915, when the Germans' devastating chemical attack using canisters of acrid, blinding chlorine gas cleared the way to this strategic point. The English war chronicler Edmund Blunden, an Ieper veteran himself, noted that this redoubt was of the highest strategic significance to the German forces, as it directly overlooked the Allied front lines. The excavation revealed a system of trenches and machine-gun positions linked to substantial wooden structures. One of the walls still bore the initials "K.W.," carved by one of the builders or soldiers stationed there. It was eerily empty except for a rusted bayonet blade and a cache of unexploded hand grenades. Luckily, the IAP team had been trained to handle such potentially dangerous finds by the bomb-disposal unit of the Belgian army. "Once we learned how to deal with the grenades, shell cases, and unexploded bombs, we had no problem with these types of finds," says archaeologist Pedro Pype.

At the second site, known in war accounts as Turco Farm, the discoveries were much more numerous and grisly. According to historical sources, this was the place where first the French and later the British established their front lines after 1915. Excavations revealed a network of narrow trenches with "duckboards"—wood planks laid to keep soldiers above the mud—that had been lined with now-rusted sheets of corrugated iron. Within these trenches, the team recovered digging tools, a copper teaspoon, shoes, a waterlogged woolen sock, and a shattered skeleton, identified as British from the distinctive uniform buttons found with it. Nearby they discovered the bones of a lower leg, with the foot still intact, inside a well-preserved military boot. The French factory marks stamped into the sole indicated the likely nationality of the fallen soldier.

The discovery of human remains changed everything. Over the years, whenever bones were found in the Ieper area, local police had been called in to determine whether they were those of battle casualties or evidence of a more recent crime. If war-related, the bones were taken to a government morgue and eventually given over to the appropriate combatant nation. Often the remains could be linked to a particular army, unit, or even individual by the equipment, uniform buttons, or personal possessions found with them. England's Commonwealth War Graves Commission (CWGC) had been particularly active in identifying the remains of British and Commonwealth soldiers and burying them with full military honors in national cemeteries. Since one of the bodies from Turco Farm was British, it was transferred to the CWGC for proper burial. Though no German archaeologists or scholars have been involved in the excavations, had the bodies of the country's soldiers been recovered, German authorities would have been contacted to repatriate the remains.

The excavation at the next site, Crossroads Farm, was not merely a battlefield recovery operation. The archaeologists were also able to verify the hellish dynamics of trench warfare. The level farmland between the outer ring of the city and the low ridges that surrounded it—through which A19 would run—had been the deadly no man's land between the Allied trenches and those of the besieging German forces on the ridges above. Here, the IAP team traced the complex trench system that the Allies had expanded in preparation for an assault on the German positions during the Third Battle of Ieper in the summer of 1917. A variety of structural details and artifacts were uncovered, including duckboards, a deep concrete bunker, a wooden dugout, and cap badges representing the Royal King's Rifle Corps, the Dorsetshire Regiment, and the East Kent Regiment known as the "Buffs." The archaeologists also examined the clearly defined shell craters that pockmarked the entire area. Within the shell craters were the shattered remains of five soldiers, two of them still wearing leather webbing, entrenching tools, pistol, bayonet, and ammunition packs. British visitors to the excavation created a temporary memorial there, marking the places where the bodies were found with the familiar poppy-decorated wooden crosses used in Ieper's military cemeteries; formal military burials were

planned for the coming months. From these remains and the location of the trenches, the archaeologists were able to trace in precise detail how the British had expanded and shifted the orientation of their trenches as they edged closer to the German front lines.

At the very start of the project, the IAP had convened a panel of military historians and preservation experts from the United Kingdom, France, and Belgium to compile a background report on the historical significance of the threatened section of the Ieper battlefield. Though the panel was cautious in expressing its political opinions about the wisdom of the proposed highway plan, they were unambiguous in their opinion about the site's enormous historical and archaeological value as one of the most important battlefields of World War I. The excavations dramatically confirmed this conclusion.

Yet for the problem of the proposed highway, there are no easy answers. The panel recommended that the area be declared a protected heritage zone, but the supporters of the road project countered that the extent of the battlefield is so vast that any attempt to shift the road's path to skirt the entire area would be too expensive and inefficient to achieve the region's development aims. Alternatively, raising the highway on pillars to protect the human remains and archaeological deposits beneath it would also be costly and, as the preservationists pointed out, would forever destroy the visual context of the open ground and low ridges where the battles of Ieper were fought. Excavating the entire four-and-a-half-mile stretch would be far beyond the capacity of the IAP—or of any similar archaeological organization—considering the hundreds of bodies, dense network of trenches and fortifications, and tons of equipment that would almost certainly be found.

Something will have to be done to prevent the total destruction of the World War I remains, says Marc Dewilde. "I am concerned about any destruction of archaeological deposits. If the highway plan is approved and the archaeological remains are in danger, it's our responsibility to excavate what we must and preserve what we can."

At the time of this writing, no decision on the A19 extension has been made, and the archaeological project goes on. More finds—and more funerals—can be expected. And with elections for the Flemish Parliament in June, no decision is anticipated soon. As the preservation and development debates continue, only one thing is certain: The pioneering project at Ieper has demonstrated archaeology's essential role in preserving and understanding the great historical trauma of modern warfare, whose gruesome traces lie beneath the surface of this now-peaceful ground.

◉ EYEWITNESS: Trench Warfare in World War I

compiled by MARK ROSE

I n the early autumn of 1914, during opening months of World War I, German troops pushed westward as the British and French armies sought to slow and contain them. Few then thought that the war would last for four long years or claim the lives of some nine million men. Patriotism ran high at the beginning of it all. It was in that atmosphere that Arthur Machen, an author with antiquarian interests, caused a sensation when he published "Bowmen" in the September 29, 1914, *Evening News*. The British had just fought a rearguard action after having to abandon positions at Mons, Belgium, when a French retreat exposed their flank. Written as a semi-official report, "Bowmen" tells of a beleaguered force facing a relentless artillery barrage and waves of oncoming Germans. In the face of certain death, the men joke with one another and recall various memories.

One man, whom Machen describes as a soldier who "happened to know Latin and other useless things" remembers a restaurant where the plates had "St. George in blue, with the motto, *Adsit Anglis Sanctus Georgius*—May St. George Be a Present Help to the English." The soldier repeats the words to himself, inadvertently summoning supernatural aid: "The roar of battle died down in his ears to a gentle murmur; instead of it, he says, he heard a great voice and a shout louder than a thunder-peal crying: 'Array, array, array!'" It is St. George, bringing with him a ghostly army of archers from the 1415 battle of Agincourt. As the Germans advance, they are slain by spectral arrow shafts as the soldier hears the phantom voices crying "St. George! St. George!" "Heaven's knight, aid us!" "St. George for merry England!"

Astonishingly, some believed Machen's tale to be a true account. It would be different, however, when the reality of trench warfare set in. Facing off behind networks of trenches and bunkers—to which the troops gave colorful names—the armies launched occasional strikes across no-man's land to capture enemy earthworks in hopes of breaking through. Muddy trenches, barbed-wire entanglements, machine guns, and poisonous "mustard" gas were the reality. Many perished for advances that could be measured in just a few yards. It was this that a number of gifted writers and poets who found themselves in the trenches wrote about. Among these were Robert Graves, a poet and classicist best known as author of *I, Claudius,* and the poet Siegfried Sassoon, who both served in the Royal Welch Fusiliers.

In his autobiography, *Good-Bye to All That,* Graves wrote matter-of-factly about harrowing experiences:

May 28, 1915. Last night a lot of German stuff was flying about, including shrapnel. I heard one shell wish-wishing towards me and dropped flat. It burst just over the trench where "Petticoat Lane" runs into "Lowndes Square." My ears sang as though there were gnats in them, and a bright scarlet light shone over everything. My shoulder got twisted in falling and I thought I had been hit, but I hadn't been. The vibration made my chest sing, too, in a curious way, and I lost my sense of equilibrium. I was ashamed when the sergeant major came along the trench and found me on all fours still unable to stand up.

It was a close call, but on July 19, Graves was less lucky:

The German batteries were handing out heavy stuff, six-and-eight-inch, and so much of it that we decided to move back 50 yards at a rush. As we did so, an eight-inch shell burst three paces behind me. I heard the explosion, and felt as though I had been punched rather hard between the shoulder blades, but without any pain. I took the punch merely for the shock of the explosion; then blood trickled into my eye and, turning faint, I called to Moodie: "I've been hit." Then I fell.

Graves was wounded in the thigh, over one eye, and in the hand, but his main injury was from a shell fragment that went in just below his right shoulder blade and exited through his chest. His commanding officer, Lt. Colonel Crawshay, who had been told the wounds were mortal, wrote to Graves' parents: "I very much regret to have to write and tell you your son has died...." Carried off the battlefield on a stretcher, Graves was placed in a corner of a first-aid station, where he remained unconscious for 24 hours. In the morning, when the dead were being removed, somebody noticed that he was still breathing.

Despite nearly being killed, Graves returned to duty. "In November, Siegfried and I rejoined the Battalion," he writes. "Siegfried said that we must 'keep up the good reputation of the poets'—as men of courage." Sassoon recalled his service in the war both in poetry and in his semi-fictitious autobiographical work *Memoirs of an Infantry Officer*, in which his descriptive prose sometimes approaches poetry:

> I can see the Manchesters down in New Trench getting ready to go over. Figures filing down the trench. ...Have just eaten my last orange. ...I am staring at a sunlit picture of Hell, and still the breeze shakes the yellow weeds, and poppies glow under Crawley Ridge where some shells fell a few minutes ago. Manchesters are sending forward some scouts. A bayonet glitters. A runner comes back across the open to their Battalion Headquarters, close here on the right. 21st Division still trotting along the sky line toward La Boisselle. Barrage going strong to the right of Contal-

maison Ridge. Heavy shelling toward Mametz.

Both Graves and Sassoon survived the war. The young poet Wilfrid Owen was less lucky. In the summer of 1917, he was in a hospital recuperating from a concussion and "trench fever." There he met Sassoon, also recovering, who encouraged his writing. Owen was sent back to France near the end of the war and was killed a week before the armistice was signed in November 1918. His poetry was collected and published by Sassoon, including "Anthem for Doomed Youth." Its opening stanza reflects the disillusionment felt by many of his generation:

> What passing-bells for these who die as cattle?
> Only the monstrous anger of the guns.
> Only the stuttering rifles' rapid rattle
> Can patter out their hasty orisons.
> No mockeries for them from prayers or bells,
> Nor any voice of mourning save the choirs—
> The shrill, demented choirs of wailing shells;
> And bugles calling for them from sad shires.

Owen's perception of the futility of war and loss of life, shared by Graves and Sassoon, is a far cry from Arthur Machen's patriotic evocation of St. George.

A Long Road Home

THE REMAINS OF A WORLD WAR II PILOT FOUND IN THE
MOUNTAINS OF PAPUA NEW GUINEA ARE BURIED IN
ARLINGTON NATIONAL CEMETERY.

by WILLIAM BELCHER *and* HELEN M. WOLS

It had been raining since mid-morning and the gray
clouds clung to the jagged ridgeline of the Finesterre
Mountains, on Papua New Guinea's north coast. From
our makeshift camp, 8,000 feet up on the mountainside, we
could still see down to the old World War II aerodrome
called Saidor, which now serves as a local airstrip. Despite the
foul weather, our team focused on excavating the scattered
remains of an aircraft, probably of a lost P-47 Thunderbolt
that took off from Saidor and never returned.

I had come here in early October 1998, as part of a
search and recovery team from the U.S. Army's Central
Identification Laboratory, Hawaii (CILHI). New Guinea was
a major theater in WWII. To the north and west were the
Japanese-occupied Philippines, to the southeast the Coral
Sea, where one of the war's pivotal naval battles was fought.
Our team had already investigated a P-47 crash site in the

central part of the island where we recovered the pilot's remains, and now we were at the second of three sites to be checked.

We had learned of this one from Alfred Hagen, a Philadelphia businessman who found it while looking for the crash site of an uncle's plane, which had also not returned from a mission during the war. In tracking down lost aircraft in Papua New Guinea, a team goes to the general area where we know, from U.S. Army records, that a plane went down, then canvasses the locals. Invariably we find hunters who use crash sites as landmarks in the jungle. Hagen heard of the site from such hunters in June 1998. He then had locals build a small, wooden landing pad for the light helicopter he was using, and flew in to check it out. Hagen identified the plane as a P-47, not the type of aircraft he was searching for, but saw that there were bones there, possibly human, which made the site a priority for us to investigate.

Local pilots are familiar with the terrain and weather, which can be treacherous in this region, so we chartered a helicopter out of Port Moresby. The site was about 20 miles from Saidor, a 15-minute ride in the chopper. It was almost impossible to see into the thick jungle canopy as we flew over, but we eventually spotted Hagen's old landing platform. The pilot tried gingerly to set the helicopter down on it, but the platform was too weak to support our heavier chopper with all of the team's gear. So I hopped out and, while the helicopter ferried up a work crew to strengthen the platform, I scouted the site.

The mountainside, thickly covered with ferns, palms, and hardwood trees, rises steeply to a flat space at the back of which is a large rocky outcrop. Most of the wreckage was scattered in a narrow ravine cut across the flat space by a small stream. I saw several large fuselage fragments, part of a wing, and the plane's 18-cylinder air-cooled Pratt-Whitney R-2800-63 engine, the type used in the P-47.

Affectionately known as "The Jug" among aviators, the P-47 was one of the most famous pursuit planes of World War II. Originally conceived as a lightweight interceptor, it developed into a heavyweight aircraft used as a high-altitude escort fighter and low-level fighter-bomber. Because of its sturdy construction, the Thunderbolt became legendary.

We made camp uphill from the crash site, rigging a large tarp between trees to form a lean-to and setting up some small tents. This would be home for the next 21 or so days. We brought our usual gear— satellite phones, laptops, global positioning systems (GPS), and excavation equipment. Our larder was a footlocker of canned goods, which we supplemented with locally bought food such as rice and, occasionally, a cuscus or tree wallaby, brought in by a hunter and cooked over a small fire.

There were six of us from CILHI, along with a Papua New Guinea National Museum representative, who was our intermediary with local officials, two Papua New Guinea Defence Force enlisted men (for protection), and four or five local workers. We established a grid over the site and mapped the visible wreckage, then began excavating, sieving the soil to ensure that we would recover any artifacts and all of the human remains.

The Great MIA Hunt

The search, recovery, and identification of the remains of American military personnel unaccounted for from World War II, the Korean War, the Cold War, and the Vietnam War— nearly 90,000 in all—is the job of the U.S. Army Central Identification Laboratory, Hawaii (CILHI), located at Hickam Air Force Base. The lab employs about 250 military and civilian personnel, including the largest staff of forensic anthropologists of any institution in the world. Their work takes them to some of the remotest places on the planet, like tiny Butaritari Island in the mid-Pacific. Working conditions vary from tropical jungles infested with leeches and possibly tigers to cold windswept plains and ridgelines. And, occasionally, they encounter live ammunition or unexploded mines, mortar shells, and bombs.

Three separate cases reported in the course of one week this past summer highlight CILHI's work. Remains of three U.S. Army servicemen, crewmembers on a helicopter that went down in Vietnam in 1969, were returned to their families for burial. At the same time, a team from CILHI was in northeastern China, investigating the wreckage of a CIA-operated plane shot down near the North Korean border 50 years ago. Aided by a 78-year-old villager, they located the wreckage but found no remains of the two crewmembers who perished. Half a world away, off the North Carolina coast, the turret of the ironclad USS Monitor, which sank in December 1862, was being raised when bones from some of the 16 sailors who went down with the ship were found. A forensic specialist from CILHI was on hand to escort them to the lab in Hawaii, where an attempt to identify them will be made, perhaps by comparing facial reconstructions based on the bones with photographs of the ill-fated crew, or by using DNA from their descendants.

The Army first began identifying and interring its dead in registered graves during the Civil War, but today's lab has its origin in the Vietnam War. Then, two army mortuaries had the job of identifying servicemembers killed in Indochina. After the United States withdrew in 1973, the Central Identification

We worked from daylight, around 6:00 a.m., until the rains came, which they did every afternoon as moisture-laden air coming in from the ocean rose up the mountainside. On good days, the rains held off until 6:00 in the evening, but often we only had a short window of time, until two o'clock, after which I would enter notes on my lap-top, work on the site map, or clean items found that day. Every afternoon, we reviewed the day's work and discussed what was to be done the next day.

Our mission was to recover any human remains and to search for crucial pieces of evidence that could identify the aircraft or the pilot, like the plane's serial number—

Laboratory, Thailand, was established to continue the work. After the fall of South Vietnam, the lab was relocated to Hawaii in 1976, where it remains today. With the move, its role expanded to include remains of American military personnel from World War II (more than 78,000 remains not recovered or identified), the Korean War (more than 8,100), and the Cold War (about 50), in addition to the Vietnam War (about 1,900).

To carry out its mission, CILHI has 18 search and recovery teams of ten to 14 people each, including forensic anthropologists, photographers, interpreters, explosive ordnance disposal specialists, radio operators, and others. Each team has an overall military leader, usually a captain, and a civilian anthropologist, who is in charge of the recovery effort. The teams work throughout Southeast Asia; in South Korea and, beginning in 1996, North Korea; on Pacific islands, such as Vanuatu or Palau in Micronesia; and in Europe.

Press releases on the lab's website (www.jpac.pacom.mil) are a barometer of the work being done. Notices of the deployment of teams to Vietnam, Laos, Cambodia, Kwajalein Island, Panama, and South Korea, appear regularly. There are also reports of remains coming to Hawaii for identification: bomber crews and fighter pilots from Papua New Guinea; a pilot shot down over Germany on September 11, 1944, in an aerial battle that resulted in the loss of 84 U.S. aircraft and 174 German fighters. And there are accounts of cases that have been resolved, the remains identified and returned to the families: sons bringing their father's remains home from Vietnam, a family receiving a call from CILHI on a Thanksgiving morning to say that remains of a sailor killed at Pearl Harbor and buried anonymously had now been identified as one of their own.

Since 1973, the lab has identified and returned to families more than 1,050 sets of remains. The hunt continues.

by WILLIAM BELCHER

most conspicuously painted on the tail—or other serial numbers such as those stamped into weapons or on a plate attached to the engine block. On our first day, I checked the engine block in hopes of quickly identifying the aircraft, but found the plate was missing, perhaps removed by the force of the impact or scavenged by a visitor to the site—it appeared that the engine had been dug out. We did recover two teeth, one with dental restorations, which, when compared with dental records, would be critical in identifying the remains. This was really exciting, because you can go days and days without finding anything. Here, on our first day, we had made an important discovery.

We found the teeth about 30 feet from the engine, in the area where the left wing and the forward fuselage had come to rest. It was here in the following days that the team recovered most of the personal effects associated with the P-47's pilot, including a 1942 Australian six-pence coin, a compass, two waterproof match cases, and a .45 caliber pistol along with bullets and magazines. This area also yielded most of the other human remains we found—portions of the skull; some shoulder, arm, and hand bones; rib fragments; a few vertebrae; some leg and foot bones; and hundreds of small fragments.

On the fourth day, we recovered the plane's four .50 caliber Browning M2 Aircraft Machine Guns perfectly preserved in anaerobic, fuel-saturated mud below the wing. I checked the serial numbers and found that all four guns matched those on Missing Aircraft Report #03308 for Second Lieutenant George P. Gaffney, Jr., who had disappeared on March 11, 1944. After leaving the Gusap aerodrome, homebase of his 41st Fighter Squadron, for a mission at Wewak, he had landed at Saidor and refueled. He then took off, and was never seen again.

We were excited to be able to identify the plane, since the P-47 was a common aircraft (it was used by Australian pilots and others, not just U.S. fliers), and I notified the lab in Hawaii immediately. Since this was a significant step toward resolving what had happened to 2nd Lt. Gaffney, the deputy commander at CILHI relayed the news to his surviving family.

Despite being elated at identifying the plane and recovering the dental evidence that might show the remains to be 2nd Lt.

Gaffney's, our mood was rather reflective. CILHI missions are difficult physically and mentally, but everybody feels they are important. The Finesterre Mountains are tricky for aircraft today, and during the war they were even more dangerous. Most of the 300 or so American planes that went down here were flying over the mountain ridges. Aviation charts were often inaccurate—you could be flying at 12,000 feet, high enough to clear a ridge according to the elevation noted on the chart, but the ridge might really be 12,600 feet. If you were in clouds and flying by instruments, you would hit the mountain without ever seeing it. That may have been 2nd Lt. Gaffney's fate.

Once our investigation was completed, we moved on to the third site, the wreckage of a B-25 bomber about 13 miles farther inland. This was just a scouting trip to assess the site for a future recovery mission. We pinpointed the crash site's location and recorded the plane's number, which could still be read on its tail. Back in Port Moresby, our team split up. I turned over the locked case holding the human remains and artifacts recovered at the crash site of 2nd Lt. Gaffney's plane to the team's sergeant, who was heading back to Hawaii with most of our group. I then boarded a plane for Vietnam to check out other sites with a different search and recovery team.

With nothing like a wallet or identification tags to prove the remains were 2nd Lt. Gaffney's, analysis of the bones at CILHI back in Hawaii was critical in making that determination. My colleague Helen Dockall was assigned the analysis of the remains and interpretation of the evidence, artifactual and skeletal. As is customary, the anthropologist who directs the recovery does not do the skeletal analysis, and the one who examines the bones works "blindly." With only limited knowledge of the case, the anthropologist evaluates the bones more objectively and there is no possibility of any unintentional bias creeping into the interpretation. So, Dockall knew only that the remains were from a World War II site in Papua New Guinea. She determined that the remains were from one person and that, based on some of the vertebrae and a lower leg bone, the individual was most likely more than 18 years old. But because of the fragmentary nature of the bones, it was impossible to make a determination as to sex, race, or stature.

After reviewing the case files, it was clear to Dockall that the remains were likely to be 2nd Lt. Gaffney's based on where they were found, but the skeletal evidence was too slight to prove this. In the end, dental identification was definitive. The two restorations on one of the teeth we found matched dental work noted in 2nd Lt. Gaffney's military records.

Dockall submitted her conclusion that the remains we had recovered were 2nd Lt. Gaffney's to Tom Holland, the lab's scientific director, who concurred. CILHI then issued an identification, consisting of reports on the excavation and the skeletal and other evidence, as well as the original report from the time of the crash. This, along with letters from Holland and the commander of CILHI explaining the identification, was taken by a U.S. Army service representative to Gaffney's wife, Ruth Kalupy, and daughter, Patricia.

Since the fall of 1998, when I handed over the remains for transport to CILHI, I have been on search and recovery missions in Laos and taken leave to excavate at Harrapa, an Indus Valley site in Pakistan. My next assignment took me to Butaritari, a mid-Pacific island, with a team searching for the remains of Marine Raiders who perished in an attack on a Japanese seaplane base in 1942. It was on my first day back from there, in late April 1999, that Patricia Gaffney-Ansel came to CILHI to escort the remains of her father to their final resting place in Arlington National Cemetery. At the lab, she spent some time alone with them. She was outwardly somber when we met, but I could see in her eyes that she was grateful; she had gotten her father back. This past summer, while in Washington, I visited 2nd Lt. Gaffney's gravesite at Arlington, so far from that remote ridgetop in the Finesterre Mountains.

World War II POWs

DISCOVERIES AND EXCAVATIONS HAVE YIELDED NEW INFORMATION ON THE TREATMENT OF PRISONERS IN EUROPE, ASIA, AND THE UNITED STATES.

*A*rchaeological discoveries have, in recent years, helped reveal how people—POWs and civilians—were treated during World War II. In some cases, investigations are uncovering evidence of massacres, such as the Polish officers killed by the Soviets at the Katyn Forest. Elsewhere, remains are coming to light that remind us of how POWs and civilians were used as forced labor, such as at the infamous bridge over the River Kwai. In other cases, however, captured soldiers were treated humanely, as shown by investigations at the "Fritz Ritz" in Texas. And, from a "relocation center" in Idaho, comes a poignant relic illustrating how some Japanese-American civilians coped with imprisonment.

Unearthing Soviet Massacres
The graves of 25,700 Polish citizens massacred by the Soviets in April and May 1940 have been unearthed at three sites in western Russia, providing evidence for a genocide indictment the Polish government plans to pursue in the Polish General Court. The excavations, carried out by

Muzeum Okregowe w Sieradzu archaeologist Marek Urbanski, yielded thousands of German-made bullets bought by the Soviets between 1930 and 1935, proof of Russian involvement in the massacres. Soviet officials had blamed the killings on Hitler. Urbanski says the executions were directed mainly at Polish army officers captured at the outset of World War II and were part of a Soviet plan to exterminate the Polish intelligentsia. Some 14,700 executed officers have been identified by means of their uniforms and other military paraphernalia.

Nearly three weeks after Hitler invaded Poland on September 1, 1939, Stalin ordered Soviet troops into the eastern part of the country. Captured Polish officers were interned in concentration camps at Kozielsk, Starobielsk, and Ostaszkow, and, six months later, were executed in Katyn and Miednoje forests and in a wooded area on the outskirts of Kharkov. The German army discovered the Katyn Forest massacre site after its invasion of the Soviet Union in 1941. Urbanski's three seasons of excavations in woods near Kharkov revealed that the majority of victims there had been shot in the back of the head with their hands tied behind their backs and their coats wrapped around their heads. A number were finished off with bayonets or a second shot.

Excavations at the massacre sites, which began in 1994, were undertaken to determine the extent of the burial grounds and how many bodies they contained, and in preparation for Polish military cemeteries. The Kharkov burial area, the most thoroughly studied, yielded more than 10,000 artifacts associated with 6,400 bodies, including 2,100 Russians, victims of Stalin's purges, as well as 4,300 Poles. Of the Poles, 3,820 were officers interned at Starobielsk; the rest were probably civilians arrested during the short-lived Soviet occupation.

by SPENCER P.M. HARRINGTON

Bones at the River Kwai

Remains of more than 900 laborers impressed by the Japanese into building the bridge memorialized in Pierre Boulle's novel *The Bridge on the River Kwai* have been excavated in western Thailand by a Buddhist group. The laborers were among some 100,000 Asians and prisoners of war who perished during the construction of a 260-mile railway that Japan hoped to use in an invasion of India during World War II.

According to Mikel Flamm, a freelance photographer traveling through Kanchanaburi, Thailand members of the Phothipawana Songkroh Foundation, a Buddhist organization based in Bangkok, cremated the remains in a ceremony conducted shortly after they were discovered in a mass grave six miles from the bridge. Most of the remains were those of Indians, Malays, and other Asians who comprised the majority of the estimated 300,000-person workforce. A Thai archaeologist, however, has determined that some of the remains were those of 61,000 British, Australian, and Dutch prisoners who were also forced to work on the bridge and railway.

According to survivors' accounts, both prisoners and laborers died of malaria, cholera, and malnutrition. To avoid the spread of infectious disease, they were often cremated and buried in mass graves. The whereabouts of other mass graves remain in doubt since many landowners in the area have refused archaeologists permission to excavate.

by DOMINIC G. DIONGSON

Fritz Ritz

A cement-lined pond that surrounded a flower garden and a moated miniature castle with clay figurines are among the decorative remains of a World War II prisoner-of-war camp recently excavated near Hearne, Texas. As many as 4,800 soldiers of Germany's Afrika Corps, divided into pro- and anti-Nazi groups, were housed here from 1943 to 1945. The site was cleared when the army closed the camp after the war. Michael Waters of Texas A&M University's department of anthropology has also found concrete slabs that supported the mess hall, storerooms, and lavatories, in addition to a concrete-lined brick fountain along the walkway to the mess hall.

In 1942 the citizens of Hearne petitioned the federal government to build the camp, believing that the prisoners could work on local cotton, onion, and peanut farms while the town's regular field hands went off to war. Only about 20 percent of the prison population agreed to work, the rest being preoccupied with softball and soccer games, language classes, reading, and the architectural embellishment of the facility, according to camp records. Among the prisoners were members of a German military orchestra captured in Tunisia who gave concerts to locals. Some residents interviewed by Waters and his graduate students felt that the POWs were treated too well,

referring to the camp as the "Fritz Ritz." Others remember sharing rationed sweets and supplies with the young men, recognizing that they were frightened and far from home, just as American soldiers were.

by JESSICA E. SARACENI

Garden Under Guard

An exquisite World War II–era Japanese rock garden has been revealed at the site of the Minidoka Relocation Center in southern Idaho, where as many as 13,000 Japanese-Americans were held from 1942 to 1945. In preparing to open the site to the public, National Park Service archaeologist Jeffrey Burton exposed and mapped the remains of an elaborate garden designed by Fujitaro Kubota, an internee at the camp who became an important figure in the development of Japanese-American landscape architecture. The garden features an arrangement of stone pathways that wind their way around several earthen mounds and basalt rock formations. Burton was also able to establish the location of the camp's honor roll board, a large wooden sign that was inscribed with the names of the nearly 1,000 internees who left the camp to fight for the United States in Europe and the Pacific.

by ERIC A. POWELL

Remembering Chelmno

HEART-WRENCHING FINDS
FROM A NAZI DEATH CAMP

by JULIET GOLDEN

I first came to Chelmno on Corpus Christi Day, a spring religious holiday when Poles flock to the streets and join long processions in cities and villages across the country. The thick fragrance of rose petals strewn across the ground mingled in the air with homilies broadcast from the village church, beckoning parishioners who knelt in prayer on the asphalt-covered main thoroughfare. From a small knoll near the church, I admired the timeless village scene, framed by the lush Ner River Valley and an agricultural landscape that has changed little over the centuries. A Russian general, obviously taken with the view, built his country estate here in the nineteenth century. Today, only a scatter of cobblestones and a granary remain from the estate, together with a few trenches dug by archaeologists and surrounded with blue memorial candles from Israel, marking the center of the Chelmno Extermination Camp.

The first camp where mass executions were carried out using gas, Chelmno was a testing ground for the Nazis looking to develop increasingly efficient methods to carry out their "final solution." Between 1941 and 1945, as many as 300,000 adults and children, mostly Polish Jews, were executed and cremated here.

Before the Nazis retreated in early 1945, they destroyed or buried much of the evidence of the camp's existence. Little remained—on the surface at least—to attest the mass exterminations.

Since the late 1980s, however, excavations by Lucja Nowak, director of the Konin Regional Museum, have uncovered traces of the camp facilities and large quantities of personal effects belonging to its victims. Her findings have led to a more complete version of the camp's history than the existing handful of eyewitness accounts provide; they also give a voice to those who died here.

"When you say that 200,000 or 300,000 people were killed here, that doesn't really say much," says Nowak, a spritely, determined woman with thick, wavy black hair and dark piercing eyes. "For me, when we find a small toy or a shoe, that represents a living person. Through these small things we re-create the history of people who had dreams and life plans."

Unlike Auschwitz, Birkenau, or Dachau, Chelmno was not a concentration camp, encircled with barbed wire and lined with barracks where prisoners lived and worked. Rather, it operated exclusively as an extermination center—in two separate phases and at two sites roughly two miles apart. In phase one (December 1941 to April 1943),

victims were transported to the estate, commonly referred to in Polish as a palace, where they were told that they were to shower before being transported to work camps. Inside the palace, victims undressed then were led to the basement, where they were forced into trucks and suffocated by redirected engine exhaust. The trucks were then driven to the forest outside the village, where the bodies were dumped in mass graves. Concerned about a typhus outbreak, the Nazis exhumed the bodies in 1942 and incinerated them in two crematories built in the forest. The Nazis razed the palace and later covered the ruins with a thick layer of soil when killings at Chelmno were temporarily halted, for unknown reasons, in the spring of 1943. In phase two (June 1944 to January 1945), victims spent the night in the village church, then were brought to barracks in the forest where they were collected and forced onto trucks to be gassed. In the second phase all the victims were cremated.

The Polish government erected a memorial to Chelmno's victims at the forest site in 1964. The land, however, was managed by the state forest service, while the palace grounds served as an agricultural cooperative. In the 1980s, Nowak and her husband, also an archaeologist and former regional museum director, wanted the two sites incorporated under the aegis of the museum.

Archaeology would provide the opportunity to do so. "People said that the Germans had liquidated all traces of the camp and that nothing was left," recalls Nowak. Work began at the forest site in 1986; it was incorporated into the museum the following year. Nowak and her team, made up of members of the museum's archaeology department and local volunteers, located the barracks and three crematories and uncovered pits where the victims' personal effects were burned. In one section of the crematory wall, excavators found metal parts of a baby carriage, used to reinforce the concrete structure.

During the Nazi occupation, most of the villagers were evacuated from Chelmno, with the exception of families near the river, away from the center of town. Older villagers agreed to talk with Nowak's team; they also provided photos carried by Chelmno's victims that were found on the grounds of the palace after the war.

Zofia Szalek was 11 when the Nazis established the camp. During the occupation, she pastured cows and goats in the ravine near the church. A small, nervous woman, Szalek recalls people being murdered in the palace. She remembers the screaming. While she supports Nowak's efforts, Szalek fears that in excavating at Chelmno, the dead will come back to haunt the living. Nonetheless, she has volunteered during the recent excavations of the palace grounds, sifting through dirt in search of minute personal effects.

The former village priest played a key role in the positive approach to the work at the site. "Father Idzi helped us a lot," says Nowak. "I spoke to the priest, and he said that while they were cleaning around the church they found strange things—scissors, spoons." These finds inspired Nowak to excavate near the church where the Germans had also burned looted goods.

The priest's decision to permit archaeologists onto church grounds paved the way for work later carried out at the palace, which at the time was owned by the agricultural cooperative. Father Idzi left the village in 2001, however, and the new priest has not taken an active role in support of the excavations. Moreover, he has not continued Father Idzi's tradition of organizing masses in which he talked about the history of the Chelmno camp.

In 1997, Nowak and her team were permitted to make a limited excavation on palace grounds. Using architectural drawings of the estate, excavators made a small three-foot-deep probe. "We hit the bull's eye," says Nowak. "We had found the small hallway where the people were actually led from the basement into the trucks."

Up to then the only source of information on the role that the palace played in the extermination process were testimonies of survivors and camp staff.

Vast amounts of property plundered by the Nazis have been uncovered. "It's a little strange, but with every movement of the shovel you unearth dozens of objects," says Przymyslaw Gaj, a 26-year-old archaeology student. "You find as many things here in one day as you would normally find in an entire season in the usual dig." The meticulous segregation of goods adds to the surreal nature of the excavation. In one place archaeologists uncovered a thick layer of medicine bottles, followed by a layer of eating utensils. Another pit was filled with combs. Archaeologists have also dug up thousands of dental bridges and false teeth picked over to recover precious metals used in dental work.

There is obviously an emotional dimension to the work at Chelmno that is seldom encountered in archaeology. Small fragments of bone catch the sunlight at the forest site where the crematories once stood. "It's one thing to hear about the crematory, it's another to stand inside an enormous pit that is filled with human bones," says Krzysztof Gorczyca, an archaeologist who directed last summer's excavation. "Only then did it occur to me just how many people were murdered here."

Many of the recovered objects speak volumes about how victims lived in the weeks and months before they arrived at Chelmno. In a pit of goods looted from victims brought in from the Lodz ghetto, two brooches, crudely fashioned from wire, bear the names of Bela and Irka. Other relics give names of victims or their hometowns and reveal their hobbies or passions. Hundreds of medicine bottles found in a single pit originated in Germany, Luxembourg, and Czechoslovakia. A charm bearing the image of a tombstone gives a family name and the burial location in a Jewish cemetery in what was once the German city of Breslau, now Wroclaw. Jozef Jakubowski carried a cigarette case he won in a 1936 edition of the "Gordon-Bennet" motorcycle race.

The most valuable artifacts, such as fragments of paper and items that can be tied to specific people or locations, are photographed immediately and sent to the Konin Museum for conservation. Because of the sheer number of objects found daily, archaeologists have to perform a sort of triage. Preliminary probes showed that one pit, for example, was full of metal cooking pots. The team decided not to excavate it.

Among the most wrenching finds for Nowak were the remains of a three-month-old baby buried on the palace grounds with a knife engraved with the words "Keep the Sabbath." Eyewitness testimonies revealed that a brothel operated inside the palace. Nowak suspects Jewish women were forced to work in it. "Somehow that child must have been kept alive," Nowak says.

Chelmno is considered holy ground by Jews, and as such is subject to Jewish laws and traditions. Jewish leaders have praised Nowak's scrupulous approach to her work. "The research at Chelmno is carried out with the absolute agreement and cooperation of the Jewish community," says Simcha Keller, head of the Jewish community in Lodz. "Dr. Nowak is a guarantor that the work is done with complete respect." Human remains found during the excavations are interred in a Jewish cemetery established in the forest. The burial ceremonies are attended by Jews from around the world.

The government agency that supervises wartime cemeteries and monuments in Poland also finances the excavations at Chelmno, which cost about $17,500 a year. The country faces a large budget deficit, however, and additional funds that would allow Nowak to realize her plans of opening a museum, visitors' center, and learning center on the palace grounds are in short supply. For now, some of the objects found at Chelmno are on display in an austere, one-room makeshift museum on the site. Articles from the Polish press and pictures from Chelmno before and during the war cover the walls. The building is not well secured and Nowak is afraid of displaying valuable items, so she has had duplicates made of some of them, such as the cigarette case from the motorcycle race. Other objects found at Chelmno are on permanent loan to Yad Vashem, the Holocaust memorial and museum in Jerusalem, and the British War Museum. Part of the crematory foundations were sent to the Holocaust Museum in Washington, D.C.

Nowak's efforts to piece together the history of Chelmno is only one element of a much larger mission: She wants young Poles to understand how generations of Jews contributed to the history and culture of the region. "I am an enemy of doing lectures focused solely on the Holocaust," she says.

In the forest near the main Chelmno memorial, Nowak has reconstructed a traditional Jewish cemetery from gravestones that once stood in the nearby town of Turek. Leveled by the Nazis in 1941, the cemetery was rediscovered by Nowak in 1990, after a vigilant factory worker informed her that stones "with strange writing on them" were being dug up on the grounds of a local dairy. Nowak learned Hebrew in order to read the stones and document the history of those buried there. For Nowak, the retelling of their lives and traditions is critical in ensuring that the Holocaust is not removed from the larger historical and cultural context.

"For young people in Poland, a Jew is an unknown quantity," she says. "They don't know about the contribution Jews made to Polish culture and history. If they understand that, then they will look at the Holocaust differently."

Proving Ground of the Nuclear Age

THE MANGLED ARTIFACTS AND LUNAR LANDSCAPE OF THE NEVADA TEST SITE ARE A VIVID TESTAMENT TO THE ADVENT OF ATOMIC WEAPONRY.

by WILLIAM GRAY JOHNSON *and* COLLEEN M. BECK

The desert flats of central Nevada offer and eerie landscape of twisted I-beams bent towers and deformed bridges, frame buildings ripped apart, and stretches of land scarred by craters—one so vast it rivals depressions of the moon. Welcome to the Nevada Test Site, 1,350 square miles of landscape indelibly marked by hundreds of atomic bomb experiments. Here, for some 40 years during the Cold War between the West and the former Soviet Union and its allies, scientists experimented with various forms of nuclear weaponry. Today, with moratoriums on both underground and aboveground testing, the test site is a silent wasteland, its devastation a legacy of that time.

We work for the Desert Research Institute (DRI), a branch of the University of Nevada system set up in 1959 to investigate arid land problems such as water availability and air quality. Since then our focus has broadened to include past environments and archaeology. Working for the U. S. Department of Energy (DOE), which owns the test site, and for state and private agencies in Nevada, we also regularly study Native American cultures as well as early settlements of miners and ranchers. The Native American ruins span some 10,000 years and include scatters of stone artifacts and pottery, occasionally associated with rock-shelters, caves, and rock outcrops decorated with petroglyphs and pictographs. Most of the mining and ranching occurred between 1905 and 1940, and claim markers and shafts can be seen in the hilly regions nearby, where springs, stone and wood cabins, outhouses, corrals, and fencing still remain.

We began recording these sites in 1978 in an effort to help the DOE comply with the National Historic Preservation Act of 1966, which directs federal agencies to inventory archaeological and historical property under their jurisdiction and to determine the effects of their activities—in the DOE's case the testing of nuclear weapons—on these properties. It soon became clear that what remained of the testing program itself was the most important component of the archeological record. Like most artifacts left unused on the landscape, the test site structures and associated debris have begun to disappear. Weathering, recycling of items, and the need to reuse areas of other activities are slowly stripping the landscape of its Cold War artifacts. In 1982 Nevada's State Historic Preservation Office acknowledged the years of testing as an important period in the state's history and recommended that specific artifacts be pre-

served as testaments to the nuclear bomb experiments spawned by the Cold War.

In 1988 we proposed to the DOE that we survey the area. The proposal was well received, and in 1991 we were asked to evaluate two structures, a 1,527-foot tower used in a study of radiation released from an unshielded reactor, and an underground parking garage tested for possible lateral and vertical displacement in a nuclear blast. We felt both were eligible for the National Register of Historic Places, the official list of the nation's cultural resources deemed worthy of preservation. Soon after we were asked to inventory all test site structures to determine their eligibility for the National Register. This program continues today. Surprisingly, many of the artifacts and even some of the structures we have researched are not recorded in any official documents. Instrumentation stands and temporary storage bunkers, for example, were important for the instruments they held of stored, but were not considered worth documenting.

Access to the Nevada Test Site is off of U.S. Highway 95 north from Las Vegas at Mercury, a complex of scientific laboratories and warehouses, a building that houses radiation monitoring equipment and staff, dormitory-style housing, a cafeteria, a post office, a fire station, a hospital, a bowling alley, and a chapel. This is where scientists and support staff lived and worked during the nuclear testing period, which began January 27, 1951, with an airdrop event code-named Able. Aboveground testing ended in 1963 with the Limited Test Ban Treaty, which prohibited atmospheric, underwater, and outer-space nuclear testing.

The current moratorium, which includes underground testing, took effect on October 2, 1992. It has been extended twice, most recently to October 1995. Scientists still work here, but their efforts are focused on tracking residual radiation in the environment and cleaning it up. Mercury is still closed to the casual tourist, and a gate is manned by guards 24 hours a day. The DOE began conducting public tours in the early 1980s in recognition of the need to to communicate the nature and extent of the testing program and in acknowledgement of the taxpayers' contributions to the program. Monthly tours continue to be available to individuals and groups.

Those who visit the site follow the Mercury Highway north. A sign indicates that cameras are not allowed in the forward areas. Another warns workers to be cautious of posted radiation areas. Driving through Checkpoint Pass, a guard station no longer used, one enters Frenchman Flat, a dry lakebed surrounded by rolling hills leading to distant mountains. Blown-out buildings and twisted metal litter the landscape. Fourteen aboveground nuclear devices were detonated here; Grable, Priscilla, and Met were the code names of three. The largest, Priscilla, left most of the wreckage. Bunkers, motels, and homes, grouped at different distances from ground zero, were subjected to a blast equivalent to 37,000 tons of TNT. A steel-reinforced, concrete-sided bank vault at the center of the blast survived pressures of 600 pounds per square inch. We have recommended that the entire area be considered a historic district.

Continuing north, the highway cuts through Yucca Pass and a collection of gray windowless buildings that once served as the Nevada Test Site's electronic Control Point. Nearby, a faded sign on a boulder-covered hill identifies the site of News Nob, "where on April 22, 1952, the American press and radio first covered, and the nation first viewed by the medium of television, the firing of a nuclear device known as 'Operation Big Shot.'" At the foot of the hill are 11 rows of weather-beaten benches where reporters and dignitaries observed multiple explosions, some as close as 14 miles away.

Yucca Flat, whose cratered surface resembles the surface of the moon, witnessed more aboveground and underground tests than Frenchman Flat. One huge crater, known as Sedan, measures 320 feet deep and 1,280 feet across, and is a regular stop on the DOE tours. It was created in the Plowshare Program, a project designed to find peaceful uses for nuclear bombs, such as large-scale excavation. (A redigging of the Panama Canal was under consideration at the time.) Sedan Crater was listed on the National Register last year, the first test site area to be so designated.

Yucca Flat bears the remains of two-story houses located 6,600 and 8,000 feet southeast from ground zero of a test code-named Apple II. They were part of "Survival Town," a 1955 Civil Defense exercise designed to study the durability of typical civilian buildings subjected to nuclear weapons. Test targets also included industrial buildings and shelters, electrical power systems, communications equipment, a radio broadcasting station, trailer homes, fire equipment, cars, and food supplies placed at varying distances from ground zero. The force of the blast was the equivalent of 29,000 tons of TNT. Only the two-story houses and the frames of a few ranch-style homes survived.

Yucca Flat was also the site of radiation experiments. Bare Reactor Experiment, Nevada, or BREN, was part of Operation Ichiban, a program intended to determine radiation exposures experienced by the survivors of the Hiroshima and Nagasaki bombings. In these tests an unshielded reactor was placed in an elevator that rode up and down a 1,527-foot tower. The reactor released radiation on a mock Japanese village whose frame houses contained dosimeters for measuring exposure. Raising or lowering the reactor enabled scientists to change the angle and range of the radiation. Ichiban data allowed scientists to determine relationships between radiation doses and health problems associated with radiation sickness. Though the tower was moved to another part of the Nevada Test Site in 1965, our research at the Japanese village and the relocated tower has determined that both are National Register candidates. Also eligible is an experimental dairy farm designed to study the effects of radioactive fallout on the fodder-cow-milk food chain. A number of small dairy farms were located downwind from the test site, and there was concern at the time that children drinking milk from these dairies might be affected by the fallout.

Farther north, Rainier Mesa rises 7,000 feet above sea level. Underground nuclear testing began here in 1957. Code-named Rainier, the first blast shook the mesa and surrounding areas with the force of 1,700 tons of TNT. Rainier Mesa and its neighbor,

Pahute Mesa, were the sites of numerous underground tests. Some nuclear devices were placed in long shafts, others in tunnels. We know of underground bunkers, similar to bomb shelters, and we have heard about structures shaped like submarines with periscoping elevators. What condition are they in today? We hope to find out. Elsewhere there are remarkable structures associated with nuclear rocket development. We believe they too are significant.

Is this archaeology? We think it is. Our instincts lead us to believe that these artifacts of the Cold War are historically important and need to be studied. Can anyone honestly call them nonarcheological? Scholars traditionally time-trek through millennia. Casually discussing similarities between the migrations of hunters and gatherers of 50,000 years ago and the peopling of the New World at the end of the last Ice Age some 10,000 years ago, they have grown accustomed to thinking in large blocks of time. It is the short blocks of time, especially our own, that we have difficulty understanding.

Diving at Ground Zero

THE SHIPS OF BIKINI ATOLL ARE A GRIM REMINDER OF THE ATOMIC AGE.

by James P. Delgado

In 1946 a fleet converged on Bikini Atoll in the South Pacific. Among the vessels were U.S. Navy ships like the battleship *Arkansas* and aircraft carrier *Saratoga*, declared surplus or obsolete after the war, as well as captured enemy ships such as the German cruiser *Prinz Eugen* and the Japanese battleship *Nagato*. (See page 8 of the photo insert.) The fleet was gathered for Operation Crossroads, in which the Navy hoped to show that its vessels could survive a nuclear attack; the results proved otherwise. Two bombs were detonated, one dropped on the fleet from a B-29 on July 1, the second exploded beneath it on July 25. Ships closest to the bombs were destroyed almost instantaneously. In the second test, a landing ship directly above the bomb was vaporized, and the nearby *Arkansas* sank less than one second after the blast. Of the 97 vessels, 22 were sunk outright. The 73 that remained afloat, such as the battleship *New York*, were hopelessly

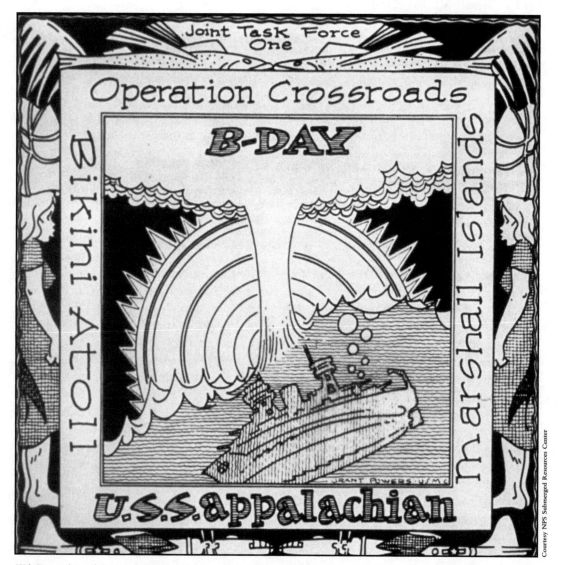

Walt Disney designed this cancellation stamp for use on mail aboard the USS Appalachian *which carried the press corps observing the 1946 atomic bomb tests at Bikini Atoll.*

irradiated. Many were later used for target practice and sunk in the Pacific. In 1989 and 1990, I participated in a survey of the vessels at Bikini undertaken by the National Park Service.

The ship that best reflects the destructive forces of the bomb is *Arkansas,* whose broken and crushed hulk lies in 180 feet of water on the bottom of Bikini lagoon, capsized and driven into the coral and sand. We made two dives on *Arkansas*. I was shocked by the inverted and broken wreck: It no longer resembles a ship. The stern was torn off, and I was astounded to find that the propeller shafts were either missing or twisted away from the hull, their 142-foot lengths yanked out of the hulk, leaving gaping holes.

More than 100 feet of superstructure and masts had towered above *Arkansas'* deck when she was afloat. Now that same deck, upside-down, rests only six to eight feet off the seabed. Swimming up from the bottom, I could see that the bomb had punched up into *Arkansas,* rolling it over to port and capsizing it. Then, millions of tons of falling silt and water had hammered it into the ocean floor, crushing and burying the superstructure and masts. The condition of the ship made it very clear that I was at ground zero, in the very maw of Armageddon.

The most famous of the ships nuked at Bikini was the aircraft carrier *Saratoga,* the focus of our work during the two years we dived on the atoll's fleet. With my colleagues, I spent hours swimming over the decks, into compartments, and down the cavernous hangar. In 1989, we made dozens of dives on *Saratoga.* A hundred feet beneath the surface, the flight deck is marked only by bits of wood adhering to the bolts that once fastened its wooden plank sheathing to the steel deck below. The flight deck, as well as the ship's stack, shows the worst bomb damage. It looked as though Godzilla had stomped the deck. When *Saratoga* rolled in the trough of the atomic bomb's tidal wave, the force of the tons of water and sand that fell out of the sky collapsed the flight deck, forming a large crease that is 70 feet wide,

200 feet long, and 20 feet deep, ending near the after end of the stack, a massive steel-plated structure that towered 80 feet above the flight deck. When it was hit by the wave, it split and fell to port across the flight deck.

Inside the bridge, many of the instruments used to navigate and conn the ship remained in place—binnacle, engine-room telegraphs and revolution indicators, chart tables, and a lighting panel on the aft bulkhead, its switches identified by black plastic labels that read "mast head" and "man overboard." Time stood still, and as I hovered over the helm, my hand rested on the simple handle that had steered *Saratoga*. It took little imagination to picture a late-night watch on the bridge, as the vessel hunted Japanese warships in the South Pacific.

The biggest thrill was swimming up to four airplanes that remain stowed, wings folded, in the carrier's hangar. The first three were navy dive-bombers—"Helldiver" single-engine aircraft, placed aboard the *Saratoga* in 1946, combat ready. Aft of the third plane, the compartment was blocked by a mound of debris where the flight deck above and wreckage from the stack had collapsed into the hangar. Beyond the shaft of elevator no. 2 we found the fourth plane, an "Avenger" torpedo-bomber. Just inside the hangar, on the starboard side, a rack of five 500-pound aerial bombs lie in the silt, next to a steel drum and a 350-pound depth bomb that rolled from port to rest against the fuses of the aerial bombs. In 1989, we all gingerly swam past the bombs. The following year I found 1946 photographs in the National Archives showing the same munitions with the word inert painted on them.

Bikini is a land of ghosts. A small stone monument records the tragic end of five Japanese weather observers who stayed on Bikini throughout the war. They commited suicide when American forces reached the island. But this small remnant of a time of war is not as haunting as the empty homes of the Bikinians. Promised that their atoll would be used for the betterment of mankind, they left in 1946 after an emotional goodbye to their ancestors. Most would never return, but in 1968 President Lyndon Johnson declared Bikini safe, and some came back. The U.S. government erected 40 prefabricated concrete houses on Bikini and planted 50,000 coconut trees. Studies in 1975, however, showed dangerous levels of contamination in the island's interior. Further studies revealed that those who had returned had ingested enormous amounts of radioactive material, and in August 1979 the island's 139 residents were again evacuated. A sad legacy remains: empty houses, concrete-lined wells that reach a plutonium-contaminated water supply, and regimented rows of radioactive coconut trees.

Courtesy NPS Submerged Resources Center

A column of water and mushroom cloud rise above a "ghost" fleet during the Baker test of Operation Crossroads.

Cold War Memories

A CRITICAL PERIOD IS COMMEMORATED IN A NEW NATIONAL HISTORIC SITE.

compiled by MARK ROSE

Some of you may share my memories of running home from school when the warning sirens sounded, of a friend or neighbor installing a bomb shelter in their back yard, of the yellow and black public fallout shelter signs posted on schools, banks, churches, and office buildings, or of the olive drab cans of crackers and drinking water stacked up in the shelters. Who can forget the pictures of missile-laden Soviet ships steaming toward Cuba, or the television newsreels of U.S. jets scrambling from their bases, darkening the air with trails of black kerosene soot during the Cuban Missile Crisis of October 1962?

—Mr. Tim J. Pavek, Minuteman II Deactivation Program Manager, Ellsworth AFB, statement before the House Subcommittee on National Parks and Public Lands, September 14, 1999

On November 29, 1999, President Clinton signed legislation creating the Minuteman Missile National Historic Site, preserving a bit of the Cold War for the benefit of future generations who did not live through it as did Mr. Pavek.

Each year tens of thousands of tourists drive along Interstate 90, heading west through South Dakota to see the state's natural wonders, national memorials, and historic sites—Badlands National Park, Mount Rushmore National Memorial, Custer State Park, the Black Hills National Forest, Wind Cave National Park, Jewel Cave National Monument, and Wounded Knee—and continue on to Yellowstone. For nearly three decades, beginning in 1963, those vacationing families drove through the 44th Missile Wing—150 Minuteman missiles buried in silos scattered across the landscape. These waving fields of grass constituted a war zone in the Cold War—and would have become ground zero if the Cold War turned hot. (See page 8 of the photo insert.)

Most of the tourists were probably unaware that the small fenced enclosures here and there marked hardened concrete missile silos or that some of the nondescript buildings away from the highway were above deeply buried capsules in which launch-control crews were on 24-hour alert. That has changed now that the National Park Service and U.S. Air Force have teamed up to add the Delta One Launch Control Facility and Delta Nine Launch Facility to the region's list of attractions. Located near the Badlands National Park, the two sites are the heart of the new Minuteman Missile National Historic Site.

The story of the Minuteman missile system and the creation of this new historic site is the story of the Cold War itself. The Soviet development of the Hydrogen bomb in 1953 and successful launch of Sputnik on an SS-6 missile in 1957 gave rise to fears the United States was falling behind. It was true that because they used volatile liquid fuel, the old Atlas and Titan missiles in the U.S. arsenal could only be fueled just before launching, a

Bill Supernaugh, Badlands National Park

Like the noses of WWII aircraft, the blast doors of ICBM facilities were painted, here in imitation of a pizza delivery box.

process that took hours. The U.S. Air Force rushed to develop a missile using stable solid fuel that could be launched at a moment's notice. The result, Minuteman, was successfully test launched at Cape Canaveral in February 1961.

Less than two years later, at the height of the Cuban Missile Crisis, President Kennedy received a bit of good news: The first ten of 150 Minuteman missiles being deployed at Malmstrom Air Force Base, Montana, had just been brought on alert. They were capable of hitting a target in the Soviet Union in 30 minutes or less (with re-entry speeds approaching 15,000 miles per hour), Kennedy later referred to the Minuteman as his "Ace in the Hole." Deployment of a second wing (150 missile silos and 15 launch control facilities) had already begun at Ellsworth Air Force Base, near Rapid City, South Dakota, and was completed the following year—crews working three shifts, seven days a week, to help meet the Soviet threat.

Ellsworth was second of six Minuteman wings. By 1967, there were 1,000 Minuteman missiles planted in silos across the upper Midwest. Each wing was divided into three squadrons (50 missiles each), which in turn were divided into five flights (ten missiles linked to a single launch control facility). Delta One and Delta Nine were part of the Delta Flight of the 66th Strategic Missile Squadron, which along with the 67th and 68th made up the 44th Strategic Missile Wing.

Over the years the Minuteman II and III were developed and deployed. Three air force bases, including Ellsworth along with Whiteman in Missouri and Grand Forks in North Dakota, received the Minuteman II but not the later version. After Mikhail Gorbachev, the Soviet head of state, and President Bush signed the Strategic Arms Reduction Treaty (START) in 1989, the 450 Minuteman II missiles at these bases were withdrawn from alert. START mandated that all Minuteman II missiles be eliminated by December 2001. Demolition at Whiteman was the first to be completed, and the 150 silos at Grand Forks were destroyed over the next two years. As for Ellsworth, the first missile was removed from its silo in December 1991, and on July 4, 1994, the 44th Missile Wing was deactivated; except for Delta One and Delta Nine, the facilities have all been destroyed.

In 1993, the U.S. Air Force and National Park Service had recognized the importance of preserving a Minuteman II launch control facility and launch facility at Ellsworth in 1993 because they were closest to the original Minuteman installations. A feasibility study concluded in 1995 that Delta One and Delta Nine, near Interstate 90 and the Badlands National Park, were suitable for inclusion in the National Park system. Since 1993 the Department of Defense Legacy Program had provided funds to preserve the two sites, and Ellsworth Air Force Base and Badlands National Park developed a plan for day-to-day maintenance as well as long-term preservation and protection of them.

Delta One is situated on 6-plus grassy acres enclosed by a security fence 0.5 miles north of I-90 at Exit 127. It consists of an aboveground building and heated garage for patrol vehicles along with an underground launch control center. The main surface structure contained a kitchen, sleeping quarters, and security systems for monitoring the ten launch facilities linked to Delta One. An example of the first version of launch control facility, Delta One had life support equipment in the aboveground building (in later versions they were contained in a buried equipment room alongside the LCC). Buried 31 feet deep, the launch control center at Delta One was connected to the surface by an elevator. It consisted of an outer, protective shell (29 feet in diameter and 54 feet long, with four-foot-thick reinforced concrete walls lined with 1/4-inch thick steel plate) in which, suspended on pneumatic shock absorbers, was a 12-by-28-foot boxlike room with the two launch control consoles and communications equipment. The launch control center (commonly called a capsule) was occupied 24 hours a day by two officers, who, if called upon, would launch the missiles. Each morning a new two-officer crew came out from Ellsworth to relieve those coming off duty; aboveground, on three-day shifts, were two security officers and two two-person armed response teams as well as a cook and a facility manager.

The most prominent feature of the unmanned Delta Nine Launch Facility, about 1.6 acres just southwest of I-90 at Exit 116, is the silo itself: 12 feet in diameter and 80 feet deep, made of reinforced concrete with a 1/4-inch steel-plate liner. The massive, hexagonal door over the silo (made of 3.5-foot-thick reinforced concrete) weighs in at more than 80 tons. This door has now been welded half-way open and given a transparent roof that protects the silo and its deactivated Minuteman Missile while letting visitors peer into its depths. The glass enclosure also allows for Russian satellite verification that the silo is non-operational, in compliance with START. At later launch facilities the power-supply structures were buried deeply, but Delta Nine retains the original configuration, set into the ground but not entirely buried.

Bill Supernaugh, Superintendent of Badlands National Park, outlined how the new historic site would be set up. A visitor center at Exit 131 on I-90 could present a broad perspective of the Cold War and the Minuteman system. Guided tours would depart from the visitor center to the Delta One Launch Control Facility at Exit 127, about four miles away. After returning, visitors could drive through the Badlands to Exit 110 then proceed to Exit 116 (about six miles) for a self-guided tour of the Delta Nine Launch Facility. For those who want more, the Ellsworth Air and Space Museum, farther west on I-90 (just outside Rapid City) has a Minuteman displayed above ground as well as a launch-control training module.

The new National Historic Site goes beyond simply archiving a sample of Cold War structures. For example, oral histories of the missileers who worked at Ellsworth Air Force Base had already been recorded. "It is the story of the people of South Dakota and other states who lived alongside military installations," says Pavek, one of those interviewed and recorded. "It is the story of a local rancher who tells of working through the bitter winter, helping mine 80-feet deep holes that would become missile silos—of a missile maintenance team battling a fierce winter blizzard to bring a missile back on alert—of a rancher who helped out an air force alert crew stranded on the backroads of the missile field—or of the elderly lady who owned the land surrounding a missile site and told us we wouldn't have to blow up her missile site, she wouldn't tell anyone, since we might need it again some day."

The new Minuteman Missile National Historic Site currently operates out of a Project Office located at Cactus Flat (Exit 131 on I-90). The National Park Service has begun offering limited daily tours of the facilities on a space available basis. Planning continues on development of the site's General Management Plan and final decision on the visitor center location. Newly appointed Minuteman Superintendent Mark Herberger anticipates the site will be fully operational, offering an expanded suite of visitor activities and experiences, in five to seven years.

For a schedule of tours or additional site information contact Minuteman Missile National Historic Site at 605-433-5552 or log onto the web site at www.nps.gov/mimi

PART VI:

Archaeology and War

Battles over Battlefields

THE FIGHT TO SAVE CIVIL WAR SITES FROM DEVELOPERS

by STEVE NASH

Hidden in a tumble of downed trees and vines on the crest of a ridge, a Confederate brigade waits. Below, the 21st Massachusetts advances through unfamiliar territory, unaware they are climbing into an ambush. As they near, the Confederates loose a terrifying volley, much of it from less than thirty feet away. They are then stunned by the speed and intensity of the return fire. But the natural advantage of the terrain allows them to stand their ground and eventually drive the federals back.

Henry Brown, a nineteen-year-old private with the 21st, later wrote of the Battle of Ox Hill, of which this was a part, in a letter home: "It was a scene I shall never forget. It was wholesale murder to stand at the muzzle of the enemy's guns and have a volley poured into us. I had a very narrow escape of my life." (A Confederate shot, likely a Minié ball, had passed through his collar.) At nearby Fairfax Station,

Clara Barton was tending Union wounded. In her journal she wrote: "Of a sudden, air and earth and all about us shook with one mingled crash of God's and man's artillery. The lightning played and the thunder rolled incessantly and the cannon roared louder and nearer each minute...with what desperation our men fought hour after hour in the rain and darkness!"

Almost nothing within the three hundred acres of the Battle of Ox Hill was preserved during the development boom that began there in the late 1980s, despite the efforts of people like amateur archaeologist Mario Espinola, who over the past quarter century has researched the battle, documented the obliteration of the site, and protested the development. Today, traffic is always heavy on West Ox Road, one of dozens of feeder routes for the endless northern Virginia urbzone, part of a familiar lattice of asphalt and strip malls. The sound of passing cars penetrates a few acres of forgotten pinewoods where the ridgeline battle took place on September 1, 1862. Recently, where the woods meet the road, there was a sign bearing notice of a public hearing to develop this last remaining parcel of battlefield. "I was wondering when that was going to happen," Espinola said. "There is no doubt that the Ox Hill battlefield was hallowed ground and should have never been developed." The next round of chain saws and bulldozers in this patch of woods is just the last chapter in an old story. In fact, it's also becoming an old story at many Civil War battlefields that are not already protected as state or federal parks.

FRANK McMANAMON, the National Park Service's chief archaeologist, has watched the progress of this disappearing act during his twenty-five-year career with the Interior Department. "The resource is finite. It's being used up," he says. "Unless there is some sort of preservation scheme for the landscapes and the sites embedded in them, they will be lost."

There is no national policy on Civil War battlefield preservation. Instead, there's a helter-skelter, high-stakes, and often high-volume debate among local and national interests: landowners, developers, Civil War reenactors, relic hunters, history buffs, highway lobbyists, tourism promoters, preservationists, the Sons of Union Veterans, and United Daughters of the Confederacy, to cite a few of the players. In deceptively simple terms, they are debating these questions: How much land do you save, and how much are you willing to spend to save it?

In its 1993 report, a Congressional commission cataloged 10,500 Civil War battle and skirmish sites, tagging 384 of them as "principal battlefields." It concluded: "This nation's Civil War heritage is in grave danger...more than one third of all principal Civil War battlefields are either lost or are hanging onto existence by the slenderest of threads...within ten years we may lose fully two thirds of the principal battlefields." Those ten years have passed. Instead of the $90 million that the commission recommended be spent for land acquisitions during that period, only some $20 million was appropriated and spent. (Congress allocated an additional $2 million in federal funds for battlefield acquisitions during 2004.) How much has been lost since 1993 won't be clear until a new study by the National Park Service is completed in a couple of years, but tens of thousands of acres is a safe estimate.

Would too much land be sequestered if more battlefields were protected? The non-profit Civil War Preservation Trust (CWPT) estimates that it will be lucky if 10 percent of the country's 249 most important unprotected battlefields, roughly 28,000 acres, can be preserved during the coming decade. Whether that looks like a bid to save everything and lock it up forever, as critics sometimes claim, depends on your point of view. Doing even this much, however, would require about $50 million from Congress, and an equal amount from state, local, and private sources. (For comparison, the total is about the same amount of money it took to produce the Hollywood Civil War epic Cold Mountain.) Meanwhile, the level of support from the Bush administration has been hard to assess. It has asked Congress for $5 million in matching funds during the 2005 fiscal year to buy Civil War battlefield sites, but critics say it hasn't done enough to support National Park Service efforts to take care of battlefields already under federal government control (see "Park Service Retirees Protest Cuts," opposite page).

Preservation advocates often point out that tourism dollars make big economic ripples, justifying more acquisitions. A recent analysis sponsored by the CWPT looked at a handful of both lesser-known and nationally known battlefield parks. At Kentucky's Mill Springs, 4,300 annual battle-site visitors support four full-time jobs, generate $83,000 in

other local income, and yield $25,000 in local and state tax revenues. At the other end of the scale, there's Gettysburg National Military Park: 1.6 million visitors, 2,653 full-time jobs, $52.2 million in local income, and $17 million in local and state tax revenues. Whether this outranks the potential income from roads, houses, office parks, or strip-mining that Civil War battlefields might also be used for is another matter, since each local economy and each site is unique. The unquantifiable part of the equation is: What price tag do you hang on your own national heritage?

BACKCOUNTRY LOUISIANA—brush fields, oaks shrouded in kudzu vine, and small, lone houses under tin roofs—laps at the edges of the sleepy hamlet of Mansfield, scene of the northernmost battle of the Union army and navy's Red River campaign in April 1864, and arguably the last major Confederate victory in the war. The federals brought 40,000 men up the river in ninety boats to try to take Shreveport. But the vessels were nearly stranded in low water, the Union troops were routed, and the campaign, says local historian Gary Joiner, was "a pretty dismal thing, primarily because the Union General Nathaniel Banks was inept. On his best day, he was inept."

At Mansfield and other sites, new technology is part of the preservationist's tool kit. Joiner is also a geographer and has worked at several Civil War sites using geographic information system (GIS) maps. These are visual displays of multiple layers of data on, for example, battle lines, archaeological finds, creeks, and fences or houses

Courtesy Steve Nash

Historian Gary Joiner observes coal-mining that threatens an 1864 Civil War battlefield at Mansfield, Louisiana.

from the Civil War period. Those layers are overlain by others, showing contemporary data on property ownerships, existing buildings, and parcels that might be available for purchase. The resulting picture often clarifies priorities: what's important historically, where there are likely to be undisturbed archaeological deposits, what's available for protection, and who owns it. The nonprofit Conservation Fund, which describes itself as a group that "creates public and private partnerships to demonstrate sustainable conservation solutions," is using the same techniques to capture local data on dozens of threatened battle sites across the Southeast. In the past couple of years it has completed forty-nine GIS-based "rapid assessments" of Civil War battlefields.

At the Battle of Mansfield, the most significant events took place on something like 1,500 acres of ground, and much of the battlefield looks today as it did then. But that's changing quickly. Only about 180 acres are protected, as a state commemorative area, and underlying the battlefield is a broad seam of lignite coal. Two enormous coal shovels have already strip-mined thousands of acres, operating with a kind of ponderous preci-

sion, hollowing out the land to a depth of about twenty feet, and producing three million tons of lignite each year to feed a power plant whose stacks are visible to the south.

The Southwestern Electric Power Company, a subsidiary of American Electric Power of Columbus, Ohio, says its mining at Mansfield is "practiced responsibly, in accordance with the wishes of those who own the property and in compliance with all federal and state laws." It argues that its strip mine helps keep down the cost of electric power in the region and provides employment for 173 people earning an annual payroll of $10 million. "Nobody working on this issue wants to harm jobs or the power plant," counters Joiner, who identifies himself as a conservative, probusiness Republican. "They've got thousands and thousands of acres of a good coal seam. All we're saying is, leave what is historically important."

Joiner and the group he organized last year, the three-hundred-strong Friends of Mansfield Battlefield—mostly locals, but now there are some business and organizational members throughout the United States and even in Europe—are challenging the mine before state and federal authorities, and courting landowners. "History, to a lot of folks, is important until the dollar sign gets in the way," he observes. "But there comes a time when you have to have a social conscience. At some point we have to figure out, as a culture, that everything does not belong in a big box—Wal-Mart or Home Depot. This is not a Confederate thing, it's not a Union thing, it's an American thing. If we don't protect this land, who's going to? Who will be the guardians of American history if the American people don't do it? It's going to have to be protected from guys in three-piece suits in boardrooms, making decisions about what they consider to be important and unimportant on a local, regional, and national scale."

AT TIMES THE National Park Service has done an outstanding job of protecting battlefields, or portions of them, already within its domain. Today, that includes sixteen designated as National Historic Landmarks and another fifty-eight in national parks. But the federal role in enlarging protected areas, limited always by available funds, also depends heavily on local sentiment.

The government is loath to involve itself where local support is lacking. For example, one of the great success stories in Civil War battlefield preservation is occurring now with the creation of the Moccasin Bend National Archaeological District along the Tennessee River. It will be added to the 9,000-acre Chickamauga and Chattanooga National Military Park, the scene of an epic contest in 1863 involving more than 100,000 troops, when the Confederates attempted, in vain, to stop the Union advance on Chattanooga, a major rail and supply center. Chattanooga archaeologist Lawrence Alexander notes that the Park Service—constrained by limited budgets and other priorities—initially opposed the idea. Pressure channeled through an enthusiastic and well-connected local Republican congressman, Zach Wamp, who serves on the House Appropriations Committee, forced its hand.

The same armies clashed a hundred miles north, at Murfreesboro, Tennessee, but there the preservation story line turns upside down. At Stone's River National Battlefield, local pressure has led to development of land that the Park Service had earmarked as crucial to understanding the December 31, 1862–January 2, 1863 battle, which involved 80,000 troops and resulted in 24,000 casualties. A lone victory during a bleak time for the Union military, it was a turning point Lincoln was able to capitalize on to maintain support for the war. The current park includes 700 acres—less than 20 percent of the battlefield. "The proposed development land is where most of the Confederate units were positioned during the battle of Stone's River," wrote a preservation-minded citizen to the Nashville Tennessean of one project. "Can you imagine this taking place next door to the Gettysburg National Battlefield, or the Saint Laurent Cemetery in Normandy, France?"

Jim Ogden, the historian at Chickamauga and Chattanooga National Military Park, has worked on many archaeological digs in the region and visits Stone's River a couple of times a year. "Every time I go, another portion of the battlefield has disappeared to some development," he says. "The [local] government there is even working to build a big medical campus on a portion of the historic battlefield as we speak. The bulldozers are pushing the dirt." House sites, fence lines, and property lines that might have helped refine our understanding of that battle are disappearing, Ogden says. Speaking personally, he poses a question: "Has the National Park Service been proactive enough to be ahead of these threats? My answer to that is no."

Park Service Retirees Protest Cuts

This past spring, a coalition of more than 250 retired career employees of the National Park Service released a report, based on their analysis of conditions at a representative sample of sites, charging that federal cutbacks are imperiling national battlefield parks as well as natural parks, despite official statements to the contrary.

The coalition includes several dozen former Park Service directors, deputy directors, regional directors, division chiefs, park superintendents, and assistant superintendents. For Gettysburg, they cite a 75 percent reduction in operating funds to hire seasonal employees and the deferring of maintenance and protection for historic structures and objects such as deteriorating cannons. And, the report charges, "the irreplaceable archival collection is now in serious jeopardy, with inadequate funds and staff to properly care for it."

In the face of advancing decay at Fredericksburg and Spotsylvania National Military Park, funds for historic masonry repair have been cut 40 percent. The park has half a million visitors a year, but the seasonal workforce paid from operating funds has declined from seventeen to two, visitor center hours are being reduced by 20 percent, and interpretive programs have declined by a third.

Elaine Sevy, a Park Service spokesperson, defends the administration, saying that National Park Service budgets have gone up every year since 2000, and maintenance budgets in particular have gone up 60 percent during that period. While conceding that there is a longstanding maintenance backlog, she also says, "We do live in a post-9/11 world. We are in a wartime situation right now, and budgets are tight throughout the federal government." But coalition spokesman Bill Wade calls that "regurgitating the party line." A thirty-year National Park Service veteran when he retired recently as a park superintendent, Wade claims that the National Park Service's own figures show that 85 percent of park sites are operating with less money this year than last.

by Steve Nash

Archaeology can supply data that are often missing from war records, newspaper stories, and personal accounts, even where these historical records about a particular battle are plentiful. But advances in archaeological techniques in recent years can't be used on sites that are sold off and paved before they're reconnoitered, notes Park Service archaeologist David Orr, who is also on the faculty at Temple University. For example: Working with Orr, Park Service archaeologists Doug Campana and Julie Steele and geophysicist Bruce Bevan measured electrical resistance and magnetism in the soils around Fort Morton at the Petersburg, Virginia, battlefield. The team also employed ground-penetrating radar. In a field, they located the fort itself, the "bombproof" shelters within the fort, battle trenches, a well full of iron artifacts, and a house near the outer fortifications. "It's a very important fort in the siege of Petersburg," he says. "We found it in only three or four days."

Such archaeological discoveries can only be made if the site is preserved, which is where the Park Service's American Battlefield Protection Program (ABPP) comes in. ABPP provides seed money as well as organizational and research expertise for local groups that have organized themselves to try to protect battle sites of all eras, not just the Civil War. It has a staff of just four, and half a million dollars a year for grants. That amount covered only about a third of the eligible requests for help last year.

The program politely excuses itself from the role of outside agitator in local fights over battle sites. Its job is to find ways to preserve them without having to spend federal money buying them. "The good news is that something is available to citizens to take advantage of," says Frank McManamon, the top federal archaeologist. But while the government provides some tools and modest funding, local initiative, he points out, is pivotal. And that's one of the lessons suggested by these fights over Civil War landscapes: Despite some federal help and the work of private, state, and national groups such as the CWPT, a grass-roots effort is indispensable for many preservation projects, especially in their initial stages.

The second point—the one archaeology can make most strongly—is that this enterprise is more than just a hobby for history buffs or a narrow academic quest. The details that come out of the ground are, advocates say, one of the few ways future generations can hope to come to grips with the meaning of a war on our own land, among our own citizens, that cost 620,000 lives.

When Kristen Stevens, staff archaeologist for the ABPP, worked at the Gettysburg National Military Park a few years ago, some human remains were discovered along a railroad cut. Public interest was exceptionally strong. "People were hounding us," she says. "They were riveted, trying to figure out whose family that soldier might have

belonged to, which side he might have represented. It's a compelling thing. I think it's just a matter of wanting to identify. You want to really understand that person's story." But the analysis was tenuous. "We based most of our observations on the slimmest of evidence, just the shadows of what was on the human remains and the bones—an undershirt button and the heel of a shoe," recalls Stevens. "To me, it really heightened the importance of every scrap of evidence. Every Minié ball counts."

Who Owns the Spoils of War?

AS GERMANY AND RUSSIA SPAR OVER THE RETURN OF WARTIME BOOTY, HISTORIANS AND LEGAL SCHOLARS TAKE A FRESH LOOK AT WHAT REALLY HAPPENED 50 YEARS AGO.

by KARL E. MEYER

What Byron called the "fatal gift of beauty" is again sowing international discord, as it has since the Trojans abducted Helen. The latest dispute concerns a dazzling collection of Old Master and Impressionist paintings, recently exhibited for the first time in half a century in Moscow and St. Petersburg. It also concerns a royal ransom in the decorative arts; several million books, including two or perhaps three Gutenberg Bibles; whole storerooms of manuscripts and archival records; and the celebrated Treasure of Priam, the Bronze Age artifacts unearthed at Troy in 1873 by Heinrich Schliemann, a symbol and metaphor of the entire dispute.

Germany claims ownership of most of these prizes, all of which were removed by Russian forces in 1945. At first glance the German case seems airtight. The Soviet Union and Germany agreed in 1990 to exchange all works uprooted from either country during World War II, an agreement confirmed two years later by President Boris Yeltsin of the new Russian Federation. A joint commission was established to compile lists of missing works and to preside over exchanges. But it soon became apparent that under such an agreement far more art would flow from Russia back to Germany than vice versa.

Hesitantly at first, then more boldly, the Russian government took up the refrain of militant nationalists and museum directors such as Irina Antonova of the Pushkin State Museum of Fine Arts in Moscow, whose vaults had hidden the Trojan treasure since 1945. Do not give back a thing, they argued, noting that Russia was still owed reparations for 20 million war dead and 400 looted museums. That Russia had approved a repatriation agreement with Germany, not to mention successive Hague conventions that bar use of cultural treasures as reparations, went unmentioned.

Hence the buzz of anticipation in New York early in 1995 when a dozen Russians turned up at a conference on "The Spoils of War." The three-day event, sponsored by the Bard Graduate Center for Studies in the Decorative Arts, was literally an eye-opener. Delegates from Germany, France, Poland, Hungary, and elsewhere gaped at Russian slides of long-missing Old Master paintings, prints, and drawings seized by Soviet forces. And for the first time at a public forum, Russian cultural officials developed their case for keeping everything. Mark M. Boguslavky of the Institute of State and Law

of the Russian Academy of Science, a legal adviser to the Russian Ministry of Culture, claimed that all art removed from Soviet soil during World War II was taken illegally. "On that we all agree," he said, but as for the art removed from Germany by the Red Army, "we cannot agree it was illegal." He reasoned that with Hitler's defeat there was no German state, and since the Soviet Union was the legitimate governing authority in its occupation zone, it had every right to remove cultural property. Besides, in vaguely defined wartime declarations the Allies had accepted the idea of "restitution in kind," and Russia was merely applying that principle to Germany. It had indeed pledged to return what had been illegally removed from Germany, but, since everything was legally removed, Russia was not obliged to return anything.

This demarche was reminiscent of earlier times when Soviet diplomacy consisted of a thump on the table and a tirade in *Pravda*. What was different at the Bard conference, the Cold War being over, was the absence of unanimity among the Russian delegates. Not only did they differ with each other on the need for compromise and an end to secrecy, they differed openly and passionately. Resistance among younger scholars to official orthodoxy was borne home by the presence of Konstantin Akinsha, an art historian and journalist, and Grigorii Kozlov, a former inspector for Russia's Department of Museums and former curator of the Museum of Private Collections affiliated with the Pushkin Museum. Akinsha and Kozlov were the first to disclose, in a 1991 *ARTnews* article, that the Schliemann treasure, along with countless other works missing from German and European collections, had been hidden for decades in Soviet "special depositories." Their report encouraged similar exposés by other young researchers, notably Alexei Rastorgouev, an art historian at Moscow University, whose specialty is the "displaced" art of World War II. Thanks to their combined work, which appeared in Russian and international art journals, it is possible for the first time to piece together what really happened 50 years ago.

Russian passions concerning captured German artworks cannot be understood without recalling the rape of European cultural treasures during the Third Reich. A failed artist himself, Hitler dreamed of building a vast art museum in Linz, near his Austrian birthplace. He recruited a Dresden museum director, Hans Posse, to gather a collection by whatever means necessary and ordered the Wehrmacht to assist a special trophy unit commanded by Nazi ideologist Alfred Rosenberg. Posse and Rosenberg competed for spoils with the sybaritic Hermann Goering, with Himmler's SS, and with thousands of officers billeted in foreign castles and estates.

In France and the Low Countries, art was harvested by seizing works from Jewish collections and state museums, or by forced sales, such as the "purchase" of superb Old Master drawings from Dutch collector Franz Koenigs. In the East, Polish museums were stripped and royal palaces destroyed. Slavs were deemed Untermenschen, their history worthless. In his first tour of the Royal Palace in Warsaw, Governor-General Hans Frank set the example by tearing silver eagles from the canopy covering the royal throne and pocketing them.

Poland's fate foreshadowed the devastation of the Soviet Union. Within weeks of Hitler's blitzkrieg on June 1941, German forces occupied czarist palaces on the outskirts of Leningrad. At the palace of Catherine the Great at Tsarskoye Selo, they dismantled the Amber Room, a great chamber whose walls were lined with precious amber, which had been given to Peter the Great by Frederick-William II of Prussia. The walls of the room were taken to Koenigsberg in East Prussia, where they disappeared, removed and hidden by the Germans or unknowingly destroyed in the Russian assault on the city. German depredations of a three-year period are graphically described in Lynn Nicholas' account of World War II plunder, *The Rape of Europa:* "They took anything they could pry loose from the myriad palaces and pavilions around Leningrad, right down to the parquet floors. They opened packed crates and helped themselves to the contents. Mirrors were smashed or machine-gunned, brocades and silks ripped from the walls. At Peterhof...the gilded bronze statues of Neptune and Samson upon which the waters played were hauled off to the smelting furnace in full view of the distraught townspeople." Not since the Goths and Vandals had Europe witnessed so spiteful an assault on other people's cultural treasures. The ancient cathedral at Novgorod was ravaged, Pushkin's house ransacked, Tolstoy's manuscripts burned, and elsewhere museums, churches, libraries, universities, and scientific institutes were robbed and destroyed. Most of the Nazi plunder has never been recovered.

Small wonder that, as the battlefront shifted toward Germany, Soviet retribution was swift and all encompassing. In November 1943 an edict of an Emergency State Committee authorized the removal of state and private libraries and art collections to Russia. A Trophy Commission was formed to comb castles, bunkers, salt mines, and caves in which Germans had hidden their own treasures as well as looted foreign art. In Dresden the Russians removed everything portable, including the jeweled contents of the famous Green Vault in the royal castle and more than 500 drawings from the Koenigs collection, which Hitler's agents had brought from Holland. By then a new vision had taken hold in Moscow—the postwar creation of a great Museum of World Art to be filled with works seized as compensation for Nazi vandalism. In January 1945 Stalin signed a directive authorizing massive removal of cultural property of all kinds, ostensibly for the supermuseum.

Four months later the trophy unit arrived in Berlin, where it seized the Pergamon Altar, with its celebrated Hellenistic frieze depicting the battle of the gods and giants, originally acquired by Germany in Turkish Asia Minor. From a bombproof bunker near the Berlin Zoo, it confiscated cases of Trojan gold that Schliemann had found at Hisarlik and presented to his native Germany in 1881. Romantically if erroneously dubbed by its finder the Treasure of Priam, the collection consists of hundreds of gold and silver objects, including a gold-beaded headdress once proudly modeled by

Schliemann's young Greek wife, Sophia. The cases were flown to the Pushkin Museum, where a receipt was signed by 28-year-old curator Irina Antonova, a tiny woman with blazing eyes who had grown up in Berlin, where her father had been a Soviet trade official. Antonova has survived six Soviet leadership upheavals and the collapse of communism, and still reigns as Pushkin director and guardian of wartime spoils.

Soviet soldiers needed little encouragement in following the Trophy Commission's lead. General Vassily Chuikoff, having settled in the estate of Otto Krebs outside Weimar, saw to it that 98 Impressionist paintings in the Krebs collection were removed to Leningrad, where they were hidden until this year. Other commanders filled railroad cars with the contents of Prussian estates. At Schloss Karnzow, Lieutenant Victor Baldin came upon soldiers in the cellar shuffling through hundreds of Old Master drawings, placed there for safekeeping by curators of the Bremen Kunsthalle. Baldin crammed into his suitcase 364 drawings, including a Dürer that he acquired in a swap for a pair of boots. Baldin, an art historian, preserved the drawings, and years later tried vainly to have them returned to Bremen.

By all these routes, a flood of art reached Russia. Soviet plans for a supermuseum, however, were stalled in good part by the long-forgotten work of a handful of soldiers in the West known as "monuments men." That archaeologists, with an interest in ruins and their preservation, might play a useful military role was not at first obvious to the British War Office. Italy unwittingly caused a change of mind in 1941 when it accused

British troops of vandalizing the classical ruins of Leptis Magna, Cyrene, and Sabratha in Libya. Lt. Colonel Mortimer Wheeler, the breezily self-assured excavator of Mohenjo-daro, who happened to be serving in North Africa, was given the job of safeguarding the sites, which he did with éclat. Wheeler was supported in London by Sir Leonard Woolley, excavator of Ur, who headed the army's Archaeological Adviser's office (consisting of Sir Leonard, Lady Woolley, and a clerk).

When the United States entered the war, influential scholars soon began lobbying for a more ambitious American counterpart to Woolley's office. William Dinsmoor, then president of the Archaeological Institute of America, was among those who met with, and apparently convinced, Chief Justice Harlan Fiske Stone, an ex-officio trustee of the newly formed National Gallery of Art, that an art and monuments unit be formed. Stone sent his recommendations to the White House on December 8, 1942. What probably tipped the scales in favor of the recommendation was Roosevelt and Churchill's decision in January 1943 to invade Sicily, with its vulnerable Greek and Roman ruins and its famous Byzantine churches.

Months later in Sicily, Captain Mason Hammond, a Harvard classics professor acting as art adviser to the Supreme Allied Commander, appropriated a battered vehicle, organized rescue groups, posted off-limits signs, and courted the annoyance of generals. Hammond was the first of several score monuments officers, men and women, most of them scholars and museum curators, who accompanied Allied armies through Italy, France, and Germany. There was little

they could do about wartime devastation: Monte Cassino was destroyed; Pompeii was bombed, as was a church in Padua with frescoes by Mantegna. There were devastating aerial assaults on Dresden, Nürnberg, and other old German cities. Nor could they be held responsible for thousands of soldiers who pocketed spoils of war. In one memorable heist, a U.S. Army artillery officer from Texas, Lieutenant Joe Tom Meador, "liberated" the cathedral treasures of Quedlinburg in the Harz Mountains of north-central Germany. He mailed home rock-crystal reliquaries, a jewel-encrusted silver casket, and the priceless *Samuhel Gospels,* written in gold ink and bound in a jeweled cover, part of a treasure associated with Henry I of Saxony, who is sometimes described as the founder of Germany. After Meador's death in 1980, his heirs tried to sell his booty, which to their astonishment was appraised at tens of millions of dollars. An enterprising *New York Times* reporter, William H. Honan, picked up rumors of the attempted sale, identified Meador, and helped bring about the repatriation of the Quedlinburg treasures, with the lubrication of a $3.75 million "finder's fee" to the heirs from the German Cultural Foundation.

The monuments officers were far more successful protecting the quantities of German art and Nazi booty hidden in castles, caves and mines. At war's end they learned that senior American officials, abetted by covetous museum directors, had proposed sequestering German art as war reparations. The idea was opposed by General Lucius Clay, commander of U.S. forces in Germany, who favored the swiftest possible return of all booty to its rightful owners, though he did suggest that some German masterpieces might be exhibited temporarily in America.

To monuments officers, even that was all too reminiscent of the Nazi policy of "temporary" removals, purportedly to "protect" other people's art. They drew up what became known as the Wiesbaden Manifesto, which soberly warned, "no historical grievance will rankle so long, or be the cause of so much justified bitterness, as the removal, for any reason, of a part of the heritage of any nation, even if that heritage may be interpreted as a prize of war." Signed in November 1945 by 25 officers and supported by five others not present, the manifesto came to the attention of Janet Flanner, whose account in *The New Yorker* was immediately cited by officials opposing any use of art as reparations.

President Truman rejected the reparation idea but did approve an exhibition of 202 masterpieces from Berlin museums. The National Gallery's first blockbuster show, it drew a million visitors in 1948, then traveled to New York and St. Louis. By then Europe was dividing into East and West, and General Clay was mounting an airlift to encircled West Berlin. Returned in 1955, the Berlin paintings were placed in the new Dahlem Museum in what was then the American sector, and there they remain today. Meanwhile, thanks to the monuments officers, some 500,000 cultural items looted by Nazis in Slavic countries and found in western Germany were repatriated, an unreciprocated restitution that is invariably ignored in Russian reckoning.

All this had its effect on Moscow. Nothing more was said about establishing a Museum of World Art, with its embarrassing resemblance to Hitler's plans for Linz. In 1945, Soviet prosecutors at Nürnberg agreed with Western victors in defining the plunder of art as a war crime. The Soviet Foreign Minister, Vyacheslav Molotov, even joined with Britain in censuring America's temporary removal of German art. But what truly complicated Soviet cultural diplomacy was the division of Germany and the emergence of a comradely ally, the German Democratic Republic. In 1958, as a goodwill gesture and to buttress the legitimacy of the new East German regime, Nikita Khrushchev returned the Pergamon Altar to its old home in East Berlin and gave back to Dresden most of its Old Masters and the bejeweled objets d'art from the Green Vault. This wise and realistic gesture was opposed by museum officials such as Irina Antonova, who at the Bard conference in New York was still deploring a decision "dictated by politics." Curators come to believe they own what is in their care. Commenting on the fate of Priam's Treasure in an interview in ARCHAEOLOGY (November/December 1993), Valery Kulishov, a member of the Russian State Commission on Restitution, noted: "You must understand the feelings of the Pushkin Museum officials. If you have it, it's part of you. Psychologically, you're so much attached and bound to what you had, even secretly, in your repository. It's very hard now to give it back, regardless of any kind of agreements."

Trophy art, however, is not exhibited or cataloged. Anybody with access to storerooms can steal and sell it. Leakage has been considerable. Of 562 drawings in the Dutch

Limits of World Law

Two remarkable people helped write the laws meant to bar warring nations from destroying or looting each other's cultural treasures. One was the German-American soldier and philosopher, Francis Lieber, author of a military code promulgated by Lincoln during the Civil War. The other was Nicholas Roerich, a Russian painter and mystic, who in 1935 persuaded the United States and 20 other countries to approve a treaty asserting the inherent neutrality of works of art in wartime.

The belief that cultural treasures need special treatment was expressed as early as 1758 by Emheric de Vattel, a legal scholar during the Enlightenment, whose treatise The Law of Nations spoke to the future: "For whatever cause a country is ravaged, we ought to spare those edifices which do honor to human society, and do not contribute to increase the enemy's strength—such as temples, tombs, public buildings and all works of remarkable beauty. . . . It is declaring one's self to be an enemy of mankind, thus wantonly to deprive them of these wonders of art." Napoleon, nonetheless, crammed the Louvre with wagonloads of conquered art. At the Congress of Vienna in 1815, the Allies ordered France to return the art, since looting, in the words of the Duke of Wellington, was "contrary to the principles of justice and the rules of modern law."

Yet those laws were unwritten. By chance, this was rectified by Francis Lieber, a Prussian-born soldier who in 1827 emigrated to America. He taught legal philosophy at Columbia College in New York, and during the Civil War President Lincoln asked him to draft a military code. Issued as General Order 100 in 1863, it called among other things for the protection during wartime of "classi-cal works of art, libraries, scientific collections or precious instruments, such as astronomical telescopes."

The Lieber code inspired a similar declaration in 1874 at the Conference of Brussels that was endorsed by the German kaiser. This declaration in turn inspired the Russian czar to promote a more ambitious conference at the Hague. In 1907, some 40 nations approved a series of conventions that expressly forbade the seizure or destruction in wartime of cultural treasures. The Hague codes proved of limited value during World War I, so in 1935 a fresh attempt was made.

This was the work of Nicholas Roerich (1874–1947), a Russian artist who designed the sets for Stravinsky's ballet Le Sacre du Printemps. As an explorer, he had led a five-year expedition to central Asia, and had also served as vice-president of the Archaeological Institute of America. A friend of Secretary of Agriculture Henry Wallace, Roerich persuaded the Roosevelt Administration to support a new treaty to protect artistic works, scientific instruments, and historic monuments. He devised a special flag, with three globes in a mystic triad, to mark protected cultural treasures.

Since World War II, insurgents have targeted the great Khmer ruins at Angkor, the walled medieval city of Dubrovnik, and the Ottoman bridges of Bosnia, as well as thousands of churches, mosques, synagogues, temples, palaces, libraries, and memorials of every kind. Nobody has yet found a way of enforcing civilized aspirations; the worst enemy of humanity's noblest works is still humanity itself.

by Karl E. Meyer

Koenigs collection seized in Dresden, 33 remained in Germany. But in 1957, the Pushkin Musuem's unpublished records listed only "337 sheets," and the total today is said to be 308. A similar attrition has taken place in the Krebs collection, which for five decades has been hidden in the Hermitage in St. Petersburg. At the Bard conference, Alexei Rastorgouev showed slides of drawings from Dresden now owned by unidentified Russian private collectors. Dealers in Europe and America routinely check the Koenigs catalog when offered drawings of suspiciously high quality.

Hence the urgent need to display and catalog all of Russia's wartime booty as soon as possible. It was this consideration that prompted the Hermitage director, Mikhail Piotrovski, to arrange the showing this past March of Impressionist and Post-Impressionist paintings from the Krebs and other private collections. A few weeks earlier Irina Antonova, not to be outdone, had quickly organized a comparable show of Old Masters from German and Hungarian collections at the Pushkin. One hopes such competition will be contagious. In Piotrovski's sensible view, it is up to the courts to decide legal title, and up to the museums to make public what they hold. In a wider sense, though, the courts can only settle claims of heirs and museums when and if Russia and Germans reach a political settlement.

In the early 1970s, I delved into the secretive antiquities market and its links with collectors and curators. The results were serialized in *The New Yorker* and published as *The Plundered Past.* If I learned any lesson, it was that on matters of acquiring cultural

treasures, no art-consuming nation has truly clean hands. Consider the United States. As Lynn Nichols recounts in *The Rape of Europe,* in 1939 the Nazis staged a scandalous auction at the Fischer Gallery in Lucerne at which allegedly "degenerate" art by Braque, Picasso, Van Gogh, and others was sold at derisory prices. The pictures had been taken from leading German museums. Among the bidders was a refugee German dealer, Curt Valentin of the Bucholz Gallery in New York, who acquired paintings by Derain, Kirchner, Klee, Lehmbruck, and Matisse. He was bidding on behalf of the Museum of Modern Art, whose director, Alfred Barr, exhibited the five works with no hint of their true provenance. No doubt the sale was legal, but it speaks volumes that the entire transaction was secret. By the same token, Harvard's acquisition of a major work by Max Beckmann, sold at the same auction, was also legal. But both institutions were extracting an advantage from a political calamity that befell German museums, a fact not advertised in accession labels.

As for Germany, everyone repudiates the cultural barbarities and wholesale brigandage that marked the Third Reich. There will be no such unanimity on Germany's legal title to the Schliemann treasure, which was spirited from Ottoman Turkey in murky circumstances, provoking a criminal suit and cash settlement at the time, and leading to a formal claim by the present Republic of Turkey. Nor is anyone talking about the controversy surrounding the bust of Queen Nefertiti, Germany's single most celebrated antiquity. Acquired in a division of finds at Amarna in 1914, the statue was hidden for a decade; Egyptians cried foul from the moment it was finally put on display in Berlin. Like other European art-importing countries, Germany has yet to ratify the UNESCO convention barring the illegal importation of cultural property. Purchase of unprovenanced antiquities, many of them clearly smuggled from their country origin, is widespread, as visitors to German museums can readily see.

As for Russia, it can indeed point to a traumatic past, but even those sympathetic to its cause will wonder whether five decades of concealment attest a confident claim of ownership. Certainly neither Poland nor Holland, Ukraine nor Hungary, ever invaded the Soviet Union, yet their claims for restitution have also gone unanswered. Ironically the Yeltsin government is seeking restitution of real estate and other properties owned by the czarist regime and its subjects in France, Italy, and Israel, appealing to the very norms of law and equity it declines to apply to its own wartime booty.

How sensible if Russia broke the ice by returning a set of rare books taken from Gotha in 1945, an act of restitution urged by a Moscow librarian speaking at the Bard conference. This gesture might be coupled with an offer to submit claims to the Trojan gold to the World Court for binding adjudication (as Germany has proposed) with the proviso that Turkey's claim also be given a full hearing. And how wise if Germany promoted an international effort to restore Russian museums and churches. Initiatives like these must be taken quickly, for it takes only a modicum of historical memory to know that it is later than the two governments think.

The Russian parliament has already given preliminary approval to legislation that would give Russia full title to all wartime booty. If that legislation is adopted, there will certainly be repercussions. German aid to Russia is reckoned at more than $73 billion since 1990, including $40 billion in loans and $14 billion in direct grants. If Bonn cuts or conditions its aid to Moscow, a likely next move, there will be a Russian outcry over German bullying and a clamor for reprisals in the Russian parliament.

Back in 1945 American monuments officers, in their Wiesbaden declaration, warned that disputes over captured spoils can sow enduring acrimony. That indeed is the theme of Homer's Iliad, which begins with Achilles' fury at the prizes of war that Agamemnon greedily bestows on himself. If no progress is made this year toward resolving the quarrel over Russian's wartime booty, positions will harden, and taking a modest step forward will be even more difficult. As evidence, consult the *Iliad*.

Probing a Landscape of Death

EVA ELVIRA KLONOWSKI'S MISSION TO RECOVER AND IDENTIFY THE VICTIMS OF ETHNIC CLEANSING

by BRENDA SMILEY

The earth shows signs of having been spaded. A covering of spring green softens the rough clumps of dirt, in some places furrowed by the treads of armored personnel carriers. Within the ridges, tiny white flowers push through the soil. Eva Elvira Klonowski, in jeans and a T-shirt, dons rubber boots for the grim task ahead. It is my first day in the field with Eva. I ask her if she thinks we'll find bodies. "If they are there, I will find them," she replies. "I'm a tough cookie."

It is also the first day of digging at a suspected mass grave near the village of Lukavica, a Serb-controlled suburb of Sarajevo that abuts the southern edge of the city's airport. Eva is chief forensic anthropologist working with a team of local experts and gravediggers. Their mission is to find and recover Bosnian Muslim victims of the ethnic cleansings of the early 1990s. Some 20,000 are still listed as missing. The work proceeds beneath the glare of the Serbs, whose hostility toward non-Serbs has surged sharply since NATO began bombing Belgrade. The local populace also simmers with resentment toward visitors from NATO-member countries. In Sarajevo, the U.S. ambassador warns Americans not to venture into Serb territories. It is those areas, where a Muslim minority once lived side by side with the Serbs, that contain most of the mass graves so far discovered.

Her close-cropped hair as white as distant snow-capped Mount Bjelasnica, Eva has recovered and identified at least 1,000 bodies during the past three-and-a-half years. Beginning in 1996, she excavated throughout Bosnia with international organizations such as the Boston-based Physicians for Human Rights, but now she prefers to work alone, free of diplomatic strictures. She returned by herself in 1998, volunteering to work directly for the Bosnian Muslims, who, she says, "have the least money, and the most dead." Now she is the only woman, and the only foreigner, working for the International Commission for Tracing Missing Persons (ICMP), established by the Bosnian state in 1996. With teams of pathologists, judges, Serb officials, police, and gravediggers, Eva travels the ravaged countryside searching for the missing and collecting evidence for The Hague War Crimes Tribunal. She is not paid for her services and survives on a small Icelandic government stipend, which she says does not even cover her accommodations and airfare. She has

kept a diary of her experiences.

July 16, 1998

 Today is the "big day"—the very first day of exhumations in the Prijedor area. There are about 3,800 missing persons in this area according to the official list. Plus about 2,200 from the nearby Omarska, Keraterm and Trnopolje concentration camps. We have permission to dig in this area until November 30. The heat is awful and the soil hard like stone. The first location is by a destroyed house where we are expected to find bodies of seven men buried in seven different graves. A young boy shows us the site. Workers dig trenches while others in our group rest in the shade of the houses and trees. I use this time to learn who is in our group, composed of Bosnian ICMP officials and their Serb counterparts. Eventually we expose three graves, but have a problem finding the next four. At the end of the day, a judge decides that we will return tomorrow with a new witness—a woman who buried all the bodies herself.

July 17, 1998

 This time, digging exactly where the woman says, we find all four bodies. They are all males. The woman recognizes her son among them. (Yesterday we exhumed another of her sons.) From there, we move down the road, some 100 meters, to yet another destroyed house alongside which she said she buried seven other bodies the same day. On the other side of the road, she shows me where her house and those of her sons and relatives used to stand. They are now all in shambles, the remaining walls disappearing daily as Serbs living in nearby Tukane come to gather the bricks for their own buildings. The rest of this second unbelievably hot day is spent digging seven more bodies from seven more graves. The woman then tells me how she and a neighbor, getting up at 2:30 in the morning, buried all 14 bodies in 13 hours. The bodies were pretty well preserved because they had been wrapped in blankets, then plastic sheets.

I FIRST MET EVA AT A forensic science conference at, of all places, Disney World in Orlando, Florida. Over iced cappuccino at a poolside table, she showed me photographs of herself in hardhat and boots digging in a dark pit full of human bones and of bodies lined up on stretchers in front of the Omarska concentration camp, where Muslims were interned and executed. I wanted to discover who this woman was who had dedicated her life to this grimmest, most unimaginable of tasks, and two-and-a-half months later I joined her in Bosnia.

Born Ewa Elvira Nowak in Bierutow, Poland, in 1946, she is a Fulbright scholar and physical anthropology Ph.D. from the University of Wroclaw. She calls herself a refugee, having fled to Iceland during the Solidarity uprising of 1981, and now lives with her engineer husband Irek and two teenage daughters in Reykjavik. In 1996, she gave up a career as an anthropology professor at the University of Iceland to pursue her human rights mission to Bosnia. Her

epiphany, she said, occurred one night as she watched the television news: shocking pictures, among the first from the former Yugoslavia, showed the site of a Serb massacre and grieving family members. She contacted Physicians for Human Rights and the International Crime Tribunal for former Yugoslavia to volunteer her services. "In 1996, when the call came from Physicians for Human Rights, I jumped at it," she says. This was also the beginning of months-long separations from her family.

Eva has since earned a position of status and respect, especially difficult for a woman, among the search officials and day laborers who work alongside her. They dig shoulder-to-shoulder with her in the trenches, joking and sweating as they uncover their missing compatriots.

"Eva, Eva, Eva," chants Amor Masovic, president of the ICMP, his arms reaching heavenward, "What would we do without her? If she had wanted to get paid for her services, we could never have afforded her. She's providing us with her expert skills, working so hard, and asking for very little in return. She has brought consolation to so many families here." But the respect of colleagues is not always enough, especially in a place so permeated with hate and distrust. A typical day may be fraught with obstacles. Bureaucratic snafus can crop up at any time. A Serb official may order an exhumation closed on the flimsiest of excuses.

The work itself is demanding, physically and psychologically. And dangerous. Unexploded land mines are everywhere. Eva's life has been threatened, once by a drunken Serb brandishing a hand grenade. Her teams are also under-equipped; in a world where ground-penetrating radar has become a common archaeological tool, Bosnian grave searchers still shove sticks in the ground to see if they come up smelling of dead bodies. Eva's family history foreshadows what would become the central focus of her life. The Soviets captured, executed, and buried her grandfather Norbert Karol Nowak in a mass grave after he was forced by the invading Germans to fight on the eastern front. She says that when she began working in Bosnia, she was jolted by the "strange coincidence" that she was now "working on exhuming victims of the worst genocide in Europe since World War II, my grandfather having been a victim of that war."

UNDER OVERCAST SKIES, our six-vehicle convoy snakes out of Sarajevo shortly after nine a.m. A few kilometers southwest of town we are joined by our escorts, a backhoe operator, UN officials, Serbian officials and police, and French Foreign Legion troops. In 25 minutes we reach our destination, Lukavica. The suburb, where Muslims and Serbs lived peacefully before the war, is now part of the Republika Srpska, or Bosnian Serb Republic, while both the airport and Sarajevo itself are within the Muslim-Croat Federation.

Lukavica's gravesite was identified by former inmates of a nearby Serbian concentration camp, who told of being forced to bury 20 executed prisoners there. After surveying the site, checking witnesses' claims, and clearing jurisdictional red tape, ICMP officials gave the go-ahead for exhumation, expecting to find 20 bodies.

The site was first swept for mines, it having been common practice during the early to mid-1990s for Serbs to boobytrap graves to discourage investigations for war-crimes tribunals. The Serbs had used broken tree limbs to hide the site, now marked off with yellow crime-scene tape. The backhoe turns up what appears to be previously disturbed earth. Eva believes this is where the bodies were dumped and orders the backhoe to enlarge the circumference of the site. Masovic motions Eva over and hands her a boot. It has a foot in it. Eva holds it up, striking a bravura pose in her oversized boots. "See?" she says. "I told you so."

Eva later calls up from the pit for more diggers. It is 3:30 p.m. and she has already uncovered one-and-a-half bodies and more small bones are surfacing. At 4:00 p.m., a skull. The searing heat requires frequent water breaks. Swigging from a plastic bottle, Eva notes that the dirt in the pit is more disturbed than elsewhere in the immediate area, suggesting that bodies have already been dug up and taken away by the Serbs. "These are just leftovers," she says.

Eva is so focused on her work that she hasn't eaten all day. "Bodies are buried all over this beautiful country," she says, "and I know that somewhere there are still relatives and friends waiting to hear [that their loved ones have been identified]," she says. "I owe it to them."

At dusk, the remains are covered with tarps to protect them from vandals and scavenging animals. We return to Sarajevo looking like farm hands coming in from the fields. We are dirty and sunburned. After a night of sleep interrupted by the sound of bombers flying to and from targets in Serbia to the northeast, we return to the site at 10:45 a.m. Eva alternates between swinging a pickax and extricating mangled bones with her trowel.

Her comments about leftovers were premature; more bodies start to appear. It's mostly hand work now since the backhoe could damage remains. Eva balances precariously on her right foot, the left one having been injured in a skiing accident ten years ago, and like an experienced rock climber, clambers out of the 15-foot-deep pit. Peeling off her muddied surgical gloves, she says, "We now have 13 bodies, but I think we will find more."

More searching, more digging. Eva finally announces that she's finished with the site. She marks the skulls with yellow flags, tags clothing with wire strips bearing case numbers, then holds up a white card with an identification number as a police photographer records the crime scene. The remains and clothing are then placed in numbered plastic bags. As lengthening afternoon shadows crisscross the gaping pit, Eva declares it clean and climbs out.

At the end of the day, Eva smells of death. With no water at hand she searches for a stream or pond in which to rinse off her boots. We spot a tethered cow in the distance and venture over a knoll to find a swampy puddle. It serves the purpose.

At a morgue south of Sarajevo, remains are laid out on tables to determine identity, if possible, and cause of death. Clothing, washed and retagged, awaits identification by relatives. It is often the only way; medical and dental records are, for the most part,

nonexistent, and few people can afford DNA testing.

When I ask what she thinks about when examining remains, she says she just concentrates on the work at hand: being objective, studying the bones carefully to find out which one goes where. "If I allowed myself to have personal feelings about the bodies I'm working on," she says, "I would never be able to do my job correctly. When the remains are commingled and in such bad shape we sometimes have to cut and mutilate them to find identity, we sometimes joke that what we are doing is worse than when they were killed, because then they were just shot. We are mutilating them in an enormous way, and I am sorry."

By week's end, Eva's team has recovered 70 bodies, 13 from the pit and 57 from an adjoining "Serb" cemetery which had been marked with Serbian orthodox crosses but actually contained Bosnian Muslims, mostly multiple burials. One body had a rope around its neck, a clear sign the person was hanged, says Eva. She has also determined that some of the victims were women. Based on clothing and documentary evidence, Eva surmises that all were civilians.

ALTHOUGH SOME FORMER COLLEAGUES at Physicians for Human Rights and the International Crime Tribunal for the Former Yugoslavia question Eva's decision to concentrate her work in Bosnia, all admire her dedication. William Haglund, director of the International Forensic Program for Physicians for Human Rights, who hired her in 1996, says he "can't deny the good she's been doing in Bosnia," but would like to see her branch out into other countries. As a human-rights archaeologist, Haglund himself travels widely to investigate war crimes and collect evidence, and is a frequent witness at UN tribunals.

It's the weekend in Sarajevo. No exhumations are scheduled and Eva is able to relax. We indulge in a Saturday afternoon stroll. Now the European sophisticate, she saunters along in little black sandals, heels clicking against the sun-dappled, cobblestone streets. We stop at sites, marked in rose-colored paint, where people were killed by snipers, artillery, and mortar attacks during the 1,395-day siege of the city in the mid-1990s. We relax at a cafe in the shade of Sarajevo's Sacred Heart Cathedral, its damaged stained-glass windows still unrepaired.

The last night before I leave, we share two glasses of Dingac, a Croatian zinfandel. The "happy little gravedigger," as she calls herself, muses about her life. She says she doesn't see herself doing anything else. "This is my gift; it's what I do best." When I ask about working elsewhere, she shakes her head, saying "I can't go anywhere else. They need me here." But in the aftermath of the NATO bombing, she did go to Kosovo, where thousands of ethnic Albanians are unaccounted for, according to a U.S. State Department estimate. There, she spent two weeks serving as an advisor to officials trying to establish a commission similar to that in Bosnia.

"People should realize that what happened in Bosnia is happening elsewhere [in the former Yugoslavia]," she says. "People are vanishing without a trace. There will be more mass graves to dig up. Where will it end?"

Museum Under Siege

EFFORTS TO RESCUE THE COLLECTIONS OF AFGHANISTAN'S NATIONAL MUSEUM

by NANCY HATCH DUPREE

When Soviet troops withdrew from Afghanistan in 1988, all but the capital of Kabul had fallen to the resistance, known as the *mujahideen*. When Kabul itself was taken in April 1992, ending the 14-year rule of the Democratic Republic of Afghanistan (DRA), mujahideen factions began warring among themselves for control of the city. Attacks were often launched from the south, and the National Museum in Darulaman, six miles south of Kabul, was often on the front line. Each time a new faction triumphed, it would loot the ruins. On May 12, 1993, a rocket slammed into the roof of the museum, destroying a fourth- to fifth-century A.D. wall painting from Delbarjin-tepe, site of an ancient Kushan city in northern Afghanistan, and burying much of the museum's ancient pottery and bronzes under tons of debris. Last November 16 another rocket hit the northwest wing of the museum, exposing storerooms to winter rain and snow and further depredations of the combatants. Despite efforts to mediate factional rivalries, the fighting and looting continues.

About 70 percent of the museum's collections are now missing. Most of its vast gold and silver coin collection, which spanned the nation's history from the Achaemenids in the sixth century B.C. through the Islamic period, has been looted. Also gone is a Greco-Bactrian hoard of more than 600 coins from Kunduz, in northern Afghanistan, dating to the third and second centuries B.C., including the largest Greek coins ever discovered. Pieces of Buddhist stucco sculptures and schist reliefs dating between the first and third centuries A.D. and Hindu marble statuary from the seventh and ninth centuries have been taken, as have carved ivories in classic Indian styles from Begram, site of the summer capital of the Kushan Empire in the early centuries A.D. Also missing are many of the museum's prized examples of the renowned metalwork of the Ghaznavids, whose sumptuous capital flourished 90 miles southwest of Kabul during the tenth and eleventh centuries. Many of these pieces are destined for sale in Islamabad, London, New York, and Tokyo.

Afghanistan's first national museum was inaugurated by King Amanullah in November 1924 at Koti Baghcha, a small palace built by the founder of Afghanistan's royal dynasty, Amir Abdur Rahman (1880–91). In 1931 its holdings were transferred to the present building in Darulaman. By this time the collection had been enriched by the work of the Délégation Archéologique Française en Afghanistan, which began after a treaty was signed with France in September 1922. After World War II, numerous archaeological missions, including those of the Italians, Americans, Japanese, British, Indians, and Soviets, conducted excavations. The first Afghan-directed work was carried out at a Buddhist site at Hadda in eastern Afghanistan in 1965. Foreign archaeological missions were bound by agreements guaranteeing that all excavated objects would be deposited with the government of Afghanistan. In 1966 the Afghan Institute of Archaeology was established in Darulaman to receive these finds; exceptional items were placed in the museum. A unique feature of the museum was the fact that more than 90 percent of its exhibits were scientifically excavated inside Afghanistan.

Claims that the Soviets had carted off the museum's treasures to the Hermitage in Leningrad arose from the April 1979 removal of the museum's collections to the center of Kabul for safekeeping. They were returned in October 1980, when the museum reopened. British and American friends still living in Kabul checked the exhibits against the 1974 museum guide and found that only two small gold repoussé elephant masks, pilfered in November 1978, were missing. According to another rumor, Victor Sarianidi of the Soviet-Afghan archaeological mission, which had excavated a hoard of more than 20,000 gold ornaments from six burial mounds called Tillya-tepe, had taken the gold to the Soviet Union. The first-century B.C. to first-century A.D. hoard, however, was shown to an international conference on Kushan studies in Kabul in

November 1978. The Kabul government also displayed it to the diplomatic corps toward the end of 1991, after which the gold was packed in boxes and placed in a vault of the National Bank inside the palace, where it is said to be today.

As unrest threatened Kabul in February 1989, following the departure of Soviet troops, the museum staff crated, packed, and stored the bulk of the collections in the museum's storerooms. Only objects too heavy to move were left in situ. Astonishingly, one of the largest and heaviest pieces, a 32-inch-high second- to fifth-century A.D. Buddhist schist relief from Shotorak, disappeared one night from an upper corridor. How thieves managed to steal it without being detected remains a mystery. Still, the museum survived the rule of the Democratic Republic of Afghanistan and the Soviet occupation relatively intact.

The subsequent breakdown of law and order has been disastrous for the museum. Although united in ridding the country of the Soviets and their DRA clients, the seven major mujahideen factions that founded the Islamic State of Afghanistan in April 1992 never formed lasting alliances, and the accord establishing the new government under President Burhanuddin Rabbani had little substance. With no common enemy, the factions have fought one another for power. In May 1993 Hezbe Wahdat, a group led by Abdul Ali Mazari, took control of the Darulaman valley. Museum staff—civil servants in President Rabbani's government—were forbidden to visit the museum because it was in enemy territory. One staff member, Najibullah Popal, risked a visit and found

crates and boxes in place, but could not check their contents or that of the many cabinets. He noted, however, that two schist reliefs were now missing. The rocket attack came the following week as fighting between Hezbe Wahdat and Rabbani's government troops intensified. Popal returned and found the Delbarjin-tepe wall painting burned beyond repair. The boxes and crates of artifacts in the basement, however, seemed untouched. At the beginning of September, CNN and BBC reporters found that the seals on the basement doors were intact, but in mid-September Popal risked another visit and saw the remains of packing cases on the ground outside the museum. Shortly thereafter a BBC correspondent returned and noted that cases had been moved and emptied; a small Buddha head had been placed near a storeroom window where protective iron bars had been bent. Outside, tire marks led directly from the window.

In late September 1993, at the request of Sotirios Mousouris, the United Nations secretary general's special representative in Afghanistan and Pakistan, I flew to Kabul to investigate these reports. Mousouris then decided to seek the support of Mazari, leader of Hezbe Wahdat, so the museum could be protected and repaired. In November the United Nations Office for the Coordination of Humanitarian Assistance to Afghanistan (UNOCHA) requested the United Nations Center for Human Resources (HABITAT) to assess the museum's condition. Investigators led by Jolyon Leslie, head of HABITAT, found that cases stood open inside every room. Barred windows in a new wing were badly damaged, providing thieves easy access. Photographs of the interior showed artifacts strewn among the rubble, and filing cabinets of museum records and catalogs indiscriminately dumped, much of the paper badly charred. Hasps had been unscrewed and locks ripped off steel storage boxes, and drawers and crates had been methodically emptied onto the floor. It appeared that most of the storage rooms had been thoroughly ransacked. HABITAT recommended securing windows with masonry, weatherproofing the flooring over the storerooms, and fitting the rooms with steel doors and stout locks. Mousouris called an emergency meeting of experts in Islamabad on November 27 at which a contribution from the Greek government, earmarked for securing the museum, was announced. Two days later he flew to Kabul. Visiting the museum, Mousouris found all 30,000 of the museum's coins missing. He secured Mazari's support for immediate repairs, and, most important, Mazari assured Mousouris that security would be provided for museum staff and workmen. Work began on December 21, 1993, under the supervision of HABITAT and with assistance from UNOCHA.

In May 1994, I returned to Kabul. The work that had been done at the museum was impressive considering the appalling conditions—intense winter cold with no electricity or heating and only a small kerosene lantern for light. The building had been weatherproofed, windows blocked, steel doors installed, and all of the corridors cleared of rubble. Some 3,000 ceramic objects recovered from the debris had been placed in storerooms. One room contained

charred, melted, mangled, and otherwise disfigured Islamic bronzes that will require extensive conservation.

As of July 1994, the staff had inventoried about 16,000 objects remaining in the storerooms. Many of these, however, are mere fragments. Some 70 percent of the finer objects were missing. The looters in 1993 were discriminating in what they took and apparently had both the time and the knowledge to select the most attractive, saleable pieces. For example, they removed from wooden display mounts only the central figures (depicting voluptuous ladies standing in doorways) of the delicate Begram ivory carvings. It is also telling that although some 2,000 books and journals remain in the library, volumes with illustrations of the museum's best pieces are missing. This suggests the museum was not plundered by rampaging gangs of illiterate mujahideen. In 1992, while the various factions fought for control of Darulaman, government soldiers guarded the museum. In early 1993 they were replaced by soldiers loyal to Hezbe Wahdat. One, or perhaps both, of these groups is probably responsible for the looting.

Some of the larger and more important pieces remain. These include a second-century A.D. statue of the Kushan king, Kanishka, and a Bactrian inscription written in cursive Greek, both from the temple at Surkh Kotal, 145 miles north of Kabul; a third-century marble statue of a bearded figure, possibly Hermes, from the Greek city of Ai Khanoum far to the northeast; and a large, seated, painted clay Buddha of the third to fourth century from Tepe Maranjan, near Kabul. Also in place is an eleventh-century A.D. ornamental wall panel from the Ghaznavid winter palace at Lashkari Bazaar in southwestern Afghanistan. Delicately sculptured stucco decorations with borders of Koranic inscriptions from a mosque, possibly added to the Lashkari Bazaar palace by Ghorid successors in the twelfth century, remain, but they are still partly buried by debris. A black marble basin, 50 inches in diameter and embellished with fifteenth- and sixteenth-century Islamic inscriptions, found in Kandahar, still dominates the foyer. About a dozen rare pre-Islamic grave effigies from Nuristan also survive.

Some 16 metal trunks containing artifacts were removed by the government to safe areas in Kabul before the mujahideen arrived. These are still untouched but their contents remain a mystery; lists of what they contain were burned in the fire caused by the 1993 rocket attack. The government assures us that the 20,000 or more gold ornaments from Tillya-tepe are still safely guarded within the presidential palace in Kabul, but because of the political instability no attempt has been made to examine these objects, although the temptation to do so is great.

Soon after the fall of Kabul in 1992, rumors claiming that the museum had been systematically emptied by gangs of mujahideen began to circulate. The bazaars of Peshawar, Islamabad, and Karachi were reportedly filled with objects. At one time I was assured that the "entire" contents of the museum were in Chitral, Pakistan, awaiting the highest bidder, but a group of European travelers who went to Chitral reported seeing only "dreadful junk." I am frequently

shown pieces, but most of those I have seen have been fakes; the genuine pieces are mainly from recently looted sites.

There is no doubt that the ivory panels excavated at Begram, located on the ancient Silk Route some 40 miles northeast of Kabul, are on the international art market. These extremely fragile pieces originally decorated various pieces of furniture dating from the first to the middle of the third century A.D. Ten small panels were shown by an unidentified Afghan to an eminent Pakistani scholar in April 1994 in Islamabad. The seller claimed to have others, including several large ivories known to be missing from the museum. The asking price for the ten panels was $300,000; later it was rumored they were being offered for $600,000 in London—or perhaps Tokyo or Switzerland. Last summer more Begram ivories were seen in Islamabad, but accurate information is nearly impossible to obtain since the highly organized Pakistani underground network for stolen art is naturally secretive. Last September the Karachi-based *Herald Magazine* quoted General Naseerullah Babar, Pakistan's Federal Interior Minister, as saying that he had purchased one Begram ivory carving for $100,000, which he would return when the political situation in Afghanistan had stabilized. The general's fondness for antiquities is well known. The magazine also reported that Prime Minister Benazir Bhutto of Pakistan intends to provide substantial funds for obtaining artifacts to be "returned to the Afghans as a gift as soon as peace is established."

While I have seen few museum pieces for sale in Pakistan, there are a number of artifacts on the market that have recently been dug up in Afghanistan. Mujahideen commanders in all parts of the country are involved in this illicit activity, most notably in the east near the Hadda museum. An important Buddhist pilgrimage site in the second through seventh centuries, Hadda has been totally stripped of its exquisite clay sculptures in the Gandhara syle, which combines Bactrian, Greco-Roman, and Indian elements. Looted artifacts from Faryab and Balkh provinces in the north allegedly include jewel-encrusted golden crowns and statues, orbs (locally described as "soccer balls") studded with emeralds and all manner of exotic ephemera, as well as fluted marble columns similar to those found at Ai Khanoum in the northeastern province of Takhar. These are being carted away to embellish the houses of the newly powerful, according to witnesses.

As far as I know, no reputable archaeologist has examined any of these finds. According to reports, one stone figurine of a winged female is similar to the gold "Bactrian Aphrodite" from Tillya-tepe. This is particularly intriguing because such reports began surfacing last June, at the same time that ornaments from Tillya-tepe were said to be for sale in Islamabad and Peshawar. An expert in antique gold confirmed that the gold jewelry in Peshawar is of the same period as the Tillya-tepe ornaments (first century B.C. to first century A.D.). Are these artifacts from the museum? Are they from new sites? Could they be from the unexcavated, seventh mound at Tillya-tepe? We have no reason not to believe the Kabul government's assurance that the Tillya-tepe

collection is safe, even though no experts have been allowed to examine it.

In Darulaman, relative calm extended through the first half of 1994, but at the end of July a splinter group from Hezbe Wahdat overran the area and began a seesaw contest with Mazari's forces. At the same time, gunners of the Hezbe Islami faction, led by Gulbuddin Hekmatyar and headquartered at Chahrasyab 15 miles to the southeast, occupied the heights overlooking the valley. For the remainder of the year fierce battles destroyed the southern edge of Kabul. Then, last February, a new force calling itself the Taliban ("religious students") seized Chahrasyab, drove out Hekmatyar's forces, and captured Mazari, who was killed in Ghazni on March 13. Government troops routed Taliban on March 23, 1995. During these eight unsettled months guards were posted at the museum by whichever faction happened to be holding the area. With each changeover, the fleeing guards took what they could. Some of the guards may have been cooperating with dealers who capitalized on the fact that the guards had the opportunity to identify saleable pieces as the museum staff worked at sorting and organizing the objects.

Five months of relative calm followed, and the central government assumed responsibility for the protection of the museum for the first time. Last April representatives of the Society for the Preservation of Afghanistan's Cultural Heritage (SPACH), an advocacy group formed in Islamabad in September 1994, met in Kabul with Sayed Ishaq Deljo Hussaini, the Minister of Information and Culture. Hussaini acknowledged the government's commitment to moving the museum to safe premises in Kabul, and SPACH agreed to seek assistance for the preparation of an inventory. The Minister also announced that government police had recently recovered 28 looted pieces, including schist reliefs, packed for shipment to Pakistan. Four pieces—two schist reliefs and two stucco heads—had been purchased by Abdullah Poyan, the ministry's President of Art, for return to the museum. In Kabul the Commission for the Preservation of Afghanistan's Cultural Heritage was organized, consisting of Afghan members of the National Museum, the Institute of Archaeology, the Academy of Sciences, Kabul University, the Ministry of Information and Culture, HABITAT, and Afghan experts. The commission advises the government, coordinates efforts with SPACH, and receives recovered artifacts, either through donation or purchase. Last September, 43 pieces, which had been purchased in Kabul, were presented to the commission by HABITAT head Jolyon Leslie. In addition to a Bronze Age steatite seal, schist reliefs, and stucco heads, this donation included four fragments of a large Bronze Age silver bowl combining Indian and Mesopotamian stylistic characteristics in depicting a frieze of bulls. The bowl is part of a hoard of five gold and 12 silver vessels found at Tepe Fullol in northern Afghanistan in 1966. Tepe Fullol, not far from the famous lapis-lazuli mines of Badakhshan, was probably on an early trade route. Badakhshi lapis adorns luxury artifacts of the same period found at Ur in Mesopotamian Iraq. The commission purchased eight additional

pieces last summer with funds provided by the government.

Last June in Kabul a joint mission of Unesco and the Musée Guimet in Paris arranged for museum specialists to spend September in Kabul preparing a photo inventory of the objects remaining in the museum. On September 3, however, the Taliban captured the western city of Herat, and security in Kabul crumbled once again. Instead of flying on to Kabul from Peshawar, the mission returned to Paris. On the night of October 10 the Taliban recaptured the military base at Chahrasyab, and rockets fell in the museum's narrow front garden. Miraculously the building did not take another direct hit. Outside the entrance, however, the head of a lion on a Kushan schist throne from the Buddhist site of Khum Zargar, 40 miles north of Kabul, was split in two. During the attack, according to an eyewitness report by Armando Cuomo, an archaeologist from the University of London, government soldiers frightened away the government police guarding the museum, blasted open doors, and ransacked the storerooms unmindful of being observed by a foreigner. Because of the ongoing fighting, the museum staff has been unable to ascertain what was taken then.

By the time of my last visit at the end of October 1995, government guards were once again on duty, and the commission was feverishly preparing its response to President Rabbani's order that the collections be removed to Kabul immediately. The professionals on the commission are against the move. Packing and moving cannot be done in a hurry without causing much damage, and most feel that it would take from two to four months to pack adequately. They also feel that Kabul is now no safer than Darulaman; on November 20, jets dropped two 1,000-pound bombs on the center of Kabul near sites under consideration for storage of the museum collections. Despite months of searching, the government has yet to decide on a suitable new location. Meanwhile, HABITAT has drawn up plans for further work to secure the museum in Darulaman, which can be carried out with additional funds contributed by Portugal and Cyprus, along with a second donation from Greece. The commission favors accepting an offer by the president of security at Khad, the secret police, to take over responsibility for protecting the museum. But the war continues; all plans are tenuous.

For updates on Afghanistan's cultural heritage after this article was first published in 1998, see www.archaeology.org/afghanistan.

Spoils of War

THE PLUNDERING OF IRAQ'S CULTURAL INSTITUTIONS DEMONSTRATES YET AGAIN HOW WARFARE FUELS THE GLOBAL TRADE IN LOOTED ANTIQUITIES.

by NEIL BRODIE

In the days following the sack of Baghdad's museums, the first question asked was: Why had coalition war planners and military commanders not done more to stop it from happening? Looking to the events of April 2003, and beyond, another and more fundamental question is: Why has no concerted international action been taken to block the trade and sale of material looted from archaeological sites and cultural institutions during wartime? The simple answer seems to be that the political will just hasn't been there.

No one can blame Iraqis for believing that their museums were modern treasure houses—in a sense, they were. A lucrative international trade in Iraqi antiquities had already emerged in the wake of the 1991 Gulf War. In the next three years, ten regional museums were attacked. Something like three thousand objects were stolen, of which few have ever been recovered. By the mid 1990s, the focus of destruction had shifted to archaeological sites, and in Europe dealers were circulating photographs of relief fragments from palaces at Nineveh and Nimrud. Cuneiform tablets, cylinder seals, and other small antiquities—more difficult to trace—were sold openly. But not everything was leaving Iraq. In 1997, it was reported that enough antiquities had been seized at Iraq's border with Jordan to form an exhibition at Baghdad's National Museum. One year later a thousand artifacts were returned from Jordan, and in 2000 the Iraqis themselves seized five thousand more of them in southern Iraq. The looting of Iraq has not been without loss of human life. At least one guard and one looter have been shot dead (at different sites) and, in 1997, ten people were executed for stealing the head from a statue of a human-headed bull at Khorsabad.

Despite the fact that, under United Nations Security Council resolutions, trade in cultural material from Iraq was illegal, the plunder of sites and museums attracted little media attention and no political action. In fact, the trade was carried on in blatant disregard of U.N. sanctions. The Iraq Department of Antiquities found itself in the invidious position of being unable to obtain photographic film to document their collections or vehicles to patrol their sites, while at the same time being forced to watch the unhindered flow abroad of looted antiquities.

What has happened in Iraq is not without precedent. In the fighting that followed the Soviet withdrawal from Kabul in 1988, Afghanistan's National Museum was ransacked. By 1996, 70 percent of the museum's collections was missing and archaeological sites throughout Afghanistan were being devastated in the search for saleable material. Early in 2001 part of what was left in the Kabul Museum was destroyed on the orders of the Taliban, and since their fall from power it is reported that there has been an upsurge in the looting of archaeological sites. Other national museums and cultural repositories around the world have also been attacked. The national museums of Somalia in Mogadishu and Hargeysa were emptied during the fighting that broke out there in 1991, and there is no news of the whereabouts of their collections. More can be said about Cambodia, where the Dépôt de la Conservation d'Angkor housed probably the finest collection of Khmer antiquities in the world. At some point during the 1970s a large part of the collection disappeared and about 150 statues were decapitated. Attacks on the Dépôt continued into the early 1990s. To date, only seven objects have been recovered.

The collections of the National Museum of Beirut largely survived (though hardly intact) the fighting that wracked the city during the 1970s and 1980s, probably because of the successful strategies of deception and physical protection that were adopted by the museum's director, who announced the removal to safe storage of material that was still, in fact, in the museum's basement, and protected larger pieces with concrete barriers. Sites in other parts of Lebanon were not so lucky, and in Somalia and Cambodia they have been the target of illegal digging. Ironically, when the Iraqis occupied Kuwait in 1990 they moved quickly to protect museums from looting before removing collections themselves. Much of the contents of Kuwait's museums was returned in 1991, but its National Museum estimates it has lost about 20 percent of its collection.

Thus the omens were there from the start for those with the wit to read them. Museums, particularly national museums, are ripe for the picking during times of conflict. But little or no practical action has been taken to block the trade and sale of material looted from sites and cultural institutions during wartime.

So, what needs to be done in Iraq? As an obvious first priority, the museums have been secured against further attack; and now sites in the countryside must similarly be protected. The nature and scale of the damage must be assessed, and work should start on the repair and reconstruction of what is left. There seems a broad measure of agreement among the international community that this work should be in the hands of the Iraqi museum and archaeology services, which have the necessary knowledge and expertise for the tasks at hand. This is not to say that there should be no injection of material or expertise from outside agencies, but we should keep firmly in mind that overall supervision is an Iraqi prerogative. The recovery program will be long term and the greatest threat it faces is loss of public interest and thus political support when the media gaze is drawn to other cultural disasters. It is important that the looting of Baghdad's museums does not become last year's news.

A second priority is to prevent looted material from moving around the world, but it is not easy to see how this can be achieved. In the decade of neglect that followed the Gulf War, illicit trade networks were established, transport routes identified, and smuggling techniques tried and tested. Nothing definite is known about how or where looted material moves out of Iraq, but routes can be guessed at. Iraq's long land frontiers are difficult to police and allow easy passage into Turkey, Iran, Jordan, Saudi Arabia, and Syria. From Turkey material can move directly to Europe, and from Saudi Arabia it can pass through the Gulf States to Europe. Jordanian customs officers have in the past intercepted Iraqi material, and have made more seizures since April 2003, but they are unable to stop the flow completely. From Jordan material can be sent directly to Europe, or pass into Israel, where there is a legal antiquities market. Presumably material moving through Iran will follow a more circuitous route but with the same European destination in mind. Thus material from Iraq will flow into Europe from all quarters, and by a variety of means, and presumably then on to the markets in Europe, Japan, and the United States.

In general, European customs officers are not trained to recognize archaeological material, and so are poorly prepared to intercept suspect shipments. The situation in the United States is better as customs officers there are accustomed to blocking the import of specific classes of archaeological material as called for by various agreements with other countries. They also have the U.S. State Department's International Cultural Property Protection website to consult, which provides links to other websites showing images of looted Iraqi antiquities.

Given the patchy nature of customs preparedness, U.S. and United Kingdom government officials are placing great reliance on the cooperation and self-policing of dealer organizations (other European countries haven't said much; presumably, they don't feel responsible). Yet can we have any confidence that they will act to obstruct the trade in material looted from Iraq? Past experience suggests not. Large numbers of antiquities from Iraq, likely looted, have been on open sale in Europe and America for the past ten years, and nothing has been done about it. On the Monday following the attacks on the National Museum it took me only half an hour to locate forty cuneiform tablets for sale on nine Internet sites from around the world. Presumably, these are only the tip of an iceberg.

No doubt dealers selling these cuneiform tablets would claim that they have been in circulation for years, and moved out of Iraq at a time long predating the Gulf War. Maybe. But it is an interesting fact that a large number of tablets have been authenticated and translated by cuneiform expert Wilfred Lambert, a fellow of the prestigious British Academy. Now it is certainly possible that one or two tablets may have been in circulation for decades or more without being previously noted or translated, but it is scarcely credible that large numbers have been hidden away for years in dusty attics and rusty footlockers only to emerge and be authenticated toward the end of the twentieth century. Yet that is exactly what we are expected to believe.

It is probably too soon to say how much looted material will be recovered, but the prognosis is gloomy. Only a handful of objects stolen from Iraqi museums after the Gulf War have been identified over the years, and the experiences of Kabul Museum and Angkor are hardly encouraging. Inside Iraq there can be little objection to otherwise innocent people being offered immunity to prosecution in exchange for the return of stolen material—presumably major figures will not come forward and would in any case be guilty of other crimes. However, the question of reward might require more careful consideration. Perhaps a small reward is acceptable, provided it is not so large as to spur further looting. Payment could be restricted to objects that are readily identifiable as museum property, and this seems a good solution. Outside Iraq, however, the situation is less clear-cut, and it is harder to justify the payment of reward money if it goes only to sustain the market. An amnesty, however, might still be in order.

The international museum community might also take a hand. The International Council of Museums is at the forefront, and with financial support from the U.S. State Department is preparing a "Red List" of Iraqi antiquities at risk. But more could be done by individual institutions. The American Association of Museums, for example, has advised that museums should research the provenance of objects in their collections that may have changed hands during the period 1933 through 1945 when the Nazis expropriated large quantities of mainly Jewish-owned art. Many leading museums have now established programs with a view to returning stolen paintings or other objects to their rightful owners. Surely now is the time for a similar lifeline to be offered to cultural objects of other nations that have been wrongfully removed during wartime.

Cambodia, Somalia, Afghanistan, and now Iraq are among the worst cases of cultural destruction during time of war. All these cases point either to flaws in international law or to its ineffective enforcement. For example, I was puzzled that the United States had not entered into agreements protecting cultural heritage with Somalia and Afghanistan, as it has with Cambodia and other countries, under the 1970 UNESCO Convention. Then I realized that neither Somalia nor Afghanistan have actually signed the convention.

Furthermore, U.S. policy is responsive—there needs to be a clear request from a recognized central authority before any action can proceed, and the authority requesting action must have an effective jurisdiction and be able to implement measures designed to protect cultural heritage. In wartime, these requirements may be compromised. The First and Second Protocols to the Hague Convention of 1954 for the Protection of Cultural Property in the Event of Armed Conflict are designed to circumvent such problems. For example, an occupying power has a duty to protect cultural property and prevent its illicit trade, which applies whether or not the occupied country has signed the convention. The Hague Convention is a strong piece of legislation drafted with the express purpose of preventing the types of destruction and theft of cultural material that have become a common feature of modern warfare. So far, however, the United Kingdom and the United States have refused to ratify it, although the reasons for their reticence have never been made clear. If the coalition partners had acceded to the Hague Convention before the invasion of Iraq, then those responsible for the failure to protect the National Museum would have taken more care to secure it.

"Tell It to the Marines..."

I have spoken of the need to protect ancient sites, museums, and antiquities in war-torn Iraq and Afghanistan in earlier columns (www.archaeology.org/iraq and www.archaeology.org/afghanistan), and during the past year the Archaeological Institute of America (AIA) has begun an innovative program to help educate troops soon to be sent to those countries. Conceived by AIA vice president C. Brian Rose, the program sends experienced lecturers to military bases to teach the basics of Middle Eastern archaeology and the importance of protecting the evidence of past cultures. The class, taken by both officers and enlisted men and women, is mandatory.

The effort is a supplement to the AIA's long-standing, nationwide lecture program in which scholars in archaeology and related fields present the latest research and developments to more than 102 local societies in the U.S. and Canada. The lectures for the troops focus specifically on the areas where military personnel will be deployed and on the specific sites, monuments, museums, and artifacts that they might be called upon to protect. The current lectures, funded in part by the Packard Humanities Institute, emphasize Mesopotamia's role in the development of writing, schools, libraries, law codes, calendars, and astronomy, as well as connections with familiar biblical figures such as Abraham and Daniel and ancient sites such as Ur and Babylon. Afghanistan's position as a crossroads of ancient civilizations and the route of Alexander the Great through the region are also discussed. Troops also learn about basic archaeological techniques, the importance of preserving context, the necessity of working with archaeologists and conservators, and how to protect sites against looters.

The first series of lectures was given at the Marine Corps base at Camp LeJeune, North Carolina, and there are plans to expand the program to other bases and services in the near future. "Many of the officers have M.A. degrees; some are reservists and high-school history teachers," says Rose, who delivered the inaugural lectures last spring. "They care a great deal about the history of the areas in which they serve; some of them have actually lived in or near Babylon on earlier tours of duty. All of us have been struck by their thirst for knowledge during and after our lectures."

Many have helped get this program up and running, including Col. Joseph Lydon, Col. Paul Hopper, and Lt. Col. Richard Allen at Camp LeJeune. U.S. Marine Colonel Matthew Bogdanos, who was instrumental in securing the return of many antiquities stolen from the Iraq Museum, did much to smooth the way. "When it comes to clearing a building, neutralizing a land mine, or making a neighborhood safe for children, we know what to do," says Bogdanos. "When it comes to protecting a country's cultural heritage, we are just as eager to do the right thing—we just don't always know the best way to do it. This is where Brian Rose's groundbreaking program will pay dividends for generations."

by JANE WALDBAUM

The Archaeology of Battlefields

A PIONEER IN THE FIELD DISCUSSES A NEW WAY TO INVESTIGATE WARFARE.

*S*ince 1983, Douglas Scott has worked at the Midwest Archeological *Center of the National Park Service, helping protect and study* *archaeological resources in the Midwest, Great Plains, and the* Rocky Mountains. Best known for his investigations of historic battlefields, he has co-authored They Died With Custer *(1998),* Archaeological Perspectives on the Battle of Little Bighorn *(2000), and* Finding Sand Creek: History, Archaeology, and the 1864 Massacre Site *(2004). Scott recently spoke with* ARCHAEOLOGY's Mark Rose.

How did you end up becoming focused on battlefield archaeology?
I have had a long and abiding interest in military history. From an archaeological and anthropological perspective my interest focused on studying the U.S. frontier army and how it adapted, in a social and material culture sense, to being placed in remote areas for the furtherance of U.S. government policy. A natural outgrowth of that interest was how the army and their protagonists, the American Indian, chose to fight or coexist. The catalyst for my focusing on battlefield archaeological studies was a range fire at Little Bighorn Battlefield, a situation that allowed us to form a multidisciplinary team and attack (excuse the pun) the site using a variety of new field

and analytical methods. Since 1984, I have been fortunate to work on more than 30 different battlefields ranging in date from fifteenth through the twentieth centuries.

What is the aim of battlefield archaeology?

Like any archaeological study of the past there are multiple goals in studying battlefields. One is the iconographic or site focused research. Most battlefield work has as one of its goals the finding of patterns of battle-related artifacts that are amenable to analysis with the outcome of understanding the details of that battle with greater precision. I find that documentary records and oral traditions of the past are usually accurate but not necessarily precise. Archaeological work recovers, records, and interprets an independent data set that can be used to compare, corroborate, or test the documentary and traditional testimonial views of a past event. In several cases of our work on American Indian war sites, we found the Indian testimony to be much more accurate in telling the battle story than the army accounts. At the same time, the details that can be teased out of the artifact analysis regarding individual behavior on the battlefield add a level of precision to site specific interpretations that is difficult to find in the written sources. This can be especially valuable for use in public interpretation as it can help bring the story to life for a visitor.

Beyond the value of site specific interpretation of a battle the field of battlefield archaeology is capable of seeking answers to larger questions—patterns of combat, if you will, over time and space. These patterns aid us in understanding how combatants use terrain, develop tactics, extend command and control, as well as the negative side of battle, the loss of command and control, identifying tactical disintegration that may result in defeat, appreciating the effect of the fog of war, and in general help us achieve a broader appreciation of the anthropology of war.

Who came up with the idea of using volunteer teams with metal detectors to survey fields? It's kind of a low-tech, low-cost remote sensing.

Metal detectors are simply low-cost near-surface electrical conductivity meters. They are a geophysical method. When Richard Fox and I began planning the first Little Bighorn investigations we were well aware of work from the 1950s on that site and others where metal detectors were used to find battle artifacts. Those initial efforts had mixed results due to detector technology of that time. By the 1980s detectors were much more sophisticated and sensitive to buried metals, so it was a natural choice of equipment to use on a battle site where firearms predominated We also realized that we did not have the time or funding to conduct a traditional archaeological inventory and testing program, so using volunteer metal detectors seemed to be a reasonable alternative. As they say, the rest is history. Later I did a computer simulation on the Little Bighorn metal-detected artifact find locations by laying a shovel test array over the field, with 5 and 10 meter spacing, to see how many of the 5,000 artifacts we would have found using traditional shovel testing methods—the results were truly surprising, with fewer than 10 falling in any of 50 cm shovel test locales. These findings have been borne out over and over again on other battlefield work throughout this country and in Europe. I, by no means, advocate replacing traditional archaeological investigations with metal detecting, rather I espouse adding the detector and a knowledgeable operator to the archaeologist's toolkit.

You've been involved in several studies that have resulted in revisions of accepted history of battles at the Little Bighorn (1876), Hembrillo (1880), and elsewhere. Does this make you wonder how much of our history is wrong?

The historical record is a truly astounding data set, but it is just one data set that should be used in studying the past. Oral tradition or historical documents are impressions of those who set them down. While they may be more or less accurate, I will reiterate that the archaeological record is often more precise about past events in space and time, as well as an independent line of evidence that can be compared and contrasted with the other lines of evidence to achieve a fuller picture and understanding of the past.

Do you think your archaeological colleagues sometimes downplay or ignore evidence of conflict in their explanations of the past?

Twenty years ago I would have said most archaeologists were downplaying the possibility that conflict evidence was present in sites. Today that has truly changed and many colleagues around the world are working to find physical evidence of warfare and conflict. I believe one of the areas where the value of historical archaeology relative to prehistoric studies in not fully utilized or appreciated is in conflict archaeology studies. The physical evidence that historic battlefield archaeologists have collected as well as some of the methods used to find battle sites are not being applied by prehistorians interested in identifying early conflicts. While the methods we often use cannot be transferred directly to prehistoric sites, our theoretical concepts along with modified methodology could provide a fertile testing ground as models on prehistoric conflict sites, in my opinion.

Has your work given you insights about human behavior, the larger picture, that is, not just what happened at a particular place and time?

Archaeology is predicated on the principle that human behavior leaves behind physical evidence that is patterned, recoverable, and interpretable. While warfare and conflict seem like they are chaotic affairs, they are behaviors that leave behind patterned evidence. We archaeologists need to be clever enough to apply the right methods backed by good theoretical constructs that will allow us to collect that evidence so we can better understand conflicts of the past. Working in the area of historic conflicts and modern conflicts demonstrates to me that we have a long history of violent human behavior. We can and should study the physical evidence of our past conflicts to better understand the evolution of war and conflict. Today we are only on the threshold of developing a true understanding of the anthropology of war. We have some good theoretical models to work with now, and we have the technology to recover physical evidence of conflict, it is only a matter of colleagues working towards gaining a greater understanding of our conflicted past.

About the Authors

Anagnostis Agelarakis is a professor of physical anthropology at Adelphi University.

Colleen M. Beck, associate research professor at the Desert Research Institute, has published on prehistoric and historic cultures in the Andes and the western United States.

William Belcher is a civilian forensic anthropologist at the U.S. Army's Central Identification Laboratory, Hawaii, and is co-director of the excavations at Harrapa. The author would like to thank CILHI colleague Helen Dockall and Patricia Gaffney-Ansel for their contributions to this article.

Alexander Benenson is an undergraduate at Yale University where he is studying Latin, Roman History, and English. He has written for various student publications. His research on the Emperor Julian is to be published in

Classical Outlook, the journal of The American Classical League.

Neil Brodie is the coordinator of the Illicit Antiquities Research Centre of the McDonald Institute for Archaeological Research at the University of Cambridge.

David R. Bush is an associate professor of anthropology at the Center for Historic and Military Archaeology of Heidelberg College in Tiffin, Ohio. He welcomes copies of any family records relating to former prisoners or guards on Johnson's Island. He would like to thank Carl Zipfel, the current owner of the property under excavation.

Hilary Cool is a director of Barbican Research Associates. The author is grateful to English Heritage for providing the funds to rescue this site. Barbican's Jerry Evans and Quita Mould studied the artifacts; Jacqueline McKinley from Wessex Archaeology the human remains; and Julie Bond and Fay Worley from the University of Bradford the animal bones.

James P. Delgado, executive director of the Vancouver Maritime Museum, is author of *Lost Warships: An Archaeological Tour of War at Sea* (Checkmark, 2001). His recollections of diving on the ships of Operation Crossroads were adapted from his book *Ghost Fleet: The Sunken Ships of Bikini Atoll* (Honolulu: University of Hawai'i Press, 1997).

Dominic G. Diongson was formerly an intern at ARCHAEOLOGY.

Nancy Hatch Dupree is a senior consultant at the Agency Coordinating Body for Afghan Relief in Peshawar, Pakistan, and is vice-chairperson of the Society for the Preservation of Afghanistan's Cultural Heritage. From 1966 to 1974 she participated in prehistoric excavations in Afghanistan conducted by her late husband Louis Dupree.

David H. Dye is an associate professor of archaeology at the University of Memphis.

Brian Fagan is emeritus professor of anthropology, University of California, Santa Barbara, and author of *The Long Summer.*

David Friedel of Southern Methodist University co-directs the Selz Foundation Yaxuná Archaeological Project.

Tom Gidwitz is a contributing editor to ARCHAEOLOGY.

Juliet Golden is a freelance writer based in southwest Poland.

Charles M. Haecker is an archaeologist with the National Park Service and a member of its Intermountain Cultural Resources Center and the Battlefield Protection Program in Santa Fe, New Mexico.

Spencer P.M. Harrington was formerly a senior editor at ARCHAEOLOGY.

J.D. Hawkins is professor of ancient Anatolian languages at the School of Oriental and African Studies, University of London.

William Gray Johnson, assistant research professor with the Desert Research Institute, is in his third year of investigating the Nevada Test Site's historic structures.

The late **Manfred Korfmann** was director of excavations at Troy and a professor of archaeology at the University of Tübingen.

Joachim Latacz is professor of Greek philology at the University of Basel in Switzerland. The English version of his book *Troy and Homer* was released by Oxford University Press in 2005.

Karl W. Laumbach is an archaeologist with the nonprofit Human Systems Research. A native New Mexican, he has spent the last 27 years pursuing a variety of research projects in New Mexico.

Steven A. LeBlanc is director of collections at Harvard University's Peabody Museum of Archaeology and Ethnology.

C. Scott Littleton is co-author with Linda A. Malcor of *From Scythia to Camelot: A Radical Reassessment of the Legends of King Arthur, the Knights of the Round Table, and the Holy Grail* (2000).

Jarrett A. Lobell is assistant managing editor of ARCHAEOLOGY.

Karl E. Meyer is the author of *The Plundered Past* and *The Pleasures of Archaeology*.

William M. Murray is chair of the History Department and director of the Interdisciplinary Center for Hellenic Studies at the University of South Florida.

Steve Nash teaches in the journalism and environmental studies programs at the University of Richmond.

Photios M. Petsas was a professor of classical archaeology at the University of Ioannina and president of the Institute of Ionian and Adriatic Studies.

Eric A. Powell is managing editor of ARCHAEOLOGY.

Nathaniel Ralston is an undergraduate student of Classical Studies at Brandeis University.

Mark Rose is executive editor/online editor of ARCHAEOLOGY.

Jessica E. Saraceni was formerly an associate editor of ARCHAEOLOGY.

Angela M.H. Schuster was formerly a senior editor of ARCHAEOLOGY.

Neil Asher Silberman is an author, a historian, and the coordinator of international programs for the Ename Center for Public Archaeology in Belgium.

Andrew Slayman was formerly a senior editor of ARCHAEOLOGY.

Brenda Smiley, writer and journalist, has published articles on Middle Eastern history and archaeology and covered the Iraq-Iran war as a radio reporter. She also has written on DNA privacy issues and is writing a book about Eva Klonowski.

David R. Starbuck teaches at Plymouth State College, University of New Hampshire. His book *The Great Warpath: British Military Sites from Albany to Crown Point* (University Press of New England, 1999) tells the full story of Fort William Henry.

Charles Suhler of Southern Methodist University co-directs the Selz Foundation Yaxuná Archaeological Project.

Jane Waldbaum is president of the Archaeological Institute of America.

James Wiseman is a contributing editor to ARCHAEOLOGY and professor of archaeology, art history, and classics at Boston University.

Foteini Zafeiropoulou is *ephor* emerita of antiquities in the Greek Archaeological Service.

Further Reading

Part I: Roots of War. See Steven A. Leblanc, *Prehistoric Warfare in the American Southwest* (1999) and *Constant Battles: The Myth of the Peaceful, Noble Savage* (2003), along with Jean Guilaine, *The Origins of War: Violence in Prehistory* (2004) and Nick Thorpe, "Origins of war: Mesolithic conflict in Europe," *British Archaeology* 52 (2000 and at www.britarch.ac.uk/ba/ba52/ ba52feat.html). For specific artifacts, sites, and cultures, see Renée Friedman, "City of the Hawk," ARCHAEOLOGY 56:6 (November/December 2003), pp. 50–56 (Narmer Palette); Aaron David Bartels, "The Rise of Uruk and Sumer" (www.usc.edu/dept/LAS/religion/arcproj/war/EssayFour.html) and Joseph Berrigan, "Early Sumerian Warfare" (http://joseph_berrigan.tripod.com/id46.html); Larry J. Zimmerman, "Crow Creek Massacre" (www.usd.edu/anth/crow/crow1.html); and Linda Schele and David Freidel, *Flintshield Maya War and the Classic Collapse* (2001).

Part II: Ancient Warfare. The histories of Egypt's New Kingdom warrior kings can be found in detail in Aidan Dodson, *Monarchs of the Nile* (2000). For more on the Troy excavations, including preliminary reports in the journal *Studia Troica*, visit the Troia Projekt homepage at www.uni-tuebingen.de/troia/eng. The careful, evocative translations of the sixth-century B.C. poet Archilochus in "Warriors of Paros" are by Anagnostis Agelarakis. On the soldiers' bones from a collective burial in Athens, see "Interactive Lab: Fallen Heroes" (www.archaeology.org/online/features/athens/index.html). For the Actium Project, see http://luna.cas.usf.edu/~murray/actium/brochure.html. On Rome's frontier in Britain, see H. Cool, *The Roman Cemetery at Brougham, Cumbria: Excavations 1966–67* (2004), and C. Scott Littleton and Linda A. Malcor, *From Scythia to Camelot: A Radical Reassessment of the Legends of King Arthur, the Knights of the Round Table, and the Holy Grail* (2000). The brief selection from a poem by Ch'ü Yüan referring to chariots like those recently excavated in Chu state tombs is from Arthur Waley, trans., *A Hundred and Seventy Chinese Poems* (1997, first edition 1919).

Part III: From the Middle Ages to the Age of Conquest. On late medieval warfare, see V. Fiorato, A. Boylston, and C. Knüsel, eds., *Blood Red Roses. The Archaeology of a Mass Grave from the Battle of Towton A.D. 1461* (2000). More on raiding vessels can be found at the web site of Norway's Viking Ship Museum (www.khm.uio.no/english/viking_ship_museum/index.shtml). Two books on the suppression of the Cathars are Joseph R. Strayer, *The Albigensian Crusades* (1992) and Jonathan Sumption, *The Albigensian Crusade* (2000). See the Danish Medieval Centre (www.middelaldercentret.dk) and Warwick Castle's siege weapon (www.warwicksiege.com) web sites for Peter Vemming's reconstructions of medieval artillery. For the crusades in the east and Constantinople, see the first-hand accounts of Nicolò Barbaro, *Diary of the Siege of Constantinople* (1969), Jean Joinville and G. Villehardouin,

Chronicles of the Crusades (1963), and Baha' al-Din Ibn Shaddad, *The Rare and Excellent History of Saladin* (2002). The ongoing conservation and continuing recovery of Henry VIII's *Mary Rose* are documented at The Mary Rose Trust web site (www.maryrose.org). The route and impact of Hernando de Soto's *entrada* are discussed in Charles Hudson, et al., "The Hernando de Soto Expedition: From Mabila to the Mississippi River," pp. 181–207 in David H. Dye and Cheryl Anne Cox, eds., *Towns and Temples Along the Mississippi* (1990), and Jerald T. Milanich and Charles Hudson, *Hernando de Soto and the Indians of Florida* (1993). On the search for Pizarro's head, see William R. Maples and Michael Browning, *Dead Men do tell Tales. The Strange and Fascinating Cases of a Forensic Anthropologist* (1994). "The Conquest of Mexico" web site (www.theaha.org/tl/LessonPlans/ca/Fitch/index.htm) has many primary documents relating to the Spanish Conquest including the account of Cortés and the "Night of Sorrows." For the ongoing recording of the remains of Kublai Khan's fleet, see http://nautarch.tamu.edu/shiplab/randall/randall%20index%20002.htm.

Part IV: The Wars of North America. For early wars in North America, see the Fort Caroline National Memorial web site (www.nps.gov/foca); Timothy B. Riordan, *The Plundering Time. Maryland and the English Civil War 1645–1646* (2004); an exhibiton companion volume from the Montréal Museum of Archaeology and History: *1690. The Siege of Québec…The Story of a Sunken Ship* (2000); the Fort Necessity National Battlefield web site (www.nps.gov/fone); and David R. Starbuck, *The Great Warpath: British Military Sites from Albany to Crown Point* (1999). See also, the archaeology section of the Fort William Henry Museum web site (www.fwhmuseum.com) and David R. Starbuck's *Massacre at Fort William Henry* (2002). More on the re-creation of the Revolutionary War submarine *Turtle* can be found at the Handshouse web site (www.handshouse.org/turtle.html). For the Benedict Arnold gunboat, check "archaeological projects" in the Maritime Research Institute section of the Lake Champlain Maritime Museum web site (www.lcmm.org/index.html). In addition to the main web site for Valley Forge (www.nps.gov/vafo), there is a separate one on the excavation there, "Discovering What Washington's Troops Left Behind at Valley Forge" (www.cr.nps.gov/logcabin/html/rd_valleyforge.html). For more about Johnson's Island Civil War POW camp see "Unlocking a Civil War Prison" (www.archaeology.org/interactive/johnsons/index.html) and "Friends and Descendants of Johnson's Island Civil War Prison" (www.heidelberg.edu/~dbush/index.html). In addition to the NOAA *Monitor* expedition website (http://oceanexplorer.noaa.gov/explorations/02monitor/monitor.html), see William Marvel, ed., *The Monitor Chronicles* (2000), and Robert E. Sheridan, *Iron from the Deep. The Discovery and Recovery of the USS Monitor* (2003). Friends of the Hunley (www.hunley.org) is a comprehensive web site about the Confederate's best-known submarine. For other Civil War vessels, see the Louisiana State Museum web site (http://lsm.crt.state.la.us/ site/submarine/ sub_history.htm) for an as-yet unidentified Confederate submarine and the Vicksburg National Military Park web site for the USS *Cairo* (www.nps.gov/vick/ cairo/cairo.htm). The web site of the nonprofit organization National Underwater and Marine Agency has information about the search for other ironclads (www.numa.net/expeditions/

manassas_louisiana_arkansas.html). Books about the battlefield archaeology of specific sites include Charles M. Haecker, *On the Prairie of Palo Alto: Historical Archaeology of the U.S.-Mexican War Battlefield* (1997), and Karl W. Laumbach, *Hembrillo, an Apache battlefield of the Victorio war: the archaeology and history of the Hembrillo battlefield* (2001).

Part V: War in Modern Times. For WWI battlefield sites including Ieper, see "The Archaeology of the Western Front 1914–1918" website (http://web.telia.com/~u86517080/BattlefieldArchaeology/ArkeologENG_3B.html). Arthur Machen's "The Bowmen" appeared in collections of his works such as *Tales of Horror and the Supernatural* (1949), and it is online with his explanation of it on the "Aftermath" web site (www.aftermathww1.com/ bowmen.asp) about WWI. See also, Robert Graves, *Goodbye to All That* (1957), Siegfried Sassoon, *Memoirs of an Infantry Officer* (1930), and Wilfrid Owen's poems online at "War Poems & Manuscripts of Wilfred Owen" (www.hcu.ox.ac.uk/ jtap/warpoems.htm). The search and recovery of U.S. MIA's is carried out by the Joint POW/MIA Accounting Command (JPAC), the merged U.S. Army Central Identification Laboratory, Hawaii, and Joint Task Force—Full Accounting. See www.jpac.pacom.mil for more. Links to web sites on the Chelmno death camp can be found at About.com (http://history1900s.about.com/ cs/chelmnocamp/). For Nevada's Nuclear Test Site, see web sites of the Department of Energy (www.nv.doe.gov/ nts/default.htm) and The Nevada Test Site Historical Foundation (www.ntshf.org/ index.htm). The sunken ships from nuclear tests at Bikini Atoll are the subject of James P. Delgado's *Ghost Fleet* (1996); see also the web site of the National Park Service Submerged Cultural

Resources Unit (http://data2.itc.nps.gov/sub-merged). For the Minuteman Missile National Historic Site, see www.nps.gov/mimi.

Part VI: Archaeology and War. For the National Park Service's American Battlefield Protection Program, see www.cr.nps.gov/hps/abpp. The Civil War Preservation Trust (www.civilwar.org) and Friends of the Mansfield Battlefield (www.mansfieldbattlefield.org) are among the many organizations seeking to preserve Civil War battlefield sites. For the battle of Ox Hill, see http://www.espd.com/oxhill. On the fate of art and antiquities taken in WWII, see Lynn H. Nicholas, *The Rape of Europa. The Fate of Europe's Treasures in the Third Reich and the Second World War* (1995). On Afghanistan, see the ARCHAEOLOGY web site (www.archaeology.org/ afghanistan) and those of the Association for the Protection of Afghan Archaeology (www.apaa.info/index.htm) and Society for the Preservation of Afghanistan's Cultural Heritage (http://spach.info). For Iraq, see the ARCHAEOLOGY web site (www.archaeology.org/iraq). The Illicit Antiquities Research Centre of the University of Cambridge (www.mcdonald.cam.ac.uk/IARC/home.htm) has information about international laws and conventions governing as well as current news about cultural heritage issues. Additional information about the AIA's troops lecture program can be found at www.archaeological.org/webinfo.php?page=10319
.

Acknowledgments

The editors of ARCHAEOLOGY have benefited greatly from the willingness of outstanding scholars to make the results of their research known in our pages and on our web site. Through their generosity, our readers have learned of discoveries that tell the history of war from an archaeological perspective. These include investigations of the prehistory of war (Steven A. LeBlanc), Maya warfare and regime change (Charles Suhler and David Freidel), Maori fortifications (Brian Fagan), the Trojan War (the late Manfred Korfmann and colleagues), an early warriors' burial on Paros (Foteini Zafeiropoulou and Anagnostis Agelarakis), the monument of Augustus at Actium (William Murray and Photios M. Petsas), evidence from Rome's frontier in Britain (Hilary Cool and C. Scott Littleton), re-creating medieval artillery (Peter Vemming), Hernando de Soto's route through the Southeast (David H. Dye), a Mongol invasion fleet off Japan and the "ghost fleet" of Bikini Atoll (James P. Delgado), the massacre at Fort William Henry (David R. Starbuck), the

battle of Palo Alto (Charles M. Haecker),
Johnson's Island Civil War POW camp
(David R. Bush), the battle at Hembrillo
Basin (Karl W. Laumbach), World War I bat-
tlefield landscapes (Neil Asher Silberman),
MIA remains (William Belcher and Helen
M. Wols), the Chelmno death camp in
Poland (Juliet Golden), Nevada's Nuclear
Test Site (William Johnson and Colleen
Beck), and the fate of cultural heritage in
Afghanistan (Nancy Hatch Dupree) and Iraq
(Neil Brodie). We have also benefited from
the work of a select number of exceptional
writers including Tom Gidwitz (the
Revolutionary War submarine *Turtle*), Karl
E. Meyer (spoils of war), Steve Nash (pre-
serving Civil War battlefields), and Brenda
Smiley (forensic archaeology in the Balkans).
Jane Waldbaum, the current AIA president,
and past president James Wiseman, have con-
tributed, respectively, columns about teaching
armed forces to recognize and respect cultur-
al heritage and the brutal suppression of a
medieval religious sect. A number of addition-
al contributions in this volume are by
ARCHAEOLOGY's own editorial staff, both past
(Dominic G. Diongson, Spencer P.M.
Harrington, Jessica E. Saraceni, Angela M.H.
Schuster, Andrew Slayman) and present
(Alexander Benenson, Jarrett A. Lobell, Eric A.
Powell, and Nathaniel Ralston). We hereby
acknowledge our debt to all of our authors.
Special thanks are due ARCHAEOLOGY's long-
time friends Anagnostis Agelarakis, David R.
Bush, James P. Delgado, Brian Fagan, David
Freidel, Neil Asher Silberman, and David R.
Starbuck for their help cover the years.
Completion of this volume was made possi-
ble in large part by the efforts of Alexander
Benenson, who in addition to authoring
several pieces researched subjects and images
during the course of the book's compilation.

Index

A

Aborigines, 6
Aboukir, Battle of, 119, 122–123
Actium, 51–57
Aeschylus, 41
Afghanistan's National Museum, collections of, 243–250, 252
Agelarakis, Anagnostis, 38–41, 43, 44, 47
Agrippa, Marcus, xvi
Akinsha, Konstantin, 229
Akita, 57
Albigensian, 79
Alexander the Great, 49–50, 54
Alföldy, Géza, 58
Alligator, 168, 171
Alligator Junior, 168
Almagro, Diego, 102
Ambrosino, James, 20
American Diver, 169
American Ram, 169
Anasazi, 3–4
Anatolia, 37
Antonova, Irina, 229, 231, 235
Antony, Mark, xvii, 52, 53, 56, 59
Arch of Titus, *insert 3*
Archilochos, xv
Aristobulus, 49
Aristogeiton, 43
Arkansas, 170, 210, 211, 212
art in wartime, 234
Arthurian Legend, 64
Arzawa, 34
atomic weaponry, advent of, 206–209
Augustus, xvi, xvii, 53, 59
Aurelius, Marcus, 61, 64, 65

B

Badlands National Park, 217
Baldin, Victor, 231
Barbican Research Associates, 61
Batraz, 64
Battesti, Michéle, 120
Battle of Ox Hill, 221–222
Battle of the Little Bighorn, 156
Beck, Colleen M., 206–209
Belcher, William, 192–197
Benedict Arnold Gunboat, 147
Benenson, Alexander, 7, 11–13, 76–78, 84–88, 93–95, 104–106, 124–125, 166–171
Bennett, Sharon, 18
Berlandier, Jean Louis, 153–154, 155
Bernadino, Don, 17
Bernier, Marc-André, 134
Betatakin, 6
Bevan, Bruce, 226
Bikini Atoll, ships of, xix, 210–213, *insert 8*
Blegen, Carl, 35
Boguslavky, Mark M., 229
Book of Judges, xv
Bosnian victims of ethnic cleansing, 238
Brainerd, George, 19, 21
Bremetennacum Veteranorum, 64
Brocavum, 61
Brodie, Neil, 251–255
Bronze Age artifacts, 228
Brougham, 60–65, 63
Brown, Rick and Laura, 142–147
Buffalo soldiers, xviii
buffalo soldiers, 172–179
burial, 24, 17, 18, 19, 20, 21
Burton, Jeffrey, 200
Burton, Robert, 173
Bush, David R., 157–163
Bushnell, David, 142–147

C

Caesar, Julius, 52
Calakmul, 8
Callisthenes, 49
Calvert, Charles, 131, 132, 133
Calvert, Leonard, 132
Calverts, 131, 132
Campana, Doug, 226
Carcassonne, 80
Carroll, Captain Henry, 172–179
Castus, Lucius Artorius, 64
Cathars, suppression of the, 79–83
Cehpech, 19
Celtic societies, 25
Cerros, 20
Chabrias, tomb of, 46
Chaco Canyon, 9
Chaney, Ed, 132
Charles V, King, 96
Chelmno Extermination Camp, xviii, 201–205
Chichén Itzá, 18, 19, 20, 22
Chinese chimes, 66–67
Chrysippos, 43
Chu period, 67
Chuikoff, Vassily, 231
Civil War
   battlefield preservation, 221–227
   espionage in the, 164–165
   warships, 167–171
   Johnson's Island, xviii, 158–16, *insert 6*
Cleitus, 50
Cleopatra, xvii, 52, 53, 59
Cliff, Maynard, 20
Cohn, Art, 147
Cold War, xix, 214–217
colonization, attempts at, 129–135
Colosseum, xvii, 58
confederate POWs, captivity of, 157–163
Conline, John, 176
Conlon, Thomas, 112
Conon, 43
Constantinople, conquest of, 89–92
Cool, Hilary, 60–65
Cortés, 104–106
Costen, Michael, 81

Creamer, Winifred, 6
Crow Creek, South Dakota, xvii, 11, 12, 13, *insert 1*
crusades, 89–92
CSS *Georgia*, 171
CSS *Jackson*, 170
CSS *Neuse*, 170
CSS *Virginia*, 167, 168, 170
Cunliffe, Barry, 5
Custer Battlefield, 176

D

Dardany, 31
Darius, 50
de Soto, Hernando, 96–100
Dean, Martin, 94
Deane, John, 94
Delgado, James P., 107–111, 111–113, 210–213
Delta Nine, 216, 217
Delta One, 216
Demetrius, fleet of, 54
Dêmosion Sêma, 43, 45
Denon, Dominique Vivant, 122–123
Denyen, 31
DePratter, Chester, 131
Dewilde, Marc, 183–188
Diaz, Bernal, 104
Dinsmoor, William, 232
Diordorus, 49
Dumas, Jacques, 120
Dupree, Nancy Hatch, 243–250
Dutour, Olivier, 115
Dye, David H., 96–100

E

Edward VI, xvi, 71
El Mirador, 8
El Morro Valley, 3
Elizabeth and Mary, xviii, 134
English Heritage, 61
espionage in the Civil War, 164–165
ethnic cleansing, 237–242
Europe's First Farmers, 5
Ewen, Charles, 97
extremadura, 101–103

F

Fagan, Brian, 23–25
Flamm, Mike, 199
Flanders Fields, artifacts in, 183–188
Flanner, Janet, 233
Fort Caroline, xviii
Fort Morton, 226
Fort William Henry, 130, 136–141
Fox, Aileen, 25
French and Indian war, massacre during the,
    136–141
Frenchman Flat, 208
Friedel, David, 17–22
Fritz Ritz, xviii, 198, 200

G

Gaj, Przymyslaw, 203
Gallo, Paollo, 122–123
Garber, James, 20
Gebusi, 10
Georgia, see CSS Georgia
Gidwitz, Tom, 142–146
Goddio, Franck, 119, 120
Goering, Hermann, 230
Gokstad Ship, 78
Golden, Juliet, 201–205
Gorczycz, Krzysztof, 204
Gorman, Rebecca, 131
Gowan, Lieutenant W.B., 159
Grabill, Captain John H., 159
Granicus, 49–50
Grant, Ulysses S., 151
Graves, Robert, 190–191
Great Wall of China, 124–125, *insert 4*
Green Vault, 231
Grossman, Joel W., 164, 165
Gutenberg Bibles, 228

H

Haas, Jonathan, 6
Hadrian's Wall, 60
Haecker, Charles M., 151–156
Hagen, Alfred, 193
Hague Convention, 255

Hammond, Mason, 232
Harmodios, 43
Hattusili III, 34
Hawkins, J.D., 34
Hayashida, Kenzo, 108, 109, 113
Hembrillo Basin, fight at, xviii, 172–179, 259
Henry VI, xvi, 71, 72, 73
Henry VIII, 93–95, *insert 5*
Hierakonpolis, 14, 15
hilltop construction, 5
Hincman, Matt, 146
Hittite, 34
Holland, Tom, 197
Homer, 36
Honan, William H., 232
Hongxing, Wang, 67
Hopi, 10
hoplite warfare, 39–40
hoplon, 39
Horus, 15
Hubei Provincial Archaeological Institute, 67
Hun-Nal-Yeh, 21
Hunley, xvii, xix, 169, 170, 171, *insert 6*

I

Ieper, artifacts in, 183–188
Iliad, setting for the, 35, 36
Indians of Mesa Verde, 5
Ingle, Richard, 132
Inuit, 6

J

Jankauskas, Rimantas, 115, 116, 117
John of Gaunt, 71
Johnson, William Gray, 206–209
Johnson's Island, xviii, 158–16, *insert 6*
Johnstone, Dave, 22
Joiner, Gary, 223, 224
Jones, Calvin, 97

K

kamikaze, 107–111
Katyn Forest, 198, 199
Keeley, Lawrence, 5

Kenner, Charles, 176
Kennewick man, xvii, 7
Kerameikos, 39
Kharkov burial site, 199
Kiet Siel, 6
King, Julia, 132
Klonowski, Eva Elvira, 237–242
Korfman, Manfred, 32–37
KOSUWA, 107–111
Kozlov, Grigorii, 229
Kublai Khan's fleet, discovery of, 107–111
Kulishov, Valery, 233
Kung Bushman, 10

L

Lagash, 16
Lambert, Wilfred, 254
Lancaster vs. York, 72
Larsen, Clark Spencer, 117
Latac, Joachim, 36
Late Bronze Age, 38
Laudonniérre, René de, 130
Laumbach, Karl W., 172–179
LeBlanc, Steven A., xvii, 3–10
Lekson, Stephen, 9
lekythoi, 44
Lelantine War, 40
Lepidus, 52
Lieber, Francis, 234
Linear Pottery culture, 13
Liston, Maria, 141
Lithuania, mass gravesite in, 114–117
Little Bighorn Battlefield, 257, 258, 259
Littleton, C. Scott, 64
Lobell, Jarett A., 66–67, 114–117
L'Orient, 118–121
Louis XIV, 133
Louisiana, 168, 170
Lukavica, 240

M

Machen, Arthur, 189–191
Maiden Castle, 24
majolica, 94
Manassas, 170

Mansfield, Louisiana, 224
Maori, 23–25
Margaret of Anjou, 72
Marines, archaeological education of, 256
Marquis Yi, 67
Martin, Joseph Plumb, 149
Mary Rose, 93–95, *insert 5*
Maya, 7, 8
Mbuti Pygmies, 10
McBride, Kevin, 145
McKee, Alexander, 94
McManamon, Frank, 222, 227
Meador, Joe Tom, 232
medieval artillery, reconstructing, 84–88
Medieval Centre, 84–88
medieval warfare, 71–75
Medinet Habu, 31
Menéndez de Avilés, 130
Mesa Verde, 5
Mesquida, Christina, 9
metal detectors, 258
Mexican-American War, 151–156
Meyer, Karl E., 228–231, 234
MIAs, search for, 194–195
Milanich, Jerald, 131
Mill Springs, 223
Minèrve, 81
Ming Dynasty, 124–125
Minidoka Relocation Center, xviii, 200
Minuteman Missile National Historic Site, xix,
    214–217, *insert 8*
Mithridates, 50
Moccasin Bend National Archaeological District,
    225
Moctezuma, 104
Monitor, see USS Monitor
Mosely, Increase, 133
Mozai, Torao, 108–109
Murray, William M., 51–59, 54
Mutawalli II, 34

N

Nagato, 210, *insert 8*
Napolean, 114–117, 118–121
Narmer Palette, 14, 15, *insert 2*

Narts, 64
Nash, Steve, 221–227
National Park Service, 226
Naxos, 40
Nefertiti, bust of Queen, 235
Nelson, Sir Horatio, 119
Nero, 58, 94
Nevada nuclear test site, 206–209
New Age, birth of the, 57
New Kingdom, 29
Newton, John, 170
Nicias, 43
Nikopolis, 53, 55, 57
Nile, Battle of the, 118–121, 122–123
Nimrud, 252
Nineveh, 252
Norse Vikings, 76–78
North Carolina, 168
Noss, Doc, 173
Novak, Shannon, 74
Nowak, Lucja, 202, 203, 204, 205
Nuckols, Lew, 145
Nueva Cadiz, 97

O

Octavius, Gaius, 52, 53, 55, 56, 59
Ogden, Jim, 225
Omar, Caliph, 89
Omarska concentration camp, 239
Operation Crossroads, 213
Orr, David, 149, 226
Oseberg Ship, 78
Ötzi the Iceman, xvii, 7, *insert 1*
Owsley, Douglas, 161
Oxford Illustrated Prehistory of Europe, 5

P

Pacal, 18
Paerora, 25
Pahute Mesa, 209
Palenque, 18
Palo Alto, battlefields of, xviii, 151–156
Paroikia, 38, 39, 41
Paros, xvii, 38–41

Parrott, R.P., 165
patera, 62
Pausanias, 43, 46, 47
Pax Chaco, 9
Peleset, 31
perfecti, 82
Pergamon Altar, 231
Pericles, 43, 46, 47
perro de guerra, 98
Peter the Hermit, 90
Petsas, Photios M., 51–59
Philadelpheus, Alexander, 53
Phips, Sir William, 133
Pioneer, 169, 171, *insert 6*
Piotrovski, Mikhail, 235
Pizarro, Francisco, 101–103
Plutarch, 46
polyandreia, 44
Pope, Nathaniel, 131, 132
Poskiene, Justina, 115
Posse, Hans, 230
Potidaca, 46
Powell, Eric A., 169, 198–200
Prague, defenestration of, xvi
Preveza, 51, 52, 55
Price, Douglas, 5
Princess Duda, 118–121
Prinz Eugen, 210
Ptolemy, 49, 54, 55
Puuc style, 22

Q

Qadesh, 30
Qin Dynasty, 67, 124
Quedlinburg treasures, 232
Quibell, James, 14

R

Ragan, Mark, 171
Rainier Mesa, 209
Ralston, Nathaniel, 148–150
Ramesses II, 30
Ramesses III, 30, 31, *insert 3*
Rastorgouev, Alexei, 230, 235

Reed, Jeff, 169
Ribault, Jean, 130
Richard, Duke of York, 72
River Kwai, 198, 199–200
Robertson, Robin, 20
Rose, Mark, xv–xix, 14–16, 29–31, 42–48,
    49–50, 71–75, 89–92, 101–103, 122–123,
    129–135, 189–191, 214–217
Rosenberg, Alfred, 230
Royal Cemetary of Ur, 15

S

sak-hunal, 18
saltpeter, 87
Samian ware, 61, 62
Samuhel Gospels, 232
Sand Creek, 257
Sanpoi, 10
Saraceni, Jessica E., 147, 161
Saratoga, 210, 212
Sarianidi, Victor, 244
Sarmatian tribes, xviii, 61, 64
Sassoon, Siegfried, 190–191
scabé, 19
Scarritt, Jeremiah M., 154
Schele, Linda, 8
Schliemann, Heinrich, xix, 32, 35, 228, 231, 235
Schuster, Angela, M.H., 118–121
Scott, Douglas, 175
Sea Peoples, 29, 31, *insert 3*
Seljuk Turks, 90
Septimius Severus, 61, 63
Shaw, Justine, 19
Shekelesh, 31
Siaures Miestelis, 114, 117
Signoli, Michel, 115
Silberman, Neil Asher, 183–188
Sioux reservation, 13
Slayman, Andrew, 164–165
Smiley, Brenda, 238–242
Smyrtoula, 57
South, Stanley, 131
Southwestern warfare, evidence of, 6
Soviet massacres, unearthing, 198–199

"Spoils of War," 228–236, 251–256
Standard of Ur, 14, 15, 16, *insert 1*
Starbuck, David, 134, 135, 136–141
Steele, Julie, 226
Stevens, Kristen, 227
Stocking, Bruce, 150
Stone's River National Battlefield, 225
Stoupa, Charalambia, 42, 44
Stratum VIIa, 35
Sub Marine Explorer, 168, 171
Suhler, Charles, 17–22
Sui Dynasty, 124, 125
Supernaugh, Bill, 217

T

taiha, 25
Talheim, Germany, xvii, 11, 13
Taylor, General Zachary, 152, 153
Tecumseh, 170, 171
Thasos, 39
Thompson, Eric S., 19
Thrasyboulos, 43
Thucydides, 45, 46
Thutmosis III, 30
Tikal, 8
Tikal stela, 31, 22
Tileston, Cornelius, 133
Titus, 58
Tjeker, 31
Tower of David, 90
Towton, xvi, xviii, 71, 73, 74
Treasure of Priam, xix, 228
trebuchet, xviii, 85–87, *insert 5*
Tremblay, Marc, 133
Trojan War, xvii, 37
Troy, xvii, 33–37, 35, 37
    walls of, *insert 3*
Tsegi Canyon, 6
Tullie House Museum, 61
Turtle, 142–147

U

Union soldiers, identification of, 161
Urbanski, Marek, 199

USS *Appalachian*, 211
USS *Cairo*, 170, *insert 7*
USS *Housatonic*, xviii, 169, *insert 6*
USS *Merrimack*, 167, 168
USS *Monitor*, xviii, xix, 167, 168, 170, *insert 7*
USS *St. Louis*, 168
Uxmal, 8

V

Valkenier, Lisa, 5
Valley Forge, 148–150
Valley of the Kings, 31
Vemming, Peter, 84–88
Vespasian, 58
Victorio Ridge, 172–179
vicus, 61
viking raids, 76–78
Vilnius, 114
Virginia, see CSS Virginia
von Steuben, Friedrich, 149
Vulture Stele, 16

W

Wakeman, Jim, 175
Waldbaum, Jane, 256
wanagi, 13
War Before Civilization, 5
War of the Roses, 71, 73
warfare in complex societies, 7
Warring States Period, xvii, 66, 67
warships, ancient, 54
warships of the Civil War, 167–171
wartime treasure, ownership of, 228–236
Warwick Castle, 84–88, *insert 5*
Washington, George, 129, 130, 142–147, 148–150
Waters, Michael, 200
Watson, Don, 5
Watts, Gordon P., 170
Waurin, Jean de, xvi
Weshesh, 31
Wheeler, Sir Mortimer, 24, 232
White, Colin, 120
Wiener, Neil, 9
Wiesbaden Manifesto, 233, 236

William of Tudela, 79, 81
Wilson, Robert, 116
Wilusa, 34
Wiseman, James, 79–83
Wols, Helen M., 192–197
women warriors, 60–65
Wood, John, 94, 146
Woods, Joe, 145
Woolley, Leonard, 15, 232
World War I
    Flanders Fields artifacts, 183–188
    trench warfare, 189–191
World War II
    Papua New Guinea, remains in, 192–197
    POWs, treatment of, 198–200

Y

Yaxuná, 8, 17, 18, 19, 20, 22
Youping, Li, 66
Yucca Flat, 208, 209

Z

Zafeiropoulou, Foteini, 38–41
Zeno, 43
Zhou Dynasty, 67